Latinas Attempting Suicide

Latinas Attempting Suicide

When Cultures, Families, and Daughters Collide

LUIS H. ZAYAS

OXFORD
UNIVERSITY PRESS

OXFORD
UNIVERSITY PRESS

Oxford University Press, Inc., publishes works that further
Oxford University's objective of excellence
in research, scholarship, and education.

Oxford New York
Auckland   Cape Town   Dar es Salaam   Hong Kong   Karachi
Kuala Lumpur   Madrid   Melbourne   Mexico City   Nairobi
New Delhi   Shanghai   Taipei   Toronto

With offices in
Argentina   Austria   Brazil   Chile   Czech Republic   France   Greece
Guatemala   Hungary   Italy   Japan   Poland   Portugal   Singapore
South Korea   Switzerland   Thailand   Turkey   Ukraine   Vietnam

Copyright © 2011 by Oxford University Press, Inc.

Published by Oxford University Press, Inc.
198 Madison Avenue, New York, New York 10016
www.oup.com

Oxford is a registered trademark of Oxford University Press

Library of Congress Cataloging-in-Publication Data
Zayas, Luis H.
  Latinas attempting suicide : when cultures, families, and daughters collide / Luis H. Zayas.
    p. cm.
  Includes bibliographical references and index.
  ISBN 978-0-19-973472-6 (hardcover : alk. paper)
  1. Hispanic American teenage girls—Suicidal behavior.
  2. Youth—Suicidal behavior—United States. I. Title.
  HV6546.Z39 2001
  362.280835'20973—dc22   2010050953

1 3 5 7 9 8 6 4 2
Printed in the United States of America
on acid-free paper

To the women in my life:

Mercedes, Marta, Maria, Lourdes, Lillian;
Stephanie, Marissa, and Amanda

You are a child and you find the world big and round and you have to find your place in it. How to do that is yet another mystery, and no one can tell you how exactly. Against ample evidence, against your better judgment, you put trust in the constancy of things, you place faith in their everydayness. One day you open your door, you step out in your yard, but the ground is not there and you fall into a hole that has no bottom and no sides and no color. The mystery of the hole in the ground gives way to the mystery of your fall; just when you get used to falling and falling forever, you stop; and that stopping is yet another mystery, for why you stop, there is not an answer to that any more than there is an answer to why you fell in the first place.

Jamaica Kincaid
The Autobiography of My Mother (1996)

Preface

In the spring of 1981, Yvette Rolon, a smart, earnest graduate social work student brought to her clinical supervision with me the case of a Puerto Rican girl who had attempted suicide, the first such case with which I would have direct contact. As a faculty field instructor for Columbia University, I supervised a group of five graduate social work students, who were assigned to a fieldwork placement in the child and adolescent psychiatric department of Metropolitan Hospital Center, which sits on 96th Street and Second Avenue in East Harlem, one of the many hospitals of the New York City Health and Hospitals Corporation. Graduate students, who worked with largely Puerto Rican clients, were placed in various units in the hospital, including the therapeutic nursery, adolescent inpatient psychiatric ward, and outpatient psychiatric clinic. It was in the inpatient service where Yvette was completing her internship, that she encountered our first young Latina adolescent suicide attempter. While I had been a professional social worker for 6 years at that point, and had heard from clinicians around the city about how often they saw Hispanic girls with recent suicide attempts being brought to their clinics and agencies, I had never dealt with one directly. Years before, social workers, psychologists, and psychiatrists whom I knew told of the staggering number of Hispanic girls, mostly of Puerto Rican heritage, attempting suicide. At local symposia and meetings, I would ask others about suicide attempts by our young girls and how many they had on their caseloads. Typically, my colleagues would mention how prevalent suicide attempts were, how many they saw in their agencies, and the numbers they treated themselves, but no one could put a precise number on the prevalence of this dangerous phenomenon. And there were no rates from epidemiological surveys that we could use to understand the true numbers, and more importantly, we had no real understanding of the reasons behind the attempts. We were at a disadvantage since there was no central repository of information on suicide attempts by people of any age. All we had were statistics for completed suicides, and in those years little was available that distinguished Hispanics from other, non-Hispanic groups.

Now Yvette brought to our attention the case of Wendy,[1] who had attempted suicide the previous weekend. Wendy, 14, had sat on the windowsill of her home threatening her mother and brother that she would jump from their fourth-floor tenement in East Harlem. Just prior to her threat, Wendy had had an intense argument with her family about seeing a boy from the neighborhood, who was a few years older than she and whom her mother and brother both knew. Her older brother, filling the vacuum left by the absence of a father, was upholding the traditional role of man of the house, which gave him authority over his younger siblings with the full support of their single mother. Wendy's mother and brother were forbidding her from seeing the boy since they considered him to be a neighborhood thug (whether he really was or not is not important to this story), and because she was too young to date or, worse, have any kind of sexual activity with him or anyone else. When her brother managed to yank Wendy from the window, he and his mother took her to the emergency room of Metropolitan Hospital. It was the following week when Yvette went about her work that she was assigned Wendy's case for intervention.

This was my first exposure to a specific case of a suicide attempt by a Latina. Through Yvette's work I learned more about this case and saw in it many similarities to the countless number of cases I had heard so much about. Within a week or two of Wendy's admission into the hospital, four other girls were admitted to either the same inpatient service or the child and adolescent outpatient psychiatric clinic. Other Columbia graduate students under my supervision were assigned some girls like Wendy, and the cases became focal discussion points for us in the students' respective individual supervisory sessions and in our group discussions. When any one of us asked veteran clinicians at Metropolitan about these girls, we were told that the cases were not uncommon and that they occurred year round, not seasonally.

Years later, in preparation for a grant proposal and a research project, I consulted a colleague who directed a mobile child crisis unit in the Bronx to find out about the number of suicidal teenagers he was seeing. My colleague, Luis R. Torres, now on the faculty of the University of Houston, and I scoured his database to find that during a 7-month period in 1999, of 141 girls seen by his child crisis team, 33 (23.4%) had attempted suicide, and 27 of these (i.e., 82%) were Hispanic. And this was just one hospital among many hospitals in that borough. We could only imagine the numbers in their entirety if we were to do a similar review of records in the other hospitals.

In the early years of my pursuit, it also became a standard question for me to ask clinicians from other hospitals, clinics, and social agencies not only if they had seen such girls, but also if they had conjured up any possible explanations. The more intrepid clinicians had homegrown theories, usually cultural, to explain the suicide attempts. Others simply said they did not know but could certainly be persuaded by the cultural and clinical conjectures that others had put forth. These answers came from Hispanic clinicians as well as non-Hispanic clinicians who knew this population well. These conversations piqued my interest even further.

Practicing and teaching in a city hospital in East Harlem in 1981 meant that most of the Hispanics coming to the hospital were Puerto Ricans, no surprise since they constituted the vast majority of the Hispanic population in New York City at the time. All of the girls that we saw at Metropolitan Hospital in the 16 months between the spring of 1981 and the summer of 1982 were Puerto Rican, save for a Dominican or Cuban girl that appeared now and then. Our observations of a limited sample of girls led us to believe that we might be witnessing a particularly Puerto Rican cultural phenomenon. There was no way of knowing much about the issue since there was no research on the topic, at least that we knew of. I came across some writings about the "Puerto Rican Syndrome" (Fernandez-Marina, 1961; Mehlman, 1961), a term coined by some military psychiatrists in the 1950s to describe frightful, agitated, sometimes violent anxiety attacks seen among young Puerto Rican soldiers. It was thought to be due to an interpersonal problem, repressed anger, and abetted by a serious psychiatric problem. Ramon Fernandez-Marina (1961) also used the term *"ataque"* to describe this experience, taking the term from the well-known Puerto Rican folk syndrome called *ataque de nervios* to underscore the similarity.[2] The *ataque de nervios* has been part of Puerto Rican culture and is now better understood through the research of anthropologist Peter Guarnaccia and psychologist Glorisa Canino (Guarnaccia, Canino, Rubio-Stipec, & Bravo, 1993; Guarnaccia, Rivera, Franco, & Neighbors, 1996; Guarnaccia, Rubio-Stipec, & Canino, 1989), psychiatrist Roberto Lewis-Fernandez (1994), and others (Liebowitz et al., 1994; Oquendo et al., 1992).

These years of inquisitiveness about the prevalence and reasons for the suicide attempts combined with my maturation as a clinician only made me want to know more. And so I sought to learn more about what it was like to be a Puerto Rican teenager, a young female, to better understand a striking and troubling pattern in our community. With a curiosity about how humans grow and change, I began doctoral studies in developmental psychology, gaining knowledge that would arm me with research and analytic skills that would serve me well in seeking to understand this phenomenon. Wendy's case stayed with me even as I began to treat other girls and families following suicide attempts.

The topic remains, in my mind, one of the most compelling clinical and cultural phenomena that I have encountered. It has taken over 30 years to get to the point—maybe even the nerve—to write this book. What I present in these pages is the culmination of those years. Even though I had no personal experience of a friend or family member who had attempted suicide under the same conditions, I had knowledge about adolescent depression and the impact of pressures brought upon teenage girls growing up in traditional Puerto Rican homes. My four sisters, by virtue of their gender, endured the cross fire of cultural restrictions at home. They matured as young women in a larger culture that was at odds with what they were told by my parents. With two very traditionally oriented Puerto Rican parents who believed that a woman should dedicate her life to her family, protect her virginity, and eschew many of her own needs for those of others, my sisters had it much harder than I. Perhaps it was the ritual evening family rosary chanted in Spanish or the presence of a strong father in the family, the deep love of our parents, or my sisters' own strong resilient characters that protected them from a suicide attempt. The little girls I saw in clinic, despite resembling my sisters in most demographics, often did not have solid, protective family ties, maternal strength and tenderness, paternal discipline and indulgence, and predictable and consistent parenting. I could well empathize with the painful hearts, distressed minds, and troubled lives they had endured. The suicidal behaviors, therefore, became the only viable option for them.

Curiosity wasn't the only factor motivating my search for explanations about the whys and hows of suicide attempts by Latinas. Rather, as a clinician, I wanted to organize my knowledge to penetrate the phenomenon and improve my practice with patients. My mission in unraveling the mysteries of the suicide attempts by Latinas was also to give clinicians, especially adolescent and family therapists, a view of what was behind the attempts, what triggered them, and how we might go about treating and preventing them.

The suicide attempts I studied as a clinician and the ones I researched as a scientist are at their core acts of communication. In actuality, the attempts are communications that stemmed from problems *in family communication*. I do not mean the kind of trite "cry for help" communication that we so often hear about in suicidal behaviors. These were suicidal communications that had profound meanings with respect to development, gender, and family. The suicide attempts, as I have come to understand them, have the contours and textures of a cultural idiom of distress. In treating the suicide attempts of Latinas as family communication problems when we distill them to their essence, I explore culture, mental health, acculturation, family functioning, and female adolescent development, and how all these streams seem to converge—indeed to collide—at times of crisis to form the suicide attempt.

This book is written for anyone who is interested in the conditions of Latinas in the United States and who wants to learn more about the communicational, cultural, social, psychological, and familial nature of the suicide attempts. I also want to make the intricacies of the topic, and how we study it, accessible to a wide readership. It is intended for undergraduate and graduate students in social work, psychology, anthropology, sociology, and women's and ethnic studies; for medical students and residents in child and adolescent psychiatry; and for marriage and family therapist and other practicing professionals in mental health, health, and education. I hope that clinicians and researchers, educators, and administrators will find ideas in this book that can inform, advance, or maybe inspire their work. Maybe there will be some young Latinas who will find in these pages something that enlightens, possibly helps them. Perhaps Latina readers might find something in this book that they can use to help other young Latinas.

The chapters that follow tell the story surrounding the phenomenon these Hispanic girls have lived. Their thoughts about attempting suicide and actually attempting are told in their words as much as possible. My part has been to put their decision to attempt suicide into context by bringing theory and research to bear on the search for more understanding of why it happens and why it happens so frequently. Stories are best told—except in the hands of gifted novelists, biographers, and oral storytellers—in simple chronological order and by topics or areas of interest. That is what I try to do in these pages.

Stories, of course, start with a beginning that sets the stage for what will unfold. This book tells a story about Latina suicidality. It includes cases from our study of Latino families, some whose daughters made suicide attempts and some who didn't. The case studies (some of which were written by members of my team) offer a glimpse into the lives of our girls and their families, a window into the interiors of the families with their distinct histories. Through family stories we learn about the intimate contours, atmospheres, experiences, and parenting nuances. The girls' and parents' own words tell their stories best, showing us how some families stumble, fall and can't get up, and how other families stumble, fall, and get up, sometimes stronger. We hope that their words and their parents' words deepen our understanding of the many facets of their suicide attempts.

Chapter One is about families of Hispanic origin or heritage, setting the ground for the examination of suicide attempts. Chapter Two is a brief history of the suicide attempt phenomenon and its neglect by public health and mental health researchers. Chapter Three considers human development so as to place the Hispanic daughter in the context of her family, gender, culture, and society. In Chapter Four, I draw on the written and spoken words of many Latinas, both those who showed suicidal impulses and those who didn't. Chapters Five and Six report on the most recent and extensive study that I have conducted on suicidal Latinas. In Chapter Five, I present the general results from the objective measures we used to understand the Latina, her family, and her suicide attempt. Chapter Six offers details about the suicide attempts, the descriptions of what occurred to the girls at the time of the attempt. We searched for feelings, thoughts, sensations, actions, and the immediate conditions of their suicidal behaviors. Chapter Seven is an integrative essay. It brings together the situation confronting Latino youth as they walk in two cultures, and also discusses the association of suicide attempts to individual psychopathology and to cultural idioms of distress. It visits the conceptual model I began with and the one I arrived at after our study. Like much of science, this model tries to advance and refine our understanding but may always be a "work in progress." Chapter Eight addresses prevention and treatment. It looks at interventions that are scientifically based and that seem to be effective with Hispanic youth, even if the interventions were not intended solely for suicidality. In this final chapter, I include ideas for clinical therapy, mostly family-centered treatment. And I point to the importance of starting early and including parents, particularly in schools, which can play powerful roles in saving young Latinas and other youth.

A Comment on Words and Terms

Finally, a note about the terminology I use in this book. I refer to adolescents and adolescence here in the female gender since it is a book about Latinas and their development and conduct. As such, whenever I refer to a teenager or adolescent process, or parent–adolescent interaction, I use "she" or "her" even though many of the issues are shared with males. Unless I am referring specifically to men or boys, the pronouns will be feminine ones.

Also, I use the terms *Hispanic* and *Latino* or *Latina* interchangeably as neither one enjoys a universal preference.[3] I recognize that each of these terms captures meanings that are important to many people. The term *Hispanic* retains its tie to the heritage left from the centuries of Spanish domination and its influence, and the links to Europe. It also harks back to the fact that one of the principal commonalities of Hispanics or Latinos is the Spanish language. The Spanish translation of Hispanic, *Hispano*, has long referred to someone who is Spanish speaking. And while many U.S. Hispanics are bilingual or monolingual English speakers, they remain tied to the sound of the Spanish language, its culture, and its people. The term *Hispanidad* (the Spanish translation of the term *Hispanicity*) has been used as a term appealing to our collective linguistic and cultural origins.

The term *Latino* is an appellation that evokes the core experience of mostly Spanish-speaking people from the Caribbean, Central America, South America, and Mexico and may be preferred by those people who see it as a way of distancing from the past colonization Spain and the hegemony of the United States. It has come to be more inclusive, and we find Brazilians who speak Portuguese to be considered a part of this group. In ideological circles, it is preferred over *Hispanic*, as the term *Latino* was self-appointed, while the term *Hispanic* is felt to have been arbitrarily foisted on us by the U.S. government.

My use of these two terms interchangeably reflects my comfort with both. When I refer to people in a specific group, they are identified by their nationality or heritage, such as Dominican, Honduran, or Colombian. *Latino, Hispanic,* or a specific term will be used when referring to original sources, as it was used by those authors in identifying their participants or population groups.

Contents

Latinas Attempting Suicide

1

First, the Family

As Nash Candelaria's 1988 story *The Day the Cisco Kid Shot John Wayne* opens, Junior's family is about to move from the country-side of New Mexico to a town five miles away so he can start first grade in a two-room school. An intense argument is underway between his father, Papá, and Uncle Luis, Papá's older brother, who vehemently opposes his brother's move. Uncle Luis, nearly apoplectic, cannot understand his brother's decision to take his wife and children somewhere else. Junior narrates the scene:

> "You think you're too good for us," Uncle Luis shouted at
> Papá in Spanish, "just because you finished high school
> and have a job in town! My God! We grew up in the country.
> Our parents and grandparents grew up in the country.
> If New Mexico country was good enough for them —"

Papá remained calm and respectful toward his older brother despite his irritation. Their blind mother, Grandma, her patience running thin, rocked faster in her chair as she smoked a hand-rolled cigarette. Finally, in exasperation, she tells Uncle Luis to leave his brother alone.

> "He's a grown man, Luis. With a wife and children. He can
> live anywhere he wants."
> "But what about the —"
> He was going to say orchard next to Grandma's house. It
> belonged to Papá and everyone expected him to build a
> house there someday. Grandma cut Uncle short: "Enough!"

3

Rather than follow his brother's expectations—and probably those of others—to stay with the extended family, Papá tells Uncle Luis and those present that by moving to town he will be nearer to his job, and his wife can have the car to go shopping. But that is only the ostensible reason that Papá gives for the move. What Papá cannot tell his brother and other family members, because they would not understand, is that the move was prompted by his desire to have Junior use English as his main language. As the young family drove to the new home, Papá acknowledged aloud:

> "Times have changed," Papá said. "He'll have to live in the
> English-speaking world."

This family drama encapsulates one of the many strains Latino families face in raising children in the United States. It is not hard to understand the choice that Papá and Uncle Luis are each making; they have different ideas about the future. Ultimately, neither brother is more right or more wrong than the other in his decision. In the push and pull of adapting to social demands that have changed from the time their parents raised them to today as they raise their families, the argument between Papá and Uncle Luis shows the fraying family ties. The argument that Junior's father and uncle are having is filled with love and resentment, attachments and separations. This is a family of three generations together, loving while laboring to take leave, choosing different paths in adapting to life's exigencies. Both brothers remain loyal to traditions forged through decades, just differently. Uncle Luis operates from strong sentiments for the family's traditions while his brother, Junior's father, takes a pragmatic approach for his children.

The brothers' argument also exemplifies the struggle within one Mexican-American family to maintain the traditional unity and proximity of family members, a tradition that urges family to live under the same roof or next door. It embodies the belief that family ties are more important than anything else the outside world has to offer. Social psychologist Rolando Diaz-Loving, of the National Autonomous University of Mexico, makes an interesting distinction between Anglo-American and Mexican families. Anglo-American families, Diaz-Loving quips, save money to send their children to college. Mexican parents, however, save money so that their children can build a house next door.

Junior's family drama helps us partially understand the situation facing Hispanic youth in the United States. It is the psychological dilemma of reaching for the larger society while holding faithfully to the family. Uncle Luis' argument personifies the either-or dilemma that some Latinos experience.

Others, embodied by Papá, see it as a process of fusing two cultures and cross-walking between them, with trepidation at first and then with growing equanimity. Papá's position is to prepare his children for both worlds, an adaptation that helps his children hold onto aspects of their culture while moving toward the mainstream as they acculturate. It is not only family nerves that are strained but also those of the individual family members. Adolescent Latinas may experience a dynamic family process that is in many ways similar to what is happening in Junior's family. For many Latinas, becoming more autonomous means dealing with the powerful emotional pull of the family. It involves the pressure to remain loyal and tied to the family. The process tears at families' strengths and resiliency. How well the family and teenager are prepared for this tense dynamic is a key determinant of whether a daughter's suicide attempt occurs or not.

"No book on Latinos would be complete," writes Kurt Organista (2007) in *Solving Latino Psychosocial and Health Problems*, "without a chapter dedicated to the central social-psychological institution in the Latino experience—*la familia*" (p. 141). This is evermore true of a book on young Latinas. The phenomenon of suicide attempts is, ultimately, about family, where children grow and learn the culture, traditions, and values of their parents. A chapter on the family speaks to the ties that bind children to families, to parents and siblings, for better *and* for worse. Exploring U.S. Hispanics and their families sets the context for unveiling the suicide attempts of young Latinas.

Origins, Heritage, and Generations

Hispanics trace their national origins or cultural heritage to most of the countries of Latin America, including Puerto Rico, a U.S. territory. They are people from Spanish-speaking countries: Argentina, Bolivia, Chile, Colombia, Costa Rica, Cuba, the Dominican Republic, El Salvador, Ecuador, Guatemala, Honduras, Mexico, Nicaragua, Panama, Paraguay, Peru, Puerto Rico, Uruguay, and Venezuela—countries with cultures and histories that are similar in some ways and distinct in others. There are 45.5 million people in the United States who identify themselves as Hispanic (U.S. Census Bureau, 2007a). Mexicans are by far the largest group, comprising almost two thirds of the Hispanic population, followed by Puerto Ricans (9.1%) and Cubans (3.5%). Other Hispanic groups that are emerging in sizable proportions of the U.S. Hispanic population are Salvadorans (3.2%), Dominicans (2.6%), Guatemalans (1.9%), Colombians (1.8%), Hondurans (1.2%), Ecuadorians (1.2%), and Peruvians (1.0%). Other groups each make up less than 1% of the Hispanic population.

To put this population growth in perspective, consider that in 1990 the Census Bureau counted 22.4 million Hispanics (U.S. Census Bureau, 2008a). Ten years later, a historic demographic milestone was reached: the Hispanic population had grown to about 33 million people or 13% of the total U.S. population, making it the largest ethnic minority. This was a growth rate of 57% compared with the 11% growth seen in the total U.S. population. Then in 2007, the Hispanic population reached 15% of the nation's total population, solidly establishing people of Hispanic origin as the nation's largest ethnic minority. It is estimated that by mid-2050 U.S. Hispanics will total 132.8 million or about 30% of the nation's population (U.S. Census Bureau, 2008b). The size of the U.S. Hispanic population should also be understood in the context of globalization. Consider this: the U.S. Hispanic population is the second largest aggregation of people of Hispanic or Spanish-speaking origin in the world. Only Mexico, with 108.7 million inhabitants, has a larger population of Hispanics (U.S. Census Bureau, 2008a, 2008d). Spain has a population of 40.4 million. There are several states with large proportions of Spanish-speaking residents, such as California, Texas, Arizona, and New Mexico. In Texas alone, 29% of the state's residents who are 5 years old and older speak Spanish at home. Texas leads all states with Spanish speakers and New Mexico follows closely, but the difference is not statistically significant (U.S. Census Bureau, 2006).

In the year between July 2006 and July 2007 alone, 1.4 million Hispanics were added to the total U.S. population, that is, one of every two persons who was born or immigrated was Hispanic. What's more is that much of the growth in the Hispanic population has come about as a result of a high birth rate of U.S.-born Hispanics, rather than just by immigration. This is made clear by the birth rate among Hispanic women, which, in 2006, was 23.4% compared with 11.6% for non-Hispanic women and 16.5% for African-American women (Hamilton, Martin, & Ventura, 2007).

Birth rates are important to report. But it is what they represent in terms of replenishing a country's population that is so vital to understanding our country's future. It has been estimated that U.S. Hispanic births are one of the strongest sources for the replacement population that the United States needs for continued economic growth and security. Respected family economists Shelly Lundberg and Robert A. Pollak (2007) view the current U.S. population growth as largely attributable to immigrants and their children. Specifically, the United States is replacing its population at a rate of 2.1 children per woman, while other major developed countries have lower population replacement rates due to fewer births per woman. Countries like Japan and France have seen the overall "graying" of their populations because women in those countries are having fewer children, at rates lower than are needed to replace the aging segment of their populations.

Lundberg and Pollak, and others (e.g., Dye, 2005), reveal that the fertility rate of native-born women, which includes U.S.-born Hispanics, is below the replacement rate of 2.1. And so, in actuality, it is foreign-born Hispanic women (with a fertility rate of 2.8 children per woman) and other immigrant women (with a fertility rate of 2.2 children per woman) who are providing our critically needed replacement population. The fact that the median age of Hispanics in 2007 was 27.6 years compared with 36.6 years for the U.S. population as a whole adds support to this finding (U.S. Census Bureau, 2008a). After all, birth rates are highest among younger women, those in the prime child-bearing years, and the birth rates drop as women age. With a generally younger population and high birth rate, Hispanics are helping replenish our nation's population.

A closer look at population figures on Hispanics helps set the context for a discussion of growing up Hispanic in the United States and pressures on young Latinas. In 2006, there were 9.9 million Hispanic family households in the United States. Of these households, 62% included children younger than 18, and 67% were made up of married couples (U.S. Census Bureau, 2007). Forty-four percent of Hispanic family households in 2006 consisted of a married couple with children who were younger than 18, and 66% of Hispanic children lived with two married parents. In 2007, 24% of Americans under the age of 5 were Hispanic (U.S. Census Bureau, 2008a). The number of children in mixed-status homes (i.e., unauthorized immigrant parents and citizen-children) grew from 2.7 million in 2003 to 4 million in 2008 (Fix & Zimmerman, 2001; Passel & Cohn, 2009).

Living in intact families among Hispanic immigrants is on average higher than in other ethnic and racial minority groups, a testament to their sense of obligation to the family structure and to their children. Low-income immigrants are more likely to be married than low-income natives (only 15% of immigrant children live with a single parent compared with 26% of U.S.-born children), and immigrant fathers are just as likely to work full-time, year-round as are native-born fathers (Hernandez, 2004). Employment rates among immigrants are often very high but not in jobs or occupations that they would prefer (Hernandez, 2004). But these jobs and their stability are a significant improvement to what is available in their home countries. Over 60% of Hispanics over 25 years of age have at least a high school education while 13% hold a bachelor's degree or higher (U.S. Census Bureau, 2008e, 2008f).

Still, poverty rates for Hispanics rose from 20.6% in 2006 to 21.5% in 2007, and 32.1% of Hispanics lacked health insurance in 2007 (U.S. Census Bureau, 2008c).

Many of the grim statistics among Hispanic youth are made worse by the deep poverty in which they live. Drug and alcohol use, for example, are prevalent among Hispanic adolescents, with Hispanic 8th and 10th graders using nearly all classes of drugs, from cigarettes to alcohol, at rates higher than White and African-American youth (Johnston, O'Malley, Bachman, & Schulenberg, 2007). Darkening this statistic is the fact that alcohol and drug initiation are associated with substance dependence (King & Chassin, 2007) and raise the likelihood of having substance-related problems, such as driving under the influence and delinquency (Hingson, Heeren, Levenson, Jamanka, & Voas, 2002; Zhang, Wieczoker, & Welte, 1997). Sexual risk taking is also related to alcohol and drugs (Zimmer-Gembeck, Sidbernruner, & Collins, 2004). And about 18% of Hispanic teens experience their first sexual intercourse while under the influence of alcohol or drugs, and 25% of sexually active teens report engaging in recent sexual activities while under the influence (National Center on Addiction and Substance Abuse, 2002). Adolescents are also less likely to use condoms when they have sex while under the influence (Dunn, Bartee, & Perko, 2003). According to the U.S. Centers for Disease Control and Prevention (CDC, 2006a, 2006b), rates of unprotected sexual intercourse and the number of sexual partners decreased between 1991 and 2005 for White and Black students but not for Hispanic students.

Not One Group. Many

Even with this description of Hispanics, there are some issues that need to be disentangled so that we understand that the Latino bloc is not a monolithic one. Their diversity has important implications for the discussion of suicidal adolescent Latinas. First, according to the statistics just cited, we clearly see that Hispanic diversity stems from the countries of origin and the heritage that Latinos claim. Second, there is immigration and generation status as well as length of residency in the United States, which reflects Hispanic diversity even more. In the American Southwest, Mexican Americans have resided for centuries and count many earlier generations. In the Northeast, the migration of Puerto Ricans in search of employment and greater opportunities, facilitated by an act of Congress in 1917 that granted U.S. citizenship to all Puerto Ricans, created a concentration in New York and the large industrial cities of Boston, Philadelphia, and Newark, New Jersey. Chicago became a settling point as did towns like Lorain, Ohio. Cubans fled their country in the 1960s for Miami, with a large contingent that settled in the northern New Jersey. Subsequent waves of Cuban refugees added to the vitality of South Florida, making Miami an international gateway. During the 1990s and the new millennium, areas that had seldom seen Latinos in large numbers began to see small communities of mostly Mexican and Central American immigrants spring up: in places like Georgia, North Carolina, Missouri, Nebraska, and Iowa. These were immigrants who found employment in towns where poultry farms and meat-packing companies needed to replenish their dwindling local workforces. This infusion of labor can be said to have saved many such towns, though this conclusion remains a point of controversy in the national immigration debate throughout the first decade of the 21st century.

Hispanics represent many generations. There is, of course, the first generation, the generation of the immigrant. The second generation is then made up of the immigrant's U.S.-children. In some families, we can count children who are part of the first generation and siblings who are part of the second generation. Finally, the third generation and beyond are comprised of the grandchildren and great-grandchildren of the first generation. Like countless millions of other immigrants since the early days of our country, each generation assimilates and acculturates in its own unique ways. Hispanics are not that different. In fact, demographers at the Pew Hispanic Center (Hakimzadeh & Cohn, 2007) show that 76% of foreign-born Latinos who arrived at 10 years of age or younger have high English fluency. About 30% of those who arrived between the ages of 11 to 17 claim high English fluency. About 16% of those who arrived between 18 and 25 years old and 11% of those who arrived at ages 26 and older reported that they can carry on an English conversation very well. It is an understandable pattern: the young acquire new language skills faster; with age this becomes harder. An impressive 88% of the U.S.-born adult children of immigrants report that they speak English very well. Among later generations of Hispanic adults, the figure rises to 94%. Moreover, not only do English-language abilities increase with each generation, but English also becomes the primary language spoken in the home (Alba, Logan, Lutz, & Stults, 2002; Portes & Hao, 1998).

There is one generation about which less is written. This is the so-called "1.5 generation," a term first used by Ruben Rumbaut and Kenji Ima (1988) to describe immigrant youth born in another country who come to the United States *at a very young age*. Most of their schooling occurs in the United States, although they may have had their early education in their original country. While it is not incorrect to label these youth as first-generation immigrants, their socialization and psychological frame of reference are more similar to those of the U.S.-born second-generation children than to those of immigrants who arrive later as adolescents or adults. The age of 13 seems to be the tipping point between what makes a child fit the profile of the 1.5 generation or the

second generation. Arriving after the age of 13 often means the person's fundamental socialization has occurred in her original culture, and she is very likely
to speak English with a Spanish accent however slight or pronounced. Those
who arrive before age 13 are more apt to be socialized to the new culture and to
speak English without an accent. The young Latinas that I discuss in this book
represent first-, 1.5-, second-, and sometimes third-generation Hispanics.

Included in the many aspects of diversity found among Latinos in the
United States is social class. While statistics show that a preponderance of U.S.
Hispanics live in poverty or slightly above, there are Hispanics with markedly
high wealth. Using wealth and income or what job a person holds as a measure
of social class is useful but not entirely correct when talking about Latinos or
any other immigrant group. A more worthwhile consideration of social class is
parents' educational level, especially prior to immigration. There are many
Latino immigrants who were well-educated professionals in their former countries, where they practiced medicine, law, nursing, or engineering or were
qualified schoolteachers and accountants. Even if they immigrated legally,
restrictions on admitting foreign graduates into U.S. licensed professions
limits their earning potential. Most people in this category find employment
below their capacities: an accountant works as a bookkeeper, a physician as a
lab assistant, and a teacher as a daycare worker.[4] Over the years, the number of
Hispanic suicide attempters I have seen in my practice and in my research
whose parents have college degrees is very small. With more education and
knowledge, parents interact with their children differently, displaying more
cognitive flexibility and engaging in verbal exchange that exposes their children to the world of words, abstractions, and logic that, in turn, enhances their
children's academic and social-emotional performance. While these educated
parents may not be highly acculturated to the majority culture, they carry with
them ideas and attitudes that may better prepare them and their daughters to
confront the challenges of adapting to a new culture. These features may alter
family and child–parent interaction patterns.

Speaking of Suicidal Latinas

At nearly every talk I give around the country on the suicide attempts of
young Latinas, someone in the audience—sometimes a Hispanic, sometimes
a non-Hispanic—states that "we" (mostly meaning me, the speaker) must be
cautious in talking about Hispanics and their adolescent daughters as if they
were monolithic groups. It is a familiar caution and I always acknowledge the
questioner's concerns. Still, I find it a peculiar admonition since the same

watchfulness is not urged when we speak about other racial and ethnic groups. It is an unassailable fact that Hispanics are diverse, not cut from one cloth but from many.

Accepting that Hispanics are not a monolithic entity, we still have the perplexing reality that, across our country, high school students who self-identify as Hispanic or Latino report having more suicidal ideation, plans, and attempts than other youth who self-identify as White, African American/Black, Asian, or other. There is something going on in this nonmonolithic group that results in very similar responses to the same set of survey questions. To respond to the reminder that Hispanics are not monolithic, I go through a deductive exercise about the suicide attempt phenomenon using empirical bases and a series of steps that are logical extensions of what we do know, as indicated in the following three paragraphs.

The high rates of suicide attempts among Latinas are not strictly a matter of social class. The surveys that have established the presence of the widespread phenomenon use a representative sample of schools and communities in the United States that presumably gives us a wide swath of the country's teenagers from all groups. We can rightly argue that, because Latinas are overrepresented in the lower social class, it is they who are inflating the rates. Well, maybe. But even if we look at only the lower social groups of Hispanics, we are still left with a very heterogeneous group: Latinos in the lower social echelons are as diverse as any other social strata of U.S. Hispanics; they represent the many cultural heritages, origins of Latin America, and generations. If it were only a matter of social class, then we would expect to see a similarly high rate of suicide attempts occurring primarily among low-income, working-class, and impoverished groups. In fact, suicide attempts are not restricted to social class.

It is not just one subgroup of Hispanics that accounts for the suicide-attempts phenomenon. High rates of suicide attempts and related behaviors have been reported among the wide range of Hispanic groups, as shown by surveys. We have no evidence at the moment that shows that, proportionally, Latinas from one subgroup are responsible for the majority of suicide attempts. That girls whom I studied and treated have been mostly Dominican, Mexican, and Puerto Rican is simply a matter of geography: I lived and worked in New York City for 30 years and now work in Saint Louis. My colleagues in, say, Arizona or New Mexico would study mostly girls of Mexican origin, whether immigrant, second, or later generation. Similarly, in Los Angeles and San Diego, clinicians and researchers see Mexican, Guatemalan, Honduran, and Salvadoran youth. If one group were responsible for Latina suicidality, then suicide attempts would be concentrated in those areas of the country where the group is more concentrated. But this doesn't appear to be the case. Judging from what research and surveys are reporting about the diverse group of Hispanics reporting higher than average suicidal behaviors, we can almost certainly eliminate the argument that one group is responsible for the phenomenon.

It is not one or two regions of the country with disproportionate rates of suicide attempts among Latino youth. Like subgroups, regional differences do not appear to account for the higher rates among both young Latinas and Latinos. If that were the case, then Latinas in one region would have to be attempting suicide at a scale that raises the overall levels for all other Hispanic youth. No survey that I have seen suggests that it is a regional problem.

Where does this leave us in regard to the questioner's concerns? It seems to me that it leaves us able to speak of Hispanic or Latino adolescent suicidality across groups without neglecting their diversity. True, Hispanics are not a monolithic group. But youth self-identifying as Latinos from different social classes and various Hispanic subgroups in all regions of the country do account for the phenomenon we are studying. These arguments, therefore, answer the concern raised that Hispanics are not a monolithic group. They may not be, but it seems that when it comes to adolescent suicidality, we can speak of them as a group.

So what then are the commonalities among this nonmonolithic Hispanic group, this population that traces its ethnic and cultural origins to the countries of Latin America? We can easily start with Spanish as one overarching commonality in the legacies that influence Hispanic youth. Spanish is a psychological and cultural organizing influence among persons with a shared linguistic history. Even for those Hispanics who do not speak Spanish or do not speak it well, it is one of the key anchors to culture, ethnicity, heritage, and identity (Pew Hispanic Center, 2009; Ramos, 2002). Another shared element among Latinos is religion, predominately Catholicism, which was once, and to a large degree still is, the dominant creed in Latin America, despite the rise of other, fundamentalist Christian denominations and the long presence of Judaism (Elkin, 1998) and indigenous religions and spiritual beliefs. Latin American Catholicism has been of a very conservative strain, even with the glorification of the liberation theology movement of the twentieth century. This conservative religious ideology has seeped deeply into the values by which people live and raise their children. It has ensconced itself in daily life such that Spanish idioms are sometimes inseparable from the culture and its values.

There is also a conjoint political and social history. Mexico and the countries of Central America, the Caribbean, and South America have had in common the direct rule of and occupation by imperial powers, mostly Spain but other European powers too (e.g., Britain, France, Portugal, the Netherlands).

The United States' imperialism has been direct by its imposition of economic, political, social, and military power, and indirect by its mere hegemonic presence in this hemisphere. Altogether, we see very similar cultural and social experiences that emigrants from these countries brought to the United States in their long-ago arrival and in their modern-day immigration. In the case of Mexican Americans, many were already in the North American Southwest long before it became the United States Southwest.

Suicide attempts could be a common generational process. This is a real possibility since the likelihood of attempts is greater among the U.S. born or second generation than those who were born outside of the United States. This may indicate a real social problem for children of immigrants dealing with two cultural traditions, one brought by parents to the United States and enforced at home (with the intention that it also be lived outside the home) and one that reflects contemporary Western values and ideals about women's comportment and self-identity. Surveys need to add more items or questions to discern the generational effects and their extent.[5]

Latinas are not homogeneous, but cultural traditions that have endured across the years and across immigration and migration, and generations, provide sufficient ground for discussing suicide attempts among them. The influence of language, religion, socialization, and family composition and interactions seems, to me, to hold many of the answers to the suicide attempt phenomenon.

Hispanic Families

The argument between Papá and Uncle Luis that opened this chapter was one fueled by love. Uncle Luis wanted to keep the family he knew united by drawing on a concept of the traditional family that he followed. Papá was no less family oriented than his older brother; he simply saw his family and the future differently. It is the *nuanced* definitions of family that each brother held that were displayed in Junior's narrative. Both brothers, no doubt, defined their family as many Hispanic cultures do: extended and embracing. For Hispanics, extended family includes those related by blood, those who marry into the family, and those who are taken in through any of a range of affiliations that Hispanic cultures have developed over the centuries to create *familia*. In her memoir of the exodus to the United States from Cuba as a young child during the Mariel boatlift of 1980, Mirta Ojito (2005) offers a moving depiction of how Cubans define family, a definition that applies to many other Hispanic cultures.

Mike took a quick look at the scene, concentrating on the teary-eyed Cubans who seemed to occupy every corner of the lobby. Several— women, mostly—were openly crying. After days at Mariel, they had just heard that their relatives would not be able to leave with them after all, either because the government did not approve their exit permits or because some families, afraid to be separated, had opted to stay put unless the entire family could leave, a nearly impossible feat given the stinginess of Cuban immigration officials and the size of what most Cubans considered family: not only parents and their kids but grandmothers and sometimes even aunts and uncles. (p. 204)

Extended Hispanic families are not composed of blood relations only. They include others who have earned a profound trust and love that make them family even if only in honorific terms. Two notable traditions highlight the permeability of these family boundaries. One is a system of godparent-hood known as *compadrazgo* (coparenthood), found across many Hispanic cultures. It is a traditional system taken very seriously by those within it. While *compadrazgo* is based on the traditional religious belief, especially Roman Catholic, of the importance of the baptismal godparents, it is not thought of as a merely honorific title. It is an indication of the person's permanent inclusion into the other's family, the joining of two families, much like marriage. Upon becoming a baptismal godmother (*madrina*) or a godfather (*padrino*), the person is given the honor of becoming a part of the family, forming a nonblood, yet binding, kinship. The child's godparents become *comadres* (comothers) and *compadres* (cofathers) and have an almost sacred duty to be part of the family, abide by its values, and contribute to the family.

In fact, among older and more traditional generations of Hispanic adults in *compadrazgo* relationships, the manner in which they address each other shifts. They might no longer use first names or even semiformal titles such as *Don* and *Doña*. Instead, older Hispanics may resort to the using the terms *comadre* (comother) and *compadre* (cofather). There is a beauty in this tradition for those of us who grew up in it, where intimacy and respect come together in a familial relationship that is socioreligious rather than legal. Children are taught to respect the *madrinas* and *padrinos*, a respect almost equivalent to that which they bestow on their parents, grandparents, aunts, and uncles.

The other notable tradition that exemplifies the inclusiveness of families in many Hispanic cultures, particularly among Puerto Ricans in decades past, was the informal child adoption system known as *hijos de crianza* (children of upbringing). In this informal system, families would take in children without legal adoption papers or other formalized procedures and treat them as their adoptive children. In the history of Puerto Rico, for example, a child might be given up for "adoption" by her parents to, say, a couple who could not bear children. In cases of severe poverty and a large family, a set of parents might arrange to have a child they could barely feed raised by a family of greater resources than their own. I'm certain that in the social history of families in Puerto Rico such arrangements were at times coerced or exploitative, but it was openly practiced in many rural areas and small towns without stigma. In fact, not unlike legal adoptions in the United States, the family taking in the *hijo* or *hija de crianza* might very well have enjoyed a community's greater respect for their selfless act. Mostly, the arrangements were open, known to the children, siblings, extended family, neighbors, and *compadres*. It was not a secret. The *hijo* or *hija de crianza* was, in almost all cases, told of the arrangement. The child would know early in life who her birth parents were and could distinguish them from her adoptive parents, much as we do today. And she may have had ongoing contact with her birth family, much like the open adoption arrangements practiced today in the child welfare system. Less well known were the psychological effects on the child of being an *hija de crianza*; there are no studies that I can find about the impact on the children. Nevertheless, it was a custom that reflected the lineal relationships that Puerto Rican and other Hispanic families preserve in their culture.[6]

Children hold a special place in Hispanic families and often are not segregated from adults when it comes to family events and parents' lives. In our work in the Hispanic healthy marriage programs across the United States in 2008 and 2009, we learned quickly that any attention to enriching a couple's relationship had to include the children. Therefore, marriage curricula that emphasized mostly or only the couple were often met with quizzical looks by those Latino participants with a traditional view of marriage and family. How could any definition of "couplehood" not include their children? After all, marriage and children are not considered separate entities, but rather, one unit. While many Hispanics have accepted the common practice among their non-Hispanic friends and colleagues of having parties in which children are not invited, others—even highly educated and acculturated Latinos—still find this practice off-putting.

Judith Ortiz Cofer (1990) adds marvelous clarity to the place of children in parents' and families' lives in her book *Silent Dancing: A Partial Remembrance of a Puerto Rican Childhood*. In describing a home movie from her childhood in the 1950s, filmed at a family's New Year's Eve party, Ortiz Cofer offers piercing observations and astute explanations:

> Here and there you can see a small child. Children were always brought to parties and, whenever they got sleepy, put to bed in

the host's bedrooms. Babysitting was a concept unrecognized by the Puerto Rican women I knew: a responsible mother did not leave her children with any stranger. And in a culture where children are not considered intrusive, there is no need to leave the children at home. We went where our mother went. (p. 92)

A contemporary and very historic reference to the vastness of extended-family networks in Hispanic families occurred one day during the writing of this book. On July 13, 2009, Judge Sonia Sotomayor began testifying before the Senate Judiciary Committee on her nomination to the U.S. Supreme Court. Senator Patrick Leahy of Vermont, who chaired the U.S. Senate's judiciary committee, started the hearings by saying, "Before we begin the opening statements of the senators, I know you have family members here. . . . Would you please introduce the members of your family?"

"If I introduced everybody who's family-like," Judge Sotomayor replied warmly, "we would be here all morning."

From the transcript published by CNN (2009), Sotomayor's introduction of her family continues:

I will limit myself to just my immediate family. Sitting behind me is my brother, Juan Sotomayor. Next to him is my mom, Celina Sotomayor. Next to her is my favorite husband of my mom, Omar Lopez. [Laughter]. Next to him is my niece, Kylie Sotomayor. And next to her is her mom and my sister-in-law, Tracey Sotomayor. Then there's Corey and Conner Sotomayor. . . . And the remainder of that row is filled with God-children and dear friends. This is my *immediate* family [emphasis added].

Senator Leahy thanked Judge Sotomayor and went on to say that he "remembered reading in newspaper accounts that the marshals at her swearing-in as a district court judge were surprised because they'd never seen such a large crowd of friends and supporters arrive." Leahy's reply reveals the truisms in Sotomayor's description of her family. Sotomayor incorporates precisely the matter of how Latinos define family, immediate and extended. Her immediate family is not just the nuclear family; it is a multilayered amalgam of blood and nonblood kin that defines her closest family. Moreover, we see reflected in Sotomayor's family the melding of Hispanics and non-Hispanics into one U.S. bicultural Latino family. We see the acculturation to and the adoption of mainstream culture through the marriage with non-Hispanics and the

Anglo names given to their children. This is a bicultural family indeed, and we see it every day in many Hispanic families across the United States.

Culture and Ethnicity

In everyday speech, we often conflate the concepts of culture and ethnicity. The same is true in much of the social and behavioral science literatures; the concepts get blurred. Anthropologists may see the two terms distinctly, but most of us don't see the sharp demarcation. It is understandable that ethnicity and culture lose their separateness since the definition of one inevitably incorporates a mention of the other. *Culture* refers to the beliefs and values that orient a people and that influence their customs, psychological processes, behavioral norms, social practices, and the institutions they create to give coherence and meaning to their lives. *Ethnicity* refers to groups of people who share some characteristics, such as a nationality, language, or culture. In referring to Hispanics or Latinos, I am talking about an ethnic group that shares a common language, namely Spanish, despite dialects and regional differences and colloquialisms. And even among those who identify as Hispanic but don't speak Spanish or speak it well (most often those who are born or raised in the United States), there is a feeling of unity in this large ethnic group.

In Latin America, the people of each country identify with their nationality and local culture. They are Argentine, or Bolivian, or Nicaraguan, or another Latin American nationality. Together, however, they are Latin Americans, holding economic, historical, and political pasts that are similar. Their cultural identity is a national one while their ethnic identity may be as Spanish-speaking Latin Americans. When Latin Americans migrate to the United States, they may retain their identification with a nationality, but the ethnic label by which they are recognized (whether they wish to be so identified or not) is Hispanic or Latino. Issues of race may be less problematic when we are parsing distinctions between culture and ethnicity. Ethnic and cultural groups can include different races. Race refers to the physical features of people, from facial structure to skin color or hair texture (Jones, 1991; Zuckerman, 1990). Most Latin American countries are multiracial societies, where descendants of African slaves, Spanish and other Europeans, Asians, and indigenous people share a common national identity.

In this book, I treat the terms *culture* and *ethnicity* as nearly indistinct. To be sure, though, in writing about Hispanic *culture* as it applies to individuals, I am referring primarily to the concept of *subjective culture* (Betancourt & Lopez, 1993; Triandis et al., 1980). Subjective culture refers to the internalized behavioral norms, social roles, emotions, values, beliefs, and attitudes that are significant to a group of people, starting with the family but elaborated through interactions with other adults and peers. Subjective culture is not just made up of ways of thinking and acting; it also includes emotions. Subjective culture includes the emotions, those deeply held feelings, sometimes in our unconscious, that surge in us when we hear our father's favorite song or touch a family heirloom. Emotional charges may cause us, for instance, to feel nostalgia, like a lump in our throat when we hear an anthem from our culture or country. Subjective culture encompasses scents and aromas that reach deep into our affective memory, the *añoranzas* (nostalgia, longing) for family, home, country, and identity.

Culture can also be objective or material, as seen in the carpentered or human-made world, the cuisine and music of a group, and the costumes and vestments of a culture. Objective culture includes the plays, books, short stories, jokes, pictures, paintings, and art. They are manifest symbols that influence our subjective culture; however, they are not directly part of our subjective culture. Undeniably, objective culture evokes emotions that are attached to the subjective culture we carry in us. For instance, it is not only the pictures or colors in a favorite childhood book that arouse deep emotional memories. Rather, the pictures and colors of the book are also mixed with memories of our parents' voices, their breath, the sense of security and safety, the warm chair or bed we shared as they read aloud to us. Or it may evoke those peaceful times that the book created as we read at home on a rainy, stormy day while our parents and siblings went about the house, creating the sounds and smells of their presence, safety.

The family's unique beliefs and values and those that are shared with their culture shape what parents communicate to children through words and actions, which also transmit messages about roles that older and younger family members play (Harkness & Super, 1996; Keller, Borke, Yovsi, Lohaus, & Jensen, 2005). A poem that our parents read to us from a book moves from objective culture into subjective culture by the memories and affect that accompany these objects. Powerful learning occurs when parents transmit culture in the interactions with children: we learn how to think, judge, reason, act, and even feel by these lessons. What emotions we may express, and where and with what intensity we experience them, are all determined by our cultural learning, our subjective culture (Bornstein et al., 2008; Kirmayer, 2001).

For the girls I write about in this book, ethnicity will refer to their overarching heritage as Latinas, as women of Hispanic descent, who have many cultural similarities despite their distinct origins. Their ethnic identity refers to their perception of "who I am" and "to what group I belong." Katrina, a 16-year-old,

U.S.-born daughter of Dominican parents, expressed her Latina identity in this way:

> Like, I'm proud of myself for being Hispanic. It's a beautiful thing being Hispanic. I feel like it's a perfect life. Not all the way perfect, but halfway perfect. I have everything that I wanted all my life. Like, I wanted to have a beautiful culture, food, dance, music. I have all of that that I wanted all my life since I was a young girl. I have it now.

Enculturation, Acculturation, and Ethnic Identity

Anchoring my discussion of growing up Hispanic in the United States and dissection of the suicide attempts of young Latinas also requires a discussion of *enculturation* and *acculturation*. *Enculturation* is the process that we undergo when we have lived in a place or with a group of people for all or most of our lives. Our learning, language and colloquialisms, cultural outlook, behaviors, beliefs, and all the cognitive, linguistic, and social attributes that are part of being a social group are absorbed in the process of growing up in that culture and in that place (Knight, Jacobson, Gonzales, Roosa, & Saenz, 2009).

To be sure, though, enculturation does not imply that we grow in a static culture, one that is frozen in time. We need to think of it as fluid, changing, often influenced by other cultures and their symbols. In a technological, electronic, and commercial age that has shrunk our globe—where we can fly to distant places within hours, watch television broadcasts of the Grammies, rap videos, and reruns of American sitcoms, eat Kentucky Fried Chicken or Burger King, and wear basketball jerseys to "be like Mike"—enculturation takes on a new meaning. It may be useful to conceive of enculturation as an assimilation of these influences and an accommodation of them to the local environment where we express them using the vernacular, traditions, and rituals of the place.

We are born into our cultures, and until we glimpse at other cultures, we may think very little about our own. In fact, the more we look at and expose ourselves to other cultures, the more we can specify our own and understand it. When we leave a familiar culture and move to another that is more dominant numerically and culturally, we change, we *acculturate*. Often we learn and adopt—sometimes purposefully, sometimes unconsciously—new cultural ways, values, languages, social skills, even cognitive styles. It is not, however, a zero-sum game: as we identify more with the new culture, there is not a corresponding loss of our identification with our original culture. It is much more of a complex and rich emotional and psychological blending of the old and new cultures that yields a sense of identity and of equilibrium (Smokowski & Bacallao, 2011). Most acculturation measures that are used in research rely on measuring the person's language usage (Spanish or English) primarily as the determinant of whether a person is high or low in acculturation to the new culture (Cabassa, 2003). But this approach leaves out the deeply psychological and emotional adaptations that people make in the self-identity that evolves in the acculturation process. Retaining some of the core values, beliefs, and cognitions of our original culture represents not only learned behaviors or brain functions but also emotional ties. To wit, we retain *subjective cultural attachment* to those things important and meaningful to us from our past.

Subjective cultural attachments join with a Latino's acculturative experiences in the United States. It is the rich, diverse cultural origins and how they have been adapted to the American context that come together in forming a Latina's *ethnic identity*. All told, these cultural experiences are melded, especially during adolescence, to form a sense of self as Hispanic (Phinney, 1989; Quintana & Scull, 2009). A rudimentary ethnic self begins in early and middle childhood as a simple matter of self-labeling or self-identification (e.g., "I am Salvadoran"), for this is the extent of young children's cognitive and emotional capacities (Quintana, 1998). Self-labeling evolves in adolescence, maturing into an ethnic identity that is mixed into the normal developmental process of establishing one's bicultural identity, too.

In *The Other Face of America: Chronicles of the Immigrants Shaping our Future*, Jorge Ramos (2002) argues for the strong, ineluctable link between our language and our identity. Ramos recognizes that many Hispanic families consider themselves to be Mexican, Cuban, Puerto Rican, or other Latin American nationality in spite of the fact that they have been living in the United States for many generations. For U.S. Latinos, Ramos writes, speaking Spanish signifies "belonging," and even Latinos with limited Spanish abilities "tend to throw a few Spanish words they learned at home into their conversations to indicate what their roots are to the person with whom they are speaking. Every conversation in Spanish reinforces their sense of identity" (p. xxix).

The connection to the Spanish language is an important part of this, but so too are cultural values and the common experience of being Hispanic in a non-Hispanic nation. Miguel Tinker-Salas (1991) notes that, every day on Spanish-language television, U.S. Hispanics get massive doses of Venezuelan, Mexican, Puerto Rican, and Brazilian soap operas, and musical and talk shows hosted by Chileans, Cubans, and Mexicans. Tinker-Salas concludes that "the dominant trend in this arena is decidedly pan-ethnic and has a definite impact on the formation of identity among recent waves of immigrants" (p. 68). It is partly what Daniel Bell (1975) terms "political ethnicity," that is, a choice—a very strategic one—based on political interests. But it is also a panethnic identity, an umbrella under which the common cultural experiences across Latinos' countries of origin or heritage and their shared experiences of discrimination and social-structural disadvantage huddle together (Sommers, 1991; Valle, 1991). Felix Padilla (1985) provided the term *Latinismo* to refer to the unity that a shared ethnicity offers, an empowering affinity for a minority group to use to move toward common goals. It is not that individual national identities are discarded; not at all. Rather, national identity is maintained while participating in a broader, inclusive identity that has its own symbols.

Think back to what Katrina said above. Her words describe a deep affection, a sense of self that comes from her Dominican background. She sees herself also as a Latina, an overarching ethnic identity that includes common experiences of living and cultural symbols that she shares with many of her peers. Yet, Katrina may not speak much Spanish and may prefer watching MTV over the popular show *Sábado Gigante* on Univisión. She may favor Maya Angelou over Gabriela Mistral, Ernest Hemingway over Gabriel Garcia Marquez. It is clear that on a social level Katrina has acculturated, but her subjective culture is that of a Dominican Latina. She has actually gained, enjoying the benefits of the Dominican cultural background and her inclusion in a pan-Hispanic ethnic identity, as well as her participation in a broader American culture and society. Acculturation may be the process of acquiring elements from the new culture or the one outside our parents' home, but it is more apt to see it as merging into a *bicultural ethnic identity* that holds dear the subjective cultures from being Hispanic and American.

* * *

All cultures in our world are based on the family as the essential social unit. It is a universal phenomenon and provides for the commonality among us. Latin Americans and U.S. Hispanics are no different from others in the regard they hold for the importance of the family. All cultural groups seem to place the family at the center of their societies. Moreover, each culture expresses its family orientation in its own unique way through its child-rearing beliefs and practices, the manner in which parents and extended family relate to one another, and the manner through which together they relate with their children. While marital dynamics are unique, the templates for the relationship between spouses and partners are cast in their cultures, learned from other couples and parents and families. The relationship among siblings and the roles and expectations of female children and male children are both cultural and idiosyncratic. Family routines and rituals are often a blend of culturally based values and beliefs and unique qualities of the family. Cultures dictate how uncles and aunts, cousins and nieces and nephews, and grandparents are to be treated, sometimes revered, and certainly incorporated into our lives. Culture even provides guidelines for how people not related by blood are integrated into families. Therefore, it is not that other cultures do not value the family, but rather, it is the manner in which the significance of the family is expressed and the meanings that family membership encompasses that are distinctly cultural.

How Hispanic cultures and family influence the parents' raising of their daughters and how as adolescents the girls view and experience their lives in the family are the seedbed for their development. The family context and manner in which the Latina is raised set the stage for how she manages the stresses she will inevitably face in life. My focus is trained on those who attempt suicide.

2

A Brief History

The rapid growth and geographic dispersal, size, youthfulness, and high birth rates of the U.S. Hispanic population have been a remarkable and, in most estimates, a beneficial phenomenon for the United States and the entire hemisphere we call the Americas. Immigration has filled manpower shortages, bolstered local and regional economies, and injected new elements to the cultural and social life of the United States. Latinos have continued to ascend the ladder of social mobility, making our nation a shining example of what hard work can yield. The home countries and certainly the countries that Hispanics hold as their source of heritage and pride have benefitted from this growth in the form of remittances and the return of educated, skilled citizens. Even with such stunning and transformative accomplishments, we still have social problems that vex scientists, educators, and clinicians, and truncate the human potential of those most deeply affected by these social ills. The suicidal and self-injurious acts of young Hispanic females are one such problem.

There is a history to be told about the suicide attempts of Hispanic girls. It starts as a mostly anecdotal history that pointed to a high risk of suicide attempts if you were young, Hispanic, and female. It is also a sparse history, one that has seen very little research attention given to this phenomenon. Suicide attempts among Latinas were being seen by communities across scores of years but it was a fact that suffered from scientific and public health neglect for most of those years. In this chapter I trace the history and provide a survey of several decades of findings.

23

Why the Concern?

Those of us working with Hispanic and other minority youth in community health centers, youth development programs, and social service agencies know all too well the many and multifaceted nature of the challenges facing Latino youth and their families. For some, the frequency of suicide attempts that was becoming increasingly more evident raised our sense of alarm. After all, suicidality and other deadly risk behaviors among youth in the age period between 15 and 24 account for the highest rates of death. Suicide, according to the CDC (2006a), is the third leading cause of death among 15- to 24-year olds (exceeded only by deaths from unintentional injuries and homicides, in that order). For non-Hispanic Whites, suicide is the second leading cause of death while it is the third leading cause of death for Hispanics and Blacks. Unintentional injuries and homicide are the number one and two causes of death among Hispanics. The pattern is inverse among young African Americans in this age group: homicide is the primary killer and is followed by unintentional injuries. For American Indians, suicide is the second leading cause of death, preceded by unintentional injuries and followed by homicide (CDC, 2006a).

But mortality data hide the reality that actions that invite death may be, in some cases, artificially separated from suicide. Unintended injuries, for instance, may mask suicidal intent if the injuries were due to acts that seem suicidal (e.g., racing a high-powered motorcycle in heavy traffic or driving while intoxicated). Homicides, though usually construed as death at the hand of another person, can also veil suicidality. Antagonizing gang members from another neighborhood or aiming a weapon at armed police ("suicide by cop") are pretty well known as suicidal in nature. Combine other risk behaviors common in the 15- to 24-year-old age group, such as excessive alcohol use and abuse, drugs, delinquency, and peer-influenced "extreme" tests of physical daring, and we can see how death by suicide may be understated in our statistics.

Returning to suicide attempts, there are between 100 and 200 attempts for every one completed suicide in the 15–24 year age group (Goldsmith, Pellmar, Kleinman, & Bunney, 2002). Further, youth who attempt once are six to eight times more likely to attempt again (Lewisohn et al., 1994; Pfeffer et al., 1993). A previous suicide attempt is also a key predictor of completed suicides (Moscicki, 1999; Shaffer & Craft, 1999). In their lifetime, women attempt suicide two to three times more often than men (Krug, Dahlberg, Zwi, Mercy, & Lozano, 2002). All told, these facts leave many unassailable reasons to be concerned with the suicidal behavior of young Latinas. It is this population that we have to save.

About Suicide

Suicide and attempts by adolescents are not new subjects in the research or popular literature; these have been explored by researchers, clinicians, theologians, educators, sociologists, and anthropologists for centuries. Even in great literary works, adolescent suicide is present: the two most notable being plays by William Shakespeare. In *Romeo and Juliet,* two star-crossed adolescent lovers from families entwined in a long-standing feud marry secretly. Juliet rejects the marriage arranged by her father and fakes a suicide with a potion she got from the friar. Hearing that his Juliet has killed herself, Romeo also takes poison but, in his case, a real and deadly one. When awakened from the bogus suicide, Juliet sees Romeo dead and stabs herself. In *Hamlet,* Shakespeare again touches on suicide through the passionate love of two teenagers. Hamlet is royalty, the son of the king, and is in love with Ophelia, who is warned by her father and brother to stay away from Hamlet since, in the end, he will be expected to marry royalty, and surely her heart will be broken. Ophelia obeys her father but is saddened by Hamlet's presumed "madness" and her brother's departure for college. Through a case of mistaken identity, Hamlet kills Ophelia's father and is sent to England by the king. Bereft of her brother and father, and Hamlet, Ophelia loses her mind and kills herself by drowning. Both stories contain many of the same adolescent elements as our description of Latina teenagers: passionate youth, forbidden romance, family drama.

In some cultures, suicide is seen not as a sin but as a virtue. Suicide in Asian cultures was an honorable means to atone for bringing shame on oneself or on one's family. In the lore of the Mayan people of the Yucatan of Mexico, the goddess of suicide, Ixtab, was pictured as a young woman dangling with rope around her neck. According to Mayan legend, suicide was a means of getting to heaven or paradise. These people would then live in heaven under the shade of the yaxche tree, free from labor and suffering (Cotterell, 1979).[7]

Sociologist Emile Durkheim (1897/2006) identified several types of suicide in his study of Protestants and Catholics at the end of the nineteenth century. *Altruistic* suicides are those in which there is a high level of social integration and the individual's needs are seen as less important than the society's needs. Examples of altruistic suicides are those committed by shamed Japanese government, military, or corporate officials when accused of malfeasance, scandal, or other dishonorable acts. *Anomic* suicides take their name from the sociological term that refers to a sense of alienation and purposelessness that a person or group of people experience. It is often due to a lack of standards, values, or ideals. Anomic suicides, according to Durkheim, come from situations of moral deregulation, where people feel disconnected from one another and the larger collective. Without a clear definition of "who I am" and "what I can be" because of constraints placed by the society, anomic suicides occur. People from groups that are marginalized, of the minority, or disenfranchised from the mainstream society may experience the alienation that accompanies anomie and so may prefer death. *Egoistic* suicides come about as a result of the weakened bonds that integrate persons into the larger collective or society. *Fatalistic* suicides are those more often associated with repressive societies where people prefer to die rather than to continue living in the society in which they have no rights or freedom. Fatalistic suicides result from too much regulation, and anomic suicides from insufficient regulation by the collective.

An example of fatalistic suicide occurred during the late 1980s in Cuba when a group of young rock musicians (*roqueros*) and aficionados deliberately injected themselves with blood tainted with the human immunodeficiency virus (HIV; Norborg & Sand, 1995). It was a fatalistic if chronic suicidal reaction to the repression they felt under Fidel Castro's government. A suicidal act like theirs gave the young Cuban rebels control over their lives. Injecting themselves with HIV-infected blood was the ultimate act of resistance against repression, an act by which they, not the government, dictated the terms of their lives and deaths, their humanity. To the young rockers and their friends, abiding by the government's demands and its continual harassment was to cease being human, to compromise one's ideals, to acquiesce to a spiritual death. The act of self-injection prevented them from succumbing to the power of the state (Prout, 1999).

Terminology on Suicide Ideation, Planning, and Attempts

Most of us can distinguish the differences between thinking about and planning suicide and actually attempting. It is said that almost all of us have thought fleetingly or seriously about what it would be like to kill ourselves. Some of us have even given thought to taking our lives but have recognized the futility of it and the aftermath that is wrought on survivors. Some of us have been frightened by the thought. Suicidal ideation can be terrifying when one is in a period of depression or despondency during emotionally turbulent times. Youths with poor coping skills are more apt to suffer depression and consider suicide when they experience emotionally turbulent times.

Thinking about, planning, and attempting suicide are terms used in mental health practice and research. *Ideation* refers to thoughts about killing oneself. We are not talking about thinking about what it would be like to kill oneself but rather thoughts that one might or one wants to kill oneself. *Planning* refers to going from thought about dying by suicide to preparing mentally, possibly materially for the act, moving from passive to active suicidal ideation. In the same manner as we define ideation, planning is not thinking about how one might takes one's life if the occasion occurred. Rather, we are referring to a plan for eventual execution of taking one's life, seriously planning the act and getting the necessary lethal agents, and determining the place and the time for the suicide. When we ask in a research or a clinical interview about plans, we are concerned with how well developed the plan is and how it evolved.

A *suicide attempt* is an action taken with the intent of killing oneself. Patrick O'Carroll, Alan Berman, Ronald Maris, Eve Moscicki, Bryan Tanney, and Morton Silverman (1996) advanced a definition of a suicide attempt so as to bring more clarity to a nomenclature that is so critical to suicide research. They defined a suicide attempt as any intentional nonfatal self-inflicted injury, no matter how medically lethal, if the person admits that her actions had suicidal intent. This definition relates specifically to a self-inflicted act with the intent to end one's life. More recently some of the same writers, Morton Silverman, Alan Berman, Nels Sanddal, Patrick O'Carroll, and Thomas Joiner, Jr. (2007b), refined the definitions to reflect the growth in knowledge and to sharpen the terminology, again mostly for research purposes. The new definition for *suicide attempt* proposed by Silverman and his group is that of a self-inflicted, potentially injurious behavior with a nonfatal outcome for which there is evidence (either explicit or implicit) of intent to die. This new definition is helpful in recognizing that a suicide attempt may or may not result in injuries to the person (or result in death). If some degree of suicidal intent is detected, then it is labeled as a *Suicide Attempt, Type I* (no injury) or a *Suicide Attempt, Type II* (with injury), regardless of the degree of injury or lethality of method. (*Suicide Attempt, Type III*, is one that results in death). Most Latinas that are seen in clinic can be categorized as Types I and II.

Notice though that the old and new definitions require that the diagnostician or researcher establish that there was suicidal *intent*. Intent is a very slippery thing to prove when the individual recants after first admitting to a Type I or Type II suicide attempt. Silverman et al. ask, "Without the individual self-report, can we infer intent, and, if so, using what criteria?" (2007a, p. 253). The authors note that there must be an intention to die but that it has to be ascertained by the individual who must also cooperate with the clinician or researcher.

Even in their definition of a suicide attempt, Silverman and colleagues add the qualifier "for which there is evidence (either explicit or implicit) of intent to die" (2007b, p. 273). As mental health specialists know from clinical practice and research, many teens deny that they intended to kill themselves, often to assuage their anguished parents or to dissuade clinicians from admitting them into the hospital. This leaves clinicians and researchers with the task of making a judgment about intent, using explicit evidence (e.g., cuts, ingestions) or implicit evidence (e.g., that the behavior was fundamentally a suicidal act) to arrive at their determination. In the clinical judgment that we make about the youthful suicide attempter we must consider how lethal the attempt was. In Type I suicide attempts in which there is no injury, we may have to assess the lethality of the attempt by the nature of the attempt, such as the type, amount, and deadliness of the agent ingested or the circumstances of the attempt (e.g., walking onto a highway of speeding cars; standing on the side of a bridge where the elevation and drop to the bottom would lead to certain death). In Type II suicide attempts in which there is injury, the degree of the injury may trump any other verbal indications by the adolescent that she did not intend to commit suicide. In either case, it is an algorithm that the clinician and researcher must conduct to assess intent.

And it is not an easy call to make. Many of the girls who have been referred to my research projects or clinical practice were classified as suicide attempters as a result of what they had told someone. They may have said, for example, "I wanted to die" or "I wanted to kill myself." Or clinicians made judgments that the girls' behaviors were simply suicidal in nature and intent. We have encountered girls, too, who told clinicians, friends, or teachers that they made a suicide attempt only to have them tell our research interviewer that they had no intention of committing suicide. Yet, when they were assessed by parents and clinicians, it was determined that intent was present in the suicide attempts. Sometimes all we have to go on is clinical judgment, that intent was present even when people are uncooperative or change their stories.

Puerto Ricans and the "Suicidal Fit"

The earliest scientific articles in the English language that I can locate on U.S. Hispanic women's suicide attempts were written by Edgar Trautman (1961a, 1961b). Trautman was a psychoanalytically trained psychiatrist working at Lincoln Hospital, a public hospital that still serves one of the poorest urban communities in our country, the South Bronx. In the 1950s and 1960s, when Trautman practiced psychiatry, the Bronx was home to one of the largest concentrations of Puerto Ricans outside of the Caribbean island. Since before World War II, Puerto Ricans had been migrating to New York City and other great urban centers of the Northeast in search of employment and better futures. The South Bronx was known for its poverty, crowding, and crime.

It became a national symbol of urban poverty and blight in our country when one of its neighborhoods served as the backdrop for President Jimmy Carter's historic visit in October 1977 to highlight both urban decay and urban redemption. Lincoln Hospital, like many such hospitals situated in violent neighborhoods in American cities at the time, was not just the first line of medical and psychiatric care for most immigrants and disadvantaged poor, but it was often the only line of care. Still today, Lincoln Hospital's emergency room, like many ERs in American cities, is often used by the poor and uninsured as a source of primary health care and psychiatric service.

It was at hospitals like the Bronx's Lincoln and Spanish Harlem's Metropolitan Hospital that Puerto Ricans and other newly arriving Hispanics went for their medical and psychiatric care. In the emergency room of Lincoln Hospital and its clinics, Trautman began to notice the frequency and uniformity of suicide attempts by mostly Puerto Rican women (and to a lesser extent, men). This prompted him to conduct a small study of 93 Puerto Ricans (76 women, 17 men) taken from a population of 131 suicide attempters admitted to Lincoln Hospital in a 19-month period between 1957 and 1958. From the data in his two publications, it appears that 70 of the 76 women were between the ages of 15 and 26. He noted that the proportion of suicide attempts among Puerto Ricans in Lincoln Hospital exceeded the proportion of Puerto Ricans in the hospital population. Trautman relied on psychiatric examinations of the patients and interviews with family members when possible to arrive at his conclusions about the suicide attempts. (As we see later, the rate of Latinas studied decades later in another Bronx public hospital continued to exceed their proportions in the local population.)

Trautman had two research questions in mind. He wondered, first, if there was a time-specific relation between the frequency of suicide attempts and the date of immigration. Second, he asked what the psychological difficulties were that gave rise to an atmosphere conducive to suicide and in what way were they connected with factors of the immigration experience. He speculated that the recency of immigration was connected to the "suicidal fit," as he called it, and found that of 80 subjects (64 women), 23% had immigrated within the preceding 2 years. Between the 2nd year and the 10th year, there were fewer than 4% who had attempted. Yet, between the 10th and 15th year, there was a spike to 17%.

Imagine the times: Young Spanish-speaking women in a teeming urban center with its ethnic and racial enclaves, enduring sweltering summers and freezing winters in tenements that had housed thousands of immigrants before them. These were young women from a primarily agrarian island country where the tropical climate made for a fluid connection between outdoors and indoors, where social interaction with others in the same language and the same cultural systems was much more accessible, where social support was but a sidewalk conversation away. Now they found themselves in a vastly different circumstance that was not just a matter of geographical relocation. It was insertion into a different social, cultural, and linguistic system in which they were the outsiders, the minority, the disenfranchised.

As to the characteristics of this so-called "suicidal fit," Trautman reported that in nearly every case, the women had acted under acute and severe emotional excitement and attempted suicide in the same manner in almost identical circumstances. The attempts were sudden, fitlike, and brought on by episodes of overwhelming anger, despair, and anxiety; sometimes they were acute depressive reactions. He also identified two phases in the suicidal fit. The first phase was the impulsive escape from the stressful scene to a place of seclusion and privacy. In the majority of cases, the precipitants were disturbances in intimate interpersonal relationships within the family, either with a spouse or with parents. The second phase was the impulsive act of grabbing whatever poisonous substance was available, whether a household cleanser, poison, or drugs. The commonality among the subjects' description of the suicide attempt was a "severe and painful emotional excitement. While experiencing mounting pain and tension, they were not able or willing to withdraw from the exciting situation. Instead, they had to go on fighting until their excitement reached a climax and they completely lost control over their feelings and actions" (1961a, p. 77). Most subjects had no thought or fear of death and often were not aware of their thoughts. None of the subjects showed psychotic symptoms on psychiatric examination. This similarity in the suicide attempts led Trautman to believe that the suicidal fit was "an instinctive urge to escape from overwhelming pains and find refuge in oblivion" (1961a, p. 78). Trautman detected no longing for death in the women's conscious thoughts or awareness of the deadliness of the actions they had taken. He saw the fuguelike dimming of thought processes and alertness as a hysterical reaction.

The two papers by Trautman remain the best descriptions of the suicide attempts by Puerto Rican women that I have found in the scientific literature. Although we have learned more about suicide attempts by Hispanic females, no report that I have read captures in better terms the characteristics and context of this tragic act. After Trautman's seminal papers, the literature fell silent for nearly two decades.

Researchers Discover Hispanic Girls

Even with Edgar Trautman's extraordinary contribution, over 20 years would pass before psychological and psychiatric researchers began to take notice of the number of Latinas who were attempting suicide. Some discussions of young Latinas attempting suicide were published in the professional literature but these were not research reports. Rather, they were calls to action for more research, reviews of the literature, clinical discussion, and syntheses of the information that was available at the time. Carl Bryant and I (Zayas & Bryant, 1984) published a paper directed to practitioners on understanding and treating Puerto Rican families with adolescent girls, a paper that came out of our common practice experiences in the Bronx and Brooklyn. We illustrated our practice suggestions with cases of suicidal teenage girls. A few years later, I proposed a research agenda that would give direction to our search for more understanding about the suicide attempts of Latinas (Zayas, 1987). In that paper, I pointed to the risk factors: young, Hispanic, and female. Woven into these three risk factors were consideration for immigration processes and acculturation, particularly the discrepancies between the rapidity with which Latino youth acculturate to mainstream U.S. culture and the slower pace of their parents. Language, behavioral, and value preferences that the adolescent girls made were often at odds with those of their parents. Cultural traditions, it seemed to me, also played a key role in the suicide attempt.

It may not be a coincidence that the next to provide important finding about Hispanic adolescents and suicidal behaviors were also a group of researchers in the Bronx, at Montefiore Medical Center, a private hospital, and North Central Bronx Hospital, a public hospital, both affiliated with the Albert Einstein College of Medicine. Their work began to verify the presence of the phenomenon and the elevated risk at which Latinas found themselves. Jill Harkavy Friedman, Gregory Asnis, Marjorie Boeck, and Justine DiFiore (1987) surveyed 382 high school students in the Bronx and found that a large proportion of Hispanic females had attempted suicide. During the same period of time, another group of researchers was examining this phenomenon in the same community. Their findings would not be reported for several years (Razin, O'Dowd, Nathan, & Rodriguez, 1991). Important as the Friedman et al. paper was to me and others, this study was not the only thing published on young Hispanic females' suicide attempts in literature on Hispanics, but they were two important research reports. In a retrospective review of Trautman's study, I continued to urge for more research that would tell us if indeed the phenomenon of suicide attempts was real in epidemiological terms (Zayas, 1989). At the close of the 1980s, there was still very little published that either confirmed our suspicion that Latinas were more apt to attempt suicide than other youth or that told us what the forces were in the lives of Latinas that created the phenomenon. What was needed was stronger epidemiological evidence.

The Phenomenon Is Confirmed

The 1990s represent a watershed moment in the history of what we know about Latina suicide attempts. During this decade, the knowledge on youth suicidal behavior and specifically Hispanic youth suicidal risks grew substantially. From 1991 and into the new millennium, research accumulated that positioned Latina teenagers as having a higher risk for suicidal behaviors than any other U.S. racial, ethnic, or cultural group.

But let's return first to the Bronx, for it was there that research into the suicide attempts of Latinas was ongoing. In 1991, a group led by Andrew Razin (Razin et al., 1991) published a clinical study of 33 adolescent Latinas who had been admitted to North Central Bronx Hospital following a suicide attempt. While the data on these girls would have been collected in the mid-to-late 1980s, it appeared several years later, and I place this report prominently in the beginning of the new decade, for it represents the turning point in the growth of knowledge on Latina suicidality.

Razin and his team found that Latinas admitted for a suicide attempt represented over 25% of all patients hospitalized for suicidal behavior. Latinas constituted the largest group of suicide attempters of any age or ethnic group in the hospital population even though adolescent girls comprised about 1.4% of the community served by North Central Bronx Hospital. Much like Trautman's women, their proportions in the suicidal-patient population exceeded their proportions in the general population. Razin et al. reported that mothers of attempters expressed the desire to receive care from their daughters, which led attempters to perceive their mother as needy for their attention and powerless in a male-oriented family culture. The imbalances in the family systems and the improper balance of cohesion and adaptability were evident to Razin and his fellow researchers.

In the same year that Razin et al.'s paper appeared, the U.S. Centers for Disease Control and Prevention (CDC) released findings of a national survey that confirmed our hunches about Latina suicide attempts. Findings supported what smaller studies were showing: that young Hispanic females were at the highest risk for attempts of any ethnic, racial, or cultural youth group (except perhaps for American-Indian youth). It was the survey that I was waiting for.

The CDC launched its Youth Risk Behavior Surveillance System in 1990. It is one of the best, most comprehensive surveys of the risk behaviors in which U.S. high school students engage. The CDC developed the surveillance system in response to calls from local and state agencies for more consistent empirical data that would help them coordinate health education programs at the state and local levels (CDC, 2004). The results of the Youth Risk Behavior Surveillance System would also be useful for measuring the progress that our nation was making toward achieving public health goals set in documents such as *Healthy People 2010* and beyond (U.S. Department of Health and Human Services, 2005). The *Healthy People* series is an effort by the government, academia, and the private sector to set health objectives for the U.S. It provides the basis for the development of state and community plans to improve our nation's health. Instead of looking at a single health risk behavior like cigarette smoking or drug and alcohol use, which other nationally administered surveys had done and were administered on only one or just a few occasions, the Youth Risk Behavior Surveillance System was structured so that it would be administered biennially to assess six health-risk categories: (1) behaviors that contribute to unintentional injuries and violence; (2) tobacco use; (3) alcohol and other drug use; (4) sexual behaviors that contribute to unintended pregnancies and STDs, including HIV infection; (5) unhealthy dietary behaviors; and (6) physical inactivity.

The surveillance system tracks all six areas using a questionnaire referred to as the Youth Risk Behavior Survey (YRBS). The YRBS is the questionnaire that has been administered every odd-numbered year since 1991, and results are published about a year later, in even numbered years. The YRBS is structured so that it captures a nationally representative sample of public and private high schools during the school day. It is a very reliable measure because the reported results of surveys administered 2 weeks apart were not statistically different from one another (Brener et al., 1995, 2002). To strengthen the value of the YRBS, the CDC checked on potential threats to the validity of its survey when collecting self-reported data on risk behaviors from adolescents. CDC found that neither situational nor cognitive factors that may affect the youths' responses had any real effect on the YRBS' validity (Brener, Billy, & Grady, 2003).

I focus on suicide-related risk data in using the results of the YRBS. There are five depression- and suicide-related questions in the section on violence and injury toward self and others (CDC, 2009). The YRBS first reaches for common indications of depression and hopelessness by asking whether the youth felt "so sad or hopeless almost every day for two weeks or more in a row that you stopped doing some usual activities?" This is followed by two yes-or-no questions: "During the past 12 months, did you ever seriously consider attempting suicide? During the past 12 months, did you make a plan about how you would attempt suicide?" The suicide attempt question that follows the ideation and planning questions is designed slightly differently, which calls for a range of attempts: "During the past 12 months, how many times did you actually attempt suicide?" It is followed by five choices ranging from no attempts to six or more. The CDC takes the responses to the last question and dichotomizes them into having made an attempt or not; basically, responding in yes-or-no fashion. Finally, the YRBS asks if any of the attempts in the preceding 12 months resulted in an injury, poisoning, or overdose that had to be treated by a doctor or nurse. The respondent can say she did not attempt or select a yes or a no response to receiving medical attention if she reports having attempted.

Epidemiology of Latina Suicide Attempts

From 1991 to the present, the trend in suicidality among America's high school students has shown a general decline in all reported ideation, planning, and attempts, although there are occasional spikes. As the CDC data show, teenage boys plan and attempt suicide much less often than teenage girls, although boys die at rates higher than girls. This is seen across time in ideation, planning, and attempting suicide, as reported on the YRBS. (In citing the CDC's reports, I used the terms Black, Hispanic, and White in this section in accordance with the racial and ethnic designations that appear in the YRBS data sources.)

Considering or Ideating Suicide

The gender differences between 1991 and 2007 ran very consistently with non-Hispanic White males recording the highest rates of responses to questions about considering suicide (ranging from 12% in 2003 to 21.7% in 1991). In general order, Whites were highest (except in 1997 when Hispanic males surged to 17.1% compared with the White males' 14.4%). Hispanic males followed in most years, and Black males were usually in third place except for a few years when they were nearly matched with Latinos.

In the same years, girls ideated more than boys. Figure 2.1 shows the trends in suicidal ideation by Black, White, and Hispanic high school girls. In the first year of the YRBSS, Hispanic females showed a rate of 34.6% while non-Hispanic White teenage girls reported a rate of 38.6%, the only year in over a decade when this occurred. Black females in high school in 1991 stood at 29.4% of ideators. In subsequent years, Hispanic girls reported continually higher rates of suicidal ideation followed by White and Black females, respectively. The trend was consistent through 2007.

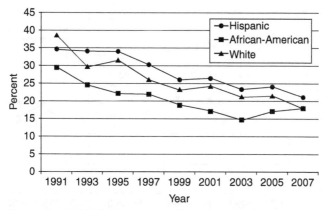

FIGURE 2.1.   Rates of suicidal ideation reported by Hispanic, African-American, and White teenage females. Source: U.S. Centers for Disease Control and Prevention.

Planning Suicide

Boys also planned suicide much less often than teenage girls during the same period of years. Hispanic males in the early years of the YRBS (1991, 1993, and 1995) generally lagged behind White males in planning suicides but ahead of Black males. Then in 1997 Hispanic males reported suicide plans more often than Black or White teenage males, exceeding their counterparts through 2007 (except in 2001 when more White males reported planning suicides).

Hispanic girls, on the other hand, planned suicides more often in all but one year—1991—and were nearly equal with White girls in 2001 (17.8% to 18%, respectively). Figure 2.2 shows that with respect to planning an attempt during the previous year, Hispanic females had a peak of 26.6% in 1993 and a low of 15.2% in 2007. In those same years, White females reported 22.8% and 12.8%, respectively, while Black females reported suicide plans at rates of 19.5% and 12%, respectively.

Attempting Suicide

Among male students from 1991 to 2007, an interesting trend emerged. Hispanic males had higher attempt rates in 5 of the 9 survey years between 1991 and 2007. Black males led in the four remaining years. In the years that Hispanic males attempted suicide more often than other males, their rates exceeded those of Black or White males from less than one percentage point up to about three percentage points.

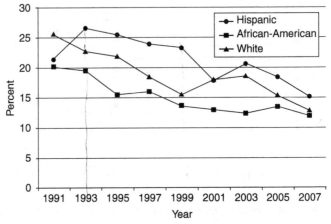

FIGURE 2.2. Rates of Hispanic, African-American, and White teenage females who planned a suicide attempt. Source: U.S. Centers for Disease Control and Prevention.

Finally, validating our concerns that Latinas attempted suicide more often than any other group of teenagers, the YRBS results showed that the rates from 1991 to 2007 were steadily higher among Hispanic female high school students than for Black or White females. The highest rate of suicide attempts among Hispanic girls was in 1995 when 21%—that's 1 in 5 girls—attempted. The lowest rate was reported in 1991 when it was 11.6% for Hispanic girls. In nearly all years, White females had the second highest rate of attempts (except

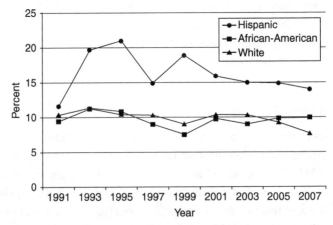

FIGURE 2.3. Rates of suicide attempts of Hispanic, African-American, and White teenage females. Source: U.S. Centers for Disease Control and Prevention.

when they were nearly tied with Black females in 1993, 1995, and 2005). As you can see in Figure 2.3, the differences ranged from 1.5 times the rate to twice the rate of Latina suicide attempts as non-Hispanic White and African-American girls.

Another survey that provided additional understanding was the National Household Survey on Drug Use (Substance Abuse and Mental Health Services Administration, 2003). This survey uncovered two additional facts about Latinas who attempted suicide. First, it showed that the odds were higher that a Latina would attempt suicide if she lived in a small metropolitan area than if she lived in a large one or in a rural or small town setting. Another revelation was that Latinas who attempted were more likely to be born in the United States than in a Latin American country.

Recently, Carolyn Garcia and her colleagues (2008) at the University of Minnesota School of Nursing published interesting findings about Latino youth suicidality that support our hunches and empirical findings. Garcia and colleagues conducted specific analyses of the 2004 Minnesota Student Survey using the data on 3,178 Latino 9th and 12th grade youths in Minnesota high schools. Although these investigators examined students who reported being either Latino (i.e., both parents of Hispanic origin) or "Latino-mixed" (i.e., one parent Hispanic origin and the other parent of a different race or ethnicity), I refer to the overall findings about Latino youth. Much of their analyses supported national survey data on Latino youth but added some interesting correlations among suicidal ideation and attempts, emotional distress, family connectedness, and parental support and caring.

In keeping with past findings, all Latino youths in the Minnesota survey reported much higher levels of communication with their mothers than with their fathers. Most Latino youths studied by Garcia and her colleagues knew that their parents cared about them "quite a bit" or "very much." As young adolescents feel a need for more independence, they often have more conflict with and a sense of alienation from parents. It is not surprising that only 68% of boys and 60% of girls in 9th grade felt that their families were closely connected. Twelfth grade Latinas and Latinos, however, reported higher pro-portions of feeling closely connected to their parents. Parents and families may have changed in response to their adolescents' needs between 9th and 12th grade, but it is certain that there was a maturation as the young teen became an older adolescent. About 34% of 9th grade girls and 18% of 12th grade Latinas reported suicidal ideation in the preceding year. And these two groups reported suicide attempts at the rate of 16% for 9th grade Latinas and about 7% for 12th grade Latinas. As often happens, adolescent suicide attempts are more evident among younger teenage girls compared with older teenage girls.

Father and mother absence—whether emotional or physical—influences the suicidal behavior of Latino and other youth. In the Garcia et al. study, suicidal ideation was more commonly reported by teens who said their parents weren't around and available to talk. Many of these same kids were significantly more likely to report a suicide attempt in the past year. Those youths who did not feel they could talk to their parents were at higher risk of suicide attempts than those who felt they could talk with their parents.

When Garcia et al. explored the odds of youth feeling emotional distress, having suicidal thoughts, or actually making attempts based on certain family factors, their results again supported past research and anyone's intuition about problems of youth. Overall, the odds of having elevated levels of emotional distress were greater for those who felt unable to talk to either parent because the parent was absent or the teen felt she couldn't talk to them. Similar odds were seen among those students who felt less parental caring and those who reported lower family connectivity. When adolescents perceived low levels of parental caring, their odds for suicidal ideation rose to between 2.5 to 5 times higher than those who saw their parents as having high levels of caring. The range of odds for suicide attempts was from 3.5 to 10 times higher for those who reported lower levels of parental care than those Latino youths who felt high levels of parenting care.

A Pan-Hispanic Phenomenon

What the YRBS verified was that suicide attempts by Latinas were not just a New York City phenomenon but rather a national one, not confined to Puerto Rican and Dominican girls in New York City, but extended to many others. The fact now became clearer that suicidal behaviors were a social problem for Hispanic youth in general. The diversity of the U.S. Hispanic population was reflected in the samples used in other studies. The sample in Razin et al.'s (1991) study was 91% Puerto Rican and 9% Dominican, reflecting the Bronx population in the late 1980s. Dominican immigration to New York City was growing, much of it to the Upper West Side of Manhattan, the area known as Washington Heights, but also to other New York City boroughs. Nationally, researchers were including increased numbers of adolescent female attempters of Cuban, Dominican, Mexican, Nicaraguan, and other Hispanic ancestry (Canino & Roberts, 2001; Roberts & Chen, 1995; Vega et al., 1993). A story in the *Miami Herald* in December of 1995, citing data from the Miami-Dade school system, reported that only 22% of public school students were Hispanic girls, mostly Cuban and an increasing number of Nicaraguans. However, Hispanic

girls made up 35% of the distric
(Robles, 1995). In California, Bernar
American adolescents who had bee
suicide attempts, 66% were female.
Wissow, Elizabeth Woods, and Elizabeth
3,365 urban teens, being a Hispanic fem
attempts. Tortolero and Roberts (2001) fo
Las Cruces, New Mexico, and Houston, T
teens to have suicidal ideation.

In published reports that did not break dc
ality or heritage, I discerned that the samples
Take, for example, the report by Lynn Rew, Na   Horner,
Michael Resnick, and Trisha Beuhring (2001), wi   0,806 7th, 9th, and
11th grade students in Connecticut. These researchers found that more Latinas
attempted suicide (19.3%) than non-Hispanic girls in the preceding 12 months.
And by looking at statistical data of the Connecticut Hispanic population at the
time, we can comfortably assume that the sample included Puerto Ricans,
Dominicans, Peruvians, Ecuadorans, and Mexicans, followed by smaller proportions of Hispanics of other national origins. In sum, adolescent suicide
attempts were seen in all Hispanic groups.

* * *

U.S. Hispanic youth do not die often by suicide, despite the higher than average rates of ideation, plans, and attempts (Canino & Roberts, 2001). Knowing
that Latinas don't die disproportionately by their own hands provides some
solace to us. However, it does not diminish the fact that our young Latina sisters are in such anguish that they see attempting suicide as a solution to their
pain and suffering To better understand the suicidal acts of the young Latina,
we have to know what the contexts are in which they develop and what most
Hispanic women say about their experiences growing up.

3

Contexts of Development

The history on Latina suicide attempts told us that the phenomenon exists, and then irrefutable evidence proved it. What this history does not answer is the question "Why?" What brings on the suicide attempts among some Latinas and not others when they have nearly identical social profiles? Why is it that they so often act to harm themselves? What meanings do the suicidal acts hold for young Latinas? In short, how can the suicide attempt phenomenon of teenage Hispanic females be explained and understood? Answering these questions requires that we understand the context of human development.

Growth and Development

To understand the person is to know that she is inseparable from the environments into which she is born, grows, develops, and thrives. One way to view the person in environment is to use developmental systems theory (Ford & Lerner, 1992; Sameroff, 1983). At its core, developmental systems theory is about reciprocal interactions between the person and her environment. The basic process of development is entirely a relational one. That is, the relationship between the person and her "ecological niche," the place she occupies in her milieu, is constantly changing (Lerner, 2002). A developmental systems approach does not side solely with biology or nature or depend on the environment or nurture alone. Instead, it recognizes that the individual is a biological, psychological and social organism, one with a particular genetic make-up, who matures physically following a natural and for the most part orderly progression, our common ontogeny.[8] Developmental systems theory observes that the person's growth and maturation occur within social, cultural, physical and architectural, economic, political, and historical structures that are themselves changing. In short, individuals are changing within environments that are always in flux.

Recognizing this reciprocal process is important. Parents do not simply raise their children following a set of values, beliefs, and practices. In actuality, parents raise their children in reaction to the child's characteristics, including gender, birth order, temperament, or some other feature. Children's temperament is a good example to use to illustrate the reciprocal process that occurs in parent–child interaction. Temperament has two dimensions that affect how parents interact with the child. One dimension is the child's dispositional reactivity, the negative emotionality that might be described as irritability and negative mood. If we add to this the level of intensity of the negative reactivity, we can see how some kids are more prone to distress and frustration than others (Rothbart & Bates, 2006; Sanson, Hemphill, & Smart, 2004). The other dimension of temperament is the self-regulation that modulates emotional reactivity. The degree to which the child can control her temperamental reactivity affects her interaction with parents and others. When the child exerts effortful control, for example, she is trying to voluntarily maintain or shift attention, or to hold back or set in motion certain behaviors. These children and adolescents tend to be less demanding of parents and are often well adjusted (Spinrad et al., 2007). But children, especially during the toddler stage, who have higher than average levels of negative emotionality and who are less able to self-regulate, are challenging for parents, particularly in the case of families with economic hardships, crowded living conditions, or mentally ill parents (Calkins, Hungerford, & Dedmon, 2004; Popp, Spinrad, & Smith, 2008). An infant or toddler—or teenager—with high negative or positive emotionality may cause parents to react to her in a distinctive way in an attempt to manage her temperament and behavior. This process of action and reaction forms a feedback loop in which the child reacts to the parents handling of her, which is in reaction to her temperament. In this sense, the child is influencing the parents probably as much as parents are influencing her. And the pattern will likely continue as the child grows into adolescence, requiring parents to adapt how they interact with their developing teenager.

At the broadest level of thinking about the suicidal actions of adolescent Latinas, we have to consider the overarching environment in which the girls have developed and function. As such, we can look at Hispanic teens, regardless of generation or level of acculturation, as sharing a common social ecology, an environment made up of people and institutions. Urie Bronfenbrenner (1979) proposed that human development is influenced by four levels in a nested environmental system, what he termed the *social ecology of human development*. The first and closest level is the *microsystem*, the one in which the person participates directly and learns and grows. The microsystem encompasses intimate family interactions, adolescent development, cultural values instruction, and the socialization process that parents and other adults undertake with their children. In examining the lives of young Latinas, I focus sharply on the microsystem of the girls, and parents, siblings, and extended family. Other influential microsystems interact with the girl's development but the family is primary.

The basic socialization of the child, in which culture and core skills of coping and living are acquired, starts in the family microsystem. The noted Russian psychologist Lev Vygotsky (1978) proposed that intimate family interactions occur within what he termed a *zone of proximal development*. In this zone, which is found within the microsystem, there are interactions between the growing person and adults and peers that might be thought of as granular, in that within the zone the finely grained, day-to-day interactions occur, and minute-by-minute teaching and learning about emotions, gestures, and other of behaviors are transmitted. It is in this zone that the most basic aspects of culture—what we believe, how we must behave, what we value—are transmitted from adults to children. This teaching and learning happens through experiences and exercises that are themselves prescribed by traditions and technologies (e.g., games, pencils, musical instruments, tools, utensils). While Vygotsky viewed cultural transmission as operating also at societal and institutional levels, such as schools, government, and museums, he took the position that culture is more directly and powerfully inculcated in the deep interactions of specific persons: parents and siblings, extended family, and immediate peers. Immersion in the microsystems that makes up her life's milieu—whether the family or other microsystems such as the classroom—provides the experiences that create a sense of subjective culture.

As the child grows, the adults around her constantly raise the bar of performance, posing new challenges so that the child stretches on "tippy toes" that are mastery-enhancing- and self-efficacy-inducing moments that stay with the child. With each developmental step, the adults expect a little more but must also, in the process, adapt flexibly to the growing child. The child grows progressively in trust, industry, competence, confidence, and identity (Erikson, 1950).

The second level of systems theory, the *mesosystem*, is comprised of the microsystems that the adolescent Latina is directly involved in at any point in her life. It is made up of clusters of microsystems in which the developing person participates directly. Besides her family, there are many other microsystems, say, church, the *colmado* (grocery store) where she works and meets other youths, the community youth center or Girl Scout troop, the after-school tutoring program, and her best friend's family. In the microsystems, she learns and displays her culture. These microsystems impact the developing girl and are themselves affected by her.

At home parents can wield more control over what happens to the young girl. But in these other microsystems, she has to handle situations in which she has much less control. These other settings don't have the same concern for her security that parents can provide at home. Kids at school or at the corner *taquería* may tease her or treat her in unkind ways with very little concern for her emotional reactions. The girl then must learn to interact in this world, unprotected by a loving family. In the process she learns and develops coping abilities, how to "take it and dish it out." A subcultural process is going on, and the girl adapts to and learns from it. As her world of microsystems expand the mesosystem, she faces new challenges.

The two other levels of development impinge on the person, but she is neither a part of them nor able to affect them. *Exosystems* are those settings in which other members of the family are involved, not the girl. What occurs to other family members in these settings can have an impact on the girl. A bad day at work for a parent, or unexpected bills that strain the family budget, can cause a stressed parent to react to the child at home in a gruff or insensitive manner (Lerner, 2002). *Macrosystems* are massive, large-scale, natural, social, political, economic, and historical influences (e.g., September 11th attack on New York's World Trade Center and the U.S. Pentagon; Hurricane Katrina in New Orleans; global economic recessions and vast unemployment) that affect the world we all inhabit and that we cannot control. My focus is on the microsystems and mesosystems that are part of the young Latina's ecological niche. In these contexts, the conditions for a suicide attempt are formed. All it takes is a spark to trigger the incident.

Adolescent Development and Parenting

Of life's developmental epochs, the one that has received more attention than almost any other, except for infancy perhaps, is the period between 11 and 20, the adolescent years. Part of the reason for this interest is that it is a period in human development that is exceedingly challenging for the person and those around the person. Early adolescence is a time of awakening for the individual, when physical changes are apparent, a person who now looks more like an adult than a child but still a child nonetheless (Steinberg, 2007). Psychologically, the teenage years are accompanied by displays of independent behaviors, from the cognitive advancements that are used in the service of questioning parents' requests, assumptions, values, and behaviors (often frustrating the parent) to novel ways of looking at the world and solving problems. Behaviorally, independence is seen as an increased orientation to the peer group and away from the family, to doing things their own way instead of the way parents have always insisted on. Romantic relationships are examples of autonomy that often strain the young Latina's interactions with her family. In fact, it is often in conflicts with and about a boyfriend, dating, and sexuality that suicide attempts occur.

The teen's increasing need for and movement toward independence places tremendous stress on parents, causing changes in parents, adolescent, their relationships, and the family as a whole. Not surprisingly, heightened levels of conflict are seen in the parent–child interaction. Conflicts tend to be more frequent and rancorous, especially in early adolescence. There is a progressive renegotiation of their relationship—and parents have to be available to negotiate (and give a little). Laurence Steinberg (1990) is correct in his appraisal that the ones who come away most stressed by the trials posed by young adolescents are their parents, less so the adolescent. It is parents who seem to be most bothered by their adolescent child's challenges, arguments, and spats.

Much of the theory on adolescence that was written in the 20th century tendered that independence or autonomy, sometimes referred in the psychoanalytic literature as the second separation–individuation phase of human development (after the first such phase in infancy), was the single most important achievement in adolescence (Blos, 1967). The increasing need for autonomy is a signal aspect of adolescence. But left in the shadows in this theoretical emphasis is the critical role of human bonding and attachment: the need for maintaining *connection* or *relatedness* to loved ones. After all, we all need the embrace of people who love us and care for us, people we want to stay close to. They give us strength, solace, and identity, succor, and refuge.

With family as the source of her identity, an anchor for her emotions, a secure haven, and a source of guidance, mentoring, and advice, it is natural for the Latina to be pulled to it. Family is, in spite of everything, the place in which one can test oneself and one's skills, including one's bids for independence. While wanting to move away, the young Latina also wants the structures that parents and families provide when novel challenges are encountered for which there is no or little experience (i.e., "How do I handle this?"). The teenager may or may not admit to the need for guidance. For in acknowledging that she still needs her family, there rests the fear of losing what little and fragile autonomy she has achieved.

Autonomy is contextual, and it is the teenager's relatedness to the family milieu that is so important. The context, however, must also be flexible and adapt to the girl's search for autonomy; it must grow with her. Parents must be willing to let go of petty injunctions while clutching jealously to the values that are important to the family. Jacqueline Eccles and her colleagues (1991) note that as the daughter matures into adolescence she will be positively motivated if her "environments change as rapidly as [she does]" (p. 55). Changing the environments too rapidly for the sake of the adolescent can be problematic. It underscores the need for parents and adults to have thoughtful conversations with the youths and make judicious decisions about how flexible they can be. In other words, parents need to respond to their daughters' needs for change but do so with the caution that comes from being more experienced in the world.

No matter the strain posed by the adolescent's efforts to become more autonomous, it is important to sustain the connection, not just to the teenager, but also her parents. Parents' willingness to allow the adolescent her autonomy while holding to their beliefs about what is valued and safe is a difficult balance. Remaining engaged with the teenager and maintaining the connection she needs should be the overriding principle. We see this in nonattempters whose parents show some flexibility but never give in entirely or as rapidly as the above quote from Eccles et al. would imply. Among the nonsuicidal girls in our research, well-functioning Latino families allow their daughters to express ideas that are different from theirs and to have friends outside the home, and they permit a modicum of privacy. Despite holding to traditional sex roles, families also showed flexible parent–parent, parent–daughter, and family interactions. When parents engage in this kind of supportive interaction with their teens and use appropriate behavioral control through firm and consistent discipline, they create buffers for the conduct problems, withdrawal, and depression that so often follow (Barber, Olsen, & Shagle, 1994). Supportive parenting bolsters adolescents' psychological well-being, their self-confidence, and their general social and academic competence (Gray & Steinberg, 1999). However, when psychological control is exercised by parents that involves inducing guilt or withdrawing affection, the effects can be very negative, fueling depression, anxiety, and low self-efficacy. Balanced parenting can be very effective.

No doubt, effective guidance by parents should respond to the heightened demands for autonomy for which the adolescent fights (Granic & Dishion, 2003). There is research to show that when parents remain engaged, even in the most stressful of times, they help their adolescents to mature. Conflict is, of course, a way of staying involved with one another: When we disagree—no matter how vehemently—we are engaged, connected to one another and showing that we care. When we are indifferent to one another or capitulate to the other's argument and acquiesce, we disconnect. This abdication of responsibility can say to the teen, "I don't care." This is driven home by the research of Colleen Dillon, Joan Liem, and Susan Gore (2003). They found that those adolescents who dropped out of high school but whose parents resisted them were much more likely to return to school, or get back "on track." Adolescents whose parents were less opposed (i.e., parents who conceded or were too permissive) either don't get back on track or return much later. In effect, locking horns in this kind of conflict is an expression of love and an unwillingness to surrender. Dillon, Liem, and Gore (2003) write that

> During high school, the parent–child connection is often described in the narratives of future on-track dropouts as conflictual as they resist the efforts of their parents to remain connected and be involved in their education and future plans. These observations are consistent with findings that conflict may not be a major problem when it occurs in the context of a strong parent–child bond; in fact, within that context it may help facilitate agency and increase autonomous functioning. It may not be unequivocally warm, but the connection to parents, including its conflictual elements, is critically linked to school- and work-related help and to the adolescent's efforts to get back on track. (p. 438)

As I found over the years of studying Hispanic families, those parents who were affectionately engaged with their daughters in times of conflict and during the push and pull of adolescence and did so with support and understanding, without name calling or derision, were much less likely to have a daughter's suicide attempt. It is not that families did not have conflict. It is that conflict in these families—from loud shouting arguments to minor spats—kept members engaged, even when they lost their "cool" and said or did things they later regretted and for which they later apologized.

Hispanic Parents Raising Adolescent Girls

Later in this book, I profile young Latinas who attempted suicide and describe their families. Most of the suicide attempters are girls whose development deviated from what we consider normal, that is, without suicide attempts or other major behavioral or psychological disorders (but with the "average" challenges of being a Latina teenager). In this chapter, I have discussed theoretical and empirical knowledge on normal adolescent development and the parenting that needs to accompany it to help us understand what it is that suicidal Latinas are deviating from. Now I turn two Hispanic families taken from those of girls in our study whose parents were using effective, growth-enhancing practices for raising their daughters. These aren't parents who discovered good parenting during their child's adolescence; in all probability they had been using good parenting techniques from the earliest years. The two families illustrate how they are raising their daughters in ways that helps the girls adjust to the vicissitudes of adolescence. (In the next chapter, we will hear more about normal childrearing and development from groups of Hispanic women and girls.)

Esmeralda: "You have to start when they are little"
BY CAROLINA HAUSMANN-STABILE

Esmeralda, a vivacious 17-year-old who entered our research project as a nonsuicidal participant, is the eldest daughter of Colombian immigrants. The household consists of her parents, Esmeralda, and a 12-year-old brother. Their parents work hard to provide for the family, father as a handyman and mother as an office clerk. A few weeks prior to her research interview, and against her mother wishes, Esmeralda got a small tattoo that ignited a difficult period for this close-knit family. When her parents learned of the tattoo, they became very upset. Her mother, with whom she had a strong, positive relationship, expressed her disappointment and withdrew her companionship for a period of time.

During ten painful days, Esmeralda endured the loneliness resulting from her acting against her parents' authority. Finally, her parents organized a family day trip in order to begin the process of healing, a truce of sorts. Esmeralda joined the family, and while in their car, they discussed the conflict, shared their points of view, and sorted things out. Esmeralda said that after that fateful car trip, "We fixed everything by talking and now we are better." Her parents also moved forward, understanding that with Esmeralda soon to be eighteen, their say in her decisions was becoming increasingly limited. In almost parallel manner, Esmeralda understands that even though she is about to become an adult, she still needs to openly negotiate her choices if she is to expect her parents' support.

From this episode, we learned that Esmeralda's family exchanges are fluid, allowing for the expression of conflict and agreement, arguments and dialogue, jokes and criticism. What strikes us the most about Esmeralda's family is that, in their interactions, the members' roles are stable and, at the same time, open to change during times of transition. For example, when Esmeralda was fourteen and started dating a boy whom both of her parents disliked, her mother convinced her father that it was in their daughter's best interest to have the boy visiting the house regularly. By offering a welcoming environment to the young couple, the parents could keep an eye on Esmeralda, did not appear to be going against her choices, and maintained the family's unity by avoiding the conflicts that would logically arise if the girl were prohibited from seeing the boy. Her mother said,

> *Yo le decía algún día se irá a dar cuenta que no le conviene.*" ["I would tell her that one day she will realize that he was not good for her."]

Her parents embraced an optimistic parenting philosophy and trusted that, with time, Esmeralda would be able to make the right decision. But it was not a decision or a strategy taken at that moment. Rather, Esmeralda's parents had set the conditions, the context in which their actions would influence their daughter by having been consistent and unified since she was very young. The mother's parenting motto, "*hay que empezar desde pequeñitos*" ["you must start when they are small"] highlights her understanding that raising a daughter is a long-term commitment.

Esmeralda and her mother discussed the significant place that support and mentoring occupy in the family interactions. More important, both agreed that support is expressed through actions, in the form of rituals. Her mother provides a clear example of her mentoring style when describing how she helped Esmeralda to address a problem at school:

> *Ella me dijo que tenía problemas con la clase de educación física. Yo le dije que fuera y hablara con su profesor, yo contacte al profesor también, me dijo cual era el problema. Entonces yo hablé con ella y ella me dijo que iba a hablar con su profesor. Yo me puse en contacto con el profesor para asegurarme que todo estaba bien.* [She told me that she had problems in the physical education class. I told her to go and talk to her teacher; I also contacted the teacher, who described the problem to me. I then spoke with Esmeralda, and she reassured me that she would speak with the teacher. I got in touch with the teacher to make sure that everything had been sorted.]

Esmeralda's parents show a practical approach in their mentoring and are realistic in assessing their children's progress: they want evidence. As Esmeralda said with a chuckle, "My parents ask: 'How is school? Let me see your report card.'"

Her mother's contrasting reactions to the tattoo and to the boyfriend speak of her understanding of her daughter's developmental needs and tempo. The risks posed by a "bad boy" are far more serious to a 14-year-old girl than those of a small tattoo to a 17-year-old adolescent.

Her mother's mentorship is gender appropriate and framed within enjoyable activities, which provides an opportunity for further bonding. Her mother says, *"Nosotras salimos mucho de compras. Yo le enseño a ella que no siempre se compra en el primer sitio"* ["We go shopping a lot together. I teach her that you do not always buy in the first place"].

Support is not something that appears briefly during times of crisis but is an integral part of their family definition. The richness and flexibility of their interactions speak of a healthy family, one in which roles are clear, and there is always room for mentoring and fun. Esmeralda confirms it when she says, "the whole family is here and everybody has fun." Their emotional closeness is paired with physical proximity. Mother says, *"Yo soy muy besadora ... la beso y le cojo sus manitas"* ["I am very much a 'kisser.' . . . I kiss her and hold her hands"]. When it comes to the girl's physical changes, the mother reports that *"yo he sido siempre muy pendiente de esas cosas"* ["I have always been very watchful of those things"]. This closeness has helped Esmeralda to be attuned with her parent's nonverbal clues. When she describes her dad, she says "he is very serious when he is mad, and he talks in a deeper voice when he is mad." This attunement is important in building the reciprocity or sense of mutuality between mother and daughter. Esmeralda is aware that her parents read into her communication style. Explaining why it is difficult to lie to her mother, she said, "Like she already knows my voice and everything."

The challenges posed by an adolescent's increasing autonomy can be anticipated, and even moderated, by a parenting style that emphasizes stability and clear roles since early childhood. As an example, Esmeralda understands now when and why her parents are upset, and what consequences will follow their disappointment. Mother and daughter agree in that rules and consequences are clear in their family. As mother says *"Si yo le doy un castigo, yo me mantengo en el"* ["If I punish her, I stick to it"]. Esmeralda puts it slightly differently, "[My mother] is stubborn, so she will stick to it."

In tune with their Hispanic background, the family model is adult centered, with the children given less room for negotiation. Esmeralda shares that "my mom taught me that when she calls me I have to say: *'Si señora,* like OK, how may I help you?" Without the cultural lenses that give meaning to this interaction, we might easily confuse it with authoritarianism. However, the mother explains that, in her family, the adults' hold of authority is a natural expression of their commitment to raise Esmeralda: *"La hemos criado con muchos sacrificios, le hemos enseñado muy buenos valores"* ["We have raised her through many sacrifices, we have taught her very good values"]. As in a traditional Latino family, father's authority is central. Esmeralda describes her father's demeanor as "'I am the dad. You have to respect me.'" Even when mother thinks that she is the strict one in the household, Esmeralda believes that her father is the tough one. Whatever the case, both parents are described by the adolescent as a source of authority, and the mother does not challenge the father's role, *"Yo le dije, si tu estas de acuerdo, yo no tengo problemas"* ["I told him, if you are in agreement, I have no problems"].

While the mother disagrees with the level of freedom that children are given in the United States, she allows Esmeralda an increasing level of autonomy commensurate with her developmental progress. The expectations for the future that Esmeralda and her mother hold resemble those of an acculturated Hispanic family. They view marriage and motherhood as developmental steps that can be put on hold until some life and professional experiences have been attained.

Esmeralda is aware that her parent's expectations are different from those of her friends' parents. She mentions that her friends and peers do not show respect to their parents or do not explain things to their parents. Esmeralda sees her relationship with her parents differently, more positively:

> I always give explanations [to my parents] because of how I was raised. To me that is being polite. I owe this to the love and respect we feel for each other. My parents always tell me that they are gonna love me, no matter what.

Ramona: A Family Anticipating Adolescence
BY LAUREN E. GULBAS

Eleven-year-old Ramona lives in a bustling household that includes her parents, eight-year-old sister, and four uncles. Within this large family unit, Ramona feels happy and content, confident she will always find support. Ramona's parents emigrated from Mexico before she was born. Ramona describes her happiest moments as those when she is spending time with her family at Mexican fiestas, baby showers, and birthday parties. Ramona's parents draw on their strong cultural identity to show Ramona love and support. Her parents both say that communication and family unity are valuable, yet many families in the United States prioritize material possessions.

Ramona's family exhibits a strong bond. Family members acknowledge their ascribed roles and responsibilities. For Ramona, this means helping her mother with household duties. Ramona does not describe these duties as chores or obligations but as contributions. She says, "I don't have chores. I *help* my mom clean the house. And if I'm done with the homework, I clean my hamster's cage." Ramona is expected to respect what her parents tell her to do. Ramona feels that this is "fair," and she rarely challenges what her parents say. Ramona notes that if she really wants something, like to go outside and play with her cousins, she might have to ask her parents twice. However, if her parents refuse, she respects their decisions. At her age, she is a budding adolescent still showing the vestiges of childhood.

Ramona's father feels that it is important that a parent always be present when Ramona arrives home from school. He explains that he does not trust another individual to watch his children because they might be mistreated. Her father also explains that the best way for Ramona to learn the difference between right and wrong is in the home. For Ramona's father, home is a safe, learning environment. Ramona's mother agrees that parents should prioritize their children.

Although both Ramona's father and mother feel it is important to have a parent stay with Ramona when she arrives home from school, deciding how they would do that proved to be difficult at first. The father wanted the mother to stay at home and promised his wife that she could work one day. And for the past eleven years, Ramona's mother has had primary child care responsibilities. Ramona's father was empathetic to his wife's frustrations, and they were able to reach a compromise. The mother now works on Saturdays in a laundromat. Ramona's father now has an opportunity to spend time with his daughters, often going to the movies together.

Ramona has an especially tight bond with her mother. She likes that her mother stays at home on school days "because whenever you come there, she's always waiting for you." These are special moments that mother and daughter get to share together. Yet Ramona also has the support of her other family members. Ramona says that the entire family helps her with her schoolwork, "from my uncles to my dad. And if my dad doesn't understand my homework, I go to my mom."

Ramona's parents anticipate her adolescence and foresee potential conflicts with her. They acknowledge that there will come a point in Ramona's life when she will want more distance from them. Her father feels that by raising Ramona in a supportive environment and by encouraging open communication now, fewer major conflicts will arise later. In the end, it is difficult to foresee what is in store for Ramona and her family. How much will Ramona push back against her parents? What will the conflicts be about? It is certain that Ramona will try to assert her autonomy, but her parents seem ready.

Family Functioning

Most of us grow up in families, or "family systems," an organization of people related to one another, mainly through biology, but also through special affection and affiliations. Members are ordered and interact to make up a functional whole, a family system. Within families, there are "subsystems," dynamic relationships made up of members based on their status in the family (e.g., spousal subsystem and parental subsystem, sibling subsystems). In families, parents act as the executive subsystem, and most often the family system is only as strong as this subsystem. When the parental or executive subsystem is impaired or weak, or contains other persons who should not be making decisions and acting like parents, the overall system can be weakened. In Ramona's family, we see a relatively well-functioning parental subsystem in which the parents communicated with one another and with their daughter.

Families, like all systems, prefer to maintain themselves in equilibrium, a steady state that helps get them through the challenges of daily life with a minimum of strife and distraction. This *homeostasis* is the point of balance for which families search in order to remain viable, functioning on a day-to-day basis. It is the point to which families and their members want to return in times of crisis and in the aftermath. However, depending on the functioning of its subsystems, and the degree to which other structural aspects of the family system are operating adequately, the homeostasis that a family falls back to during and after critical episodes may be less than optimal; in fact, it may return to a dysfunctional balance. Think of the family that cannot resume a helpful homeostasis after the death of a parent and shows deterioration in its functioning. This malfunction in its postcrisis balance is usually evidenced by problems in individual members. Others in the family are affected and a dysfunctional aftermath may be set. For example, the roles that persons play in the family and the relationships among the surviving parent and children may be altered significantly.

Boundaries are those lines or demarcations between the family and external systems and within the family members. External boundaries keep out and let in influences from the world outside the family whether nuclear or extended. Internal boundaries keep family members organized and in roles. Boundaries define systems and subsystems and insure the separation of family members into roles and statuses. Boundaries are a very interesting element of family systems: They must be strong but not brittle, elastic but not breakable. Boundaries must allow for entry into and for exit from the family but also restrain, at times, those who want to enter or want to leave if the integrity of the family is to be preserved. In essence, the boundaries need to be porous at times, impervious at others, and to open a little or a lot to permit exit and entry of people, ideas, and influences. *Roles* are the patterns of behaviors that have been determined by the culture of the system. Individual family members and family subsystems have roles, patterns of behavior that are typically "expected" of them. In the case of a parent's death, the distinctive place that the person held in the family need now be filled. Males and females and children at different ages will have expected roles, and with changes in the family system, roles will be altered, expanded, or shortened. Changes in roles touch off changes in the *relationships* that family members have. The emotional exchange and the dynamic interactions that occur in a family are changed. Family relationships are the affective, cognitive, and behavioral connection among members.

In arguing as I do that the family upheavals that come with having an adolescent are best met by effective parenting to avoid untoward outcomes, we have to take into consideration that there is a constant process of *differentiation* in family systems. Differentiation is but another term for the development of the family, its evolution. A family system has a natural tendency to become more and more differentiated as family members grow, age, and develop, change physically and psychologically, and adapt to new social expectations. This unstoppable sequence continually makes demands on the family to adapt, to move from a relatively simple system to a more complex one. The relationships among members, the family situation, and the interaction among family members change, particularly as new members (e.g., children's spouses, grandchildren) enter the family.

As we penetrate family systems, we find several dimensions that are critical to how families function in the cases of suicidal Latinas and, in fact, under all circumstances. These dimensions—cohesion, flexibility, and communication—are essential in evaluating and treating families (Olson, 2000). Family *cohesion* represents the emotional bonds among family members and is akin to what the Hispanic value of familism espouses. As emotional bonding, boundaries, and coalitions among family members vacillate, cohesion balances the separateness and togetherness of family members. Families can reside on a continuum from disengaged to enmeshed, a range of how cohesive families might be. At one extreme, families can be *disengaged,* showing very low cohesion among members. In such families, there is little in the way of an "emotional glue" to keep the members together. Members may not care about each other, and each does whatever he or she wishes without concern for the family. At the other extreme from disengaged are the *enmeshed* families, those that have very high levels of cohesion, so much so, that they are restrictive to the growth and development of their members. In enmeshed families, there is great psychological coercion toward conformity and remaining tied to the family at the expense of individual freedom. In the middle range are families that show different levels of cohesion. Some families have moderate levels of cohesion (separated), and some have moderate to high cohesion (connected). The more balanced the family systems—those in the separated and connected groups—the likelier they are to function well across the life cycle. In balanced families separation and connection are equally managed, and members can exercise independence from each other but still have profound emotional ties and rituals that keep them together.

Adaptability or flexibility refers to another dimension of how much change a family system can tolerate in its leadership, roles, and relationships. It is the way the family answers the question: "How much stability and change can we manage simultaneously and still stay balanced?" Family theorist David Olson (2000) observes that flexibility has four levels across a range. There are *rigid* families that lack or show very low capacity to be flexible to novel experiences. Rigid families have difficulty solving the common problems of human development and family evolution. *Structured* families with low to moderate levels of flexibility and *flexible* families who have moderate to high flexibility are the two middle-range groups. These two family types show more health through their capacity to adapt to change while remaining unified. *Chaotic* families, those with very high levels of flexibility that change direction and structure with virtually every soft breeze that life's challenges blows on them and leaves them with very little structure onto which they can hold, are the other extreme of families. Moving to either extreme on the continuum (to rigidity or to chaos) creates problems for families. Balanced levels of adaptability, that is, when they are structured and flexible, are better for family functioning. As children age, enter adolescence, progress into early young adulthood, and establish separate lives, all members of the family, most especially parents, must negotiate their roles and relationships in developmentally flexible, adaptive ways.

Both cohesion and adaptability are core dimensions in studying the families of Latina suicide attempters. These important ingredients may be unbalanced in such families. The third dimension—communication—is actually the means by which cohesion and flexibility occur. Communication is about how much family members, especially leaders (i.e., parents, elders), listen, speak, and disclose their beliefs, thoughts, and feelings; how clearly they communicate them; and what levels of respect and regard they demonstrate to one another. Attention and empathy involve important listening skills, a critical aspect of reciprocal, mutual interaction. As we see in the suicide attempts of young Latinas, all these dimensions of family functioning, particularly communication, are disturbed.

Where families have warm affective bonds, clear boundaries that keep members within their appropriate roles, open communication, firm but democratic parental authority, solid coparenting, and rituals that convey the family's identity, there are apt to be healthy interactions and outcomes. Negative family environments that violate some of these critical dimensions of family systems raise the potential for suicide attempts and other problems. For adolescents of all ethnic, racial, socioeconomic, religious, or cultural groups, dysfunctional families that are low in cohesion, in which there is family and marital conflict, low parental support and warmth, and higher parent–adolescent conflict, have negative consequences on the teenager. Where negative parenting, physical or sexual abuse, and less active and communicative parent–child relationships are present, we witness higher than average risks for suicide attempts. We know all too well from research that when poor communication between parents and daughters and between fathers and mothers exist, the risks for suicide attempts and other psychologically and socially problematic behaviors are raised (Johnson et al., 2002).

The possibility for healthy cohesion, adaptability, and communication are not limited to two-parent families. Many single-parent families facing the many challenges in their paths manage to succeed in maintaining healthy balanced family systems, although not without the natural struggles that a single parent encounters when raising children alone.

Two Latino Family Systems

In the cases of Esmeralda and Ramona we witnessed good parenting and sound family functioning in spite of challenges. I present now the case of Hilda's family and of Yolanda's family, two systems whose differences in functioning are pronounced. First is Hilda's family, one showing how serious dysfunction in its flexibility, boundaries, roles, and communication can have serious effects on the adolescent. Then Yolanda's family is presented as an example of positive systems interactions.

Hilda: Family Unity or Family Tyranny?

BY ALLYSON P. NOLLE

Fifteen-year-old Hilda lives with her mother and father, and two of her three older brothers. The family retains strong ties with extended family members, and Hilda says that she likes to celebrate her Puerto Rican heritage. Her father values family time and respect and tries to maintain traditional family reunion days. Both parents emphasize communication among the family members. Hilda's father states that he tries to understand teenagers today, to learn "about what they do, about what music they listen to, their language, what it means. That way you're able to talk to them. You talk to them at their level."

He speaks with his daughter every day about her school day and advises her on academic matters. He tells Hilda how she should behave, especially with regard to relationships and boys. He reflects very traditional values about virginity and marriage and holds Hilda to very high expectations. Her mother seizes every opportunity—while they shop or get their nails done—to talk to Hilda about relationships, sex, or birth control.

Beneath the surface this family is more troubled. As the youngest child, and the only girl in the family, Hilda receives special attention, albeit sometimes unwelcome. Her parents speak affectionately about her. Her mother says that she spoils Hilda at times, and that she relates more to her than to her sons because she is a girl. Her father calls her "Daddy's little girl." Her mother says that she is so close to her daughter that they are "like two flowers growing up together in the same pot." Yet there is a lack of trust. Her father, a former police officer, is overprotective, spying on Hilda to make sure she is behaving properly. He admits that she has never given him reason to not trust her.

This imbalance between strong ties and mistrust seems to have given root to more serious problems: Hilda has been unable to walk for 2 months, her legs completely numb. Doctors are unable to find a medical diagnosis for her "paralysis" and believe it to be a psychological problem, probably brought on by stress. And Hilda has attempted suicide by cutting.

Although parents insist on open communication, Hilda often feels that she has no one she can talk to, except her best friend. She feels that everyone around her tries to control her. She does not feel supported and she struggles for privacy. Her parents think that they know what is going on in her life, yet they do not know that she has cut herself over 10 times, sometimes with the intent to die.

The immobility in Hilda's legs reflects the emotional paralysis she feels in her relationship with her parents. Their overwhelming overprotection and control leave her feeling that she cannot move or be an autonomous person, free to experience the world on her own terms. Understandably, the parents are very distressed. They seem to genuinely want to be involved but are unable to understand what Hilda is actually going through. They may notice the emotional toll that the paralysis has taken on her, but they do not try speaking directly with Hilda to understand how she is feeling. The parents' constricted capacity to communicate openly without controlling was evident when Hilda was first admitted to the hospital for numbness in her legs. At that time, the attending psychologist informed her father that his daughter had been cutting herself. He seemed skeptical of his daughter's confirmed self-injurious behavior, and instead of addressing the issue directly with Hilda, he tried to look for marks on her arms while she slept. Hilda's father has never told his wife.

These parents overestimate their mutuality with Hilda. They do not know what has caused Hilda so much distress, though her father may have a dim awareness about it. He says that Hilda has "mentioned a lot of family activity, you know, maybe because she felt alone, she felt stressed out. So a lot of family activity, you know." Communication in this family is used as a means of control rather than as a means for full engagement with one another. Contrary to the father's repeated words of "you know," is not clear if anyone really knows for sure.

Yolanda: Teaching Good Boundaries and Good Judgment

Yolanda, a thirteen-year-old Puerto Rican girl who entered our study as part of the comparison group of Latinas who had not attempted suicide,[9] lives with her mother, brother, and stepfather. Like any protective family member, Yolanda gets upset when her stepfather criticizes her brother or her maternal grandmother. It is fairly clear to her mother that Yolanda does not get along with the stepfather. In fact, Yolanda once encouraged her mother to divorce him. But the mother is happy in her marriage, and the animosity between Yolanda and her stepfather is not so pronounced as to lead her to question their marriage. Her mother was not about to take her daughter's suggestion simply because her daughter was upset.

In contrast, Yolanda talks to her mother about her biological father, who abandoned them when Yolanda was four. Yolanda says the bonds with her father are broken; he has only been involved in Yolanda's life intermittently and less so now. Knowing Yolanda's struggle about her father, her mother avoids making derogatory comments about him that might add to Yolanda's burden. Her mother is sensitive that Yolanda is upset with him:

> He doesn't look for her. She ends up always looking for him. She writes a lot
> of poems about it, like very angry poems about it, how hurt she is with him.
> I always try to make him look good [despite the fact that he is a drug addict].
> I give excuses for him so then she won't hurt.

Yolanda also complains that her older brother got to date when he was fourteen and her mother expects Yolanda to wait until she is sixteen. Both mother and daughter agree that this is a normal conflict in families, and Yolanda feels that her mother, overall, treats them fairly. This is corroborated by the mother:

> I don't [follow the belief that] the woman has to obey and the woman has to
> be at home and the man can do whatever he wants, and you have to take it
> because you're female. This is not true. In my household my boy gets to do
> more than my girl but it's not because he's a boy; it's because he's sixteen
> and she's thirteen. Let it be the other way around it would be you doing more
> than him. In my house I can't have that *boy-thing* [male prerogatives]. I have
> issues with that because I feel that that stops a woman or a young girl from
> being what they can be. How do you expect to help her defend herself
> against the world if you're already putting in her head that because "you're a
> female you got a point against you, honey. You can't do this, and you can't do
> that." And I talk about sex with both of them, it's not because you are boy
> and you are a girl I can't talk to you. No, I talk to both of them the same.

Yolanda describes several positive and influential sources in her life. Yolanda has people who she can talk with: friends, a male teacher she confides in (a positive male model in her life who listens and exchanges ideas and advice), and her brother with whom she can complain about her mother.

Like her mother, Yolanda recognizes that, despite all the fights they may have, they have a close relationship. Yolanda describes her mother as a friend within limits:

> Well, I can call her a friend, 'cause I can talk to her. But, not about every-
> thing; sometimes she will agree with me, sometimes I won't agree with her,
> we get into an argument. But I am pretty close with my mom, yeah.

What is important in the relationship is that her mother—like a good mentor—is reliable and empathic. Yolanda's family struggles with the right balance of cohesion, flexibility, and communication. In terms of their communication, Yolanda is resistant to sharing certain things with her mom, but this is not due to an absence (or lack) of trust. Rather, she says, it is because her mother tries to fix her problems, to take action that flows from her love. Yolanda, however, wants to be independent and fix them herself. Yolanda's mother agrees with her daughter's assessment. The mother's insights and reactions are thoughtful, an indication that she is listening to and hearing her daughter:

> I would say 90% of the time she'll tell me things, she'll talk to me. If she's feeling really, really sad, that's when she'll cry and it's a rare moment. When she does cry, it's a very emotional cry; it's an "I can't talk" kind of cry. So I'll just let her vent, that's the first thing. I let her cry, I'll let her vent. I feel people make the mistake of, "Why you crying? Be quiet. Listen to me, talk to me. Don't cry." I'll just let her cry. When she calms down, she'll tell me, and she usually does, 90% of the times. (Only when she's trying to get away with something is when she won't communicate with me.)

Yolanda lives with the knowledge that her family will help her, including her stepfather. As a result of the relationships in the home and her upbringing, and her own fortitude, Yolanda feels good about herself and exudes confidence. Her ethnic identity is robust:

> I should be proud of my heritage. In the research I seen, like presidents and governments, and stuff I've read even in school about who else is Puerto Rican and the good things they've done (we studied that in Spanish). Even my teacher is Puerto Rican. It's nice to visit San Juan and the little town where my grandmother was born. My great-grandfather had a barber shop there and now it's a museum. I read about that in 5th grade.

Her mother's influence is evident in Yolanda's words and pride in herself and in her cultural heritage. This is how mother describes what she wants to impart to Yolanda:

> We're perceived . . . a Hispanic woman is always perceived a certain way by others. I want her how can I explain it to you? I want her to hold the culture

in her; I do. I want her to know what it is to be a proud Latina, to be very proud of herself. It's not about the Puerto Rican flag. It's about the culture; it's about knowing your past, knowing what you can. I have a whole family tree and it's like I want her to know that you were made of all these different parts. . . . Latinas grow up in a way where *familia es uno*, and the bond has to be there. And it's very easy for other girls to go into college and call once a month, or twice a month or you know, not call at all for 6 months. And many of the mothers I see don't have that "Oh, my God, why my daughter hasn't called me" or really worry. With Latinas it's the bond, "Let me call my mom. Mom, is she OK?" Or "Let me call my daughter, is she all right?" Or we can be on the same wavelength and know immediately that something's wrong with one of them. I know when something's wrong with my daughter, and she'll know something's wrong with me. But I don't want her to become so independent that she can't even call or appreciate who she is and where she comes from.

The "Cultural Range" on the Family Continuum

In the social sciences there is a perspective that espouses a view of cultures as either collectivistic or individualistic (see, for example, Triandis, Bontempo, Villareal, Asai, & Lucca, 1988). In collectivistic societies and cultures, this point of view says, the emphasis is on the group, the family, the collective, and much less so on the individual. In individualistic cultures, such as the United States and some Western European countries, the primary orientation is on the person. In the individualistic view, the development of the person is toward becoming increasingly separate and independent of those around her. This view does not dismiss the importance of the family; it sees the family as secondary to the individual.

Dichotomizing cultures and families in this way is far too narrow and possibly misleading. By putting the two orientations in separate silos, we make attributions that too often overshadow the fact that no culture is exclusively one of the other. More often than not, we see both collectivism and individualism in a society, not just one. What we might see is the *tendency* in cultures to tilt toward one orientation or the other without eliminating the presence of either orientation. Groups are not as polarized as this perspective might at first glance suggest. Indeed, some cultures socialize their members toward independence, seeing the adult as an individual agent, unique and separate from others. And it is also the case that other cultures emphasize more interdependence in which the person is a "coagent," interconnected to others (Keller & Lamm, 2005, p. 238).

In actuality, families and cultures tend to cover *a span on the continuum* from independence to interdependence, from individualistic to collectivistic. A similar scenario is seen in differences between families who are enmeshed and those who are disengaged. Families of one culture or another do not simply sit at one pole or the other. There are exceptions in all groups, of course, where extreme polarizations in families occur. But wholly enmeshed or totally disengaged often points to family pathology and dysfunction.

Instead of thinking of families as just sitting on one end or the other of the continuum, we need to appreciate that families actually reside at different points on this continuum, covering a span on a range, and that they do so within what we might call a "cultural range." Latino families and others from Mediterranean and Southeast Asian cultures, for example, tend to be found toward the collectivistic, interdependent, enmeshed end of the continuum as shown by their family centeredness, high emphasis on family obligations, and intrafamily socializing. But these families appear on a wide span of that continuum, including dysfunctionally enmeshed or disengaged. In other words, within cultures there is diversity among families. It is not, therefore, useful to say that German or North American families are exclusively focused on independence (Keller & Lamm, 2005; Lamm & Keller, 2007). Rather, their childrearing and socialization practices may be located on that part of the continuum that is more individualistic and independent than at the other end. There are families in Germany and North America that may be more enmeshed or independent than others in the same cultures.

Ian Canino and Glorisa Canino (1980) make a similar and persuasive argument on Puerto Rican families. These authors view the traditional Puerto Rican family as positioned on the normative end of the enmeshed range. They postulate that at times of extreme stress such families may become more enmeshed or interdependent as part of the family system's attempt to regain its homeostasis, or a sense of dynamic balance. This is important for clinicians and researchers to take note of as a modicum of interdependence; enmeshment is not in and of itself pathological. And more disengagement or more independence-oriented families do not reflect dysfunction, except at the extremes.

Culture and Traditions

Culture is a mighty part of who we are as individuals and as family; culture has untold influence on making us who we are. Through culture, the ways of representing our thoughts and our feelings are planted, even in terms of which feelings may be expressed and which ones are to be kept opaque (Kirmayer, 2001). Culture also provides us with the beliefs about how our emotions and mental stress begin and how we can explain them. Moreover, it dictates to some degree the forms that distress takes. We approached the study of adolescent Latinas' suicide attempts from the perspective that the attempts constitute a *form* provided by culture for experiencing overwhelming distress, a special kind of interpersonal stress.

Cultures provide the contexts and rules for how persons in the group interact with others. It sets the way our families are structured and composed and how people in them interact. Through family life, through the interactions with our parents and siblings, friends, coworkers, and others, our affects or emotions are primed and shaped. Culture gives us categories for our emotional expression and words that accompany the emotions, particularly idiomatic expression of our pain or the emotion, known as "idioms of distress."

Hispanic family traditions may influence how the adolescent girl and her parents respond to psychosocial stress, and dysfunctional families may be considerably more challenged than well-functioning families. In traditionally structured Hispanic families, the emphasis on restrictive, authoritarian parenting, especially for girls, affects the family's capacity to respond flexibly during a crucial developmental period. Specific family cultural issues may emerge in the differences between the traditional values, beliefs, and socialization practices of the family's original culture and those of the majority culture and between the rapidly acculturating and developing adolescent girl and her less acculturated, more traditional parents.

There is often a tendency to glorify and celebrate culture for all its beauty. Many of the values that are written about (even in this book) may tend to be presented as positive attributes. Not to be neglected, however, is the reality that some of these same values create constraints on people, subjugating persons into roles and beliefs (Dyche & Zayas, 1995). Cultural traditions can help explain the difficulty that some families have in adapting to their daughters' increased autonomy. We can recognize that traditional cultures—let's use Mexican culture as an example—differ in many vital ways from mainstream American culture. With success comes the need to make adaptations that some families are more prepared to make than others. As immigrant Mexican families improve their economic condition in the United States, shifts must be made in the customary ways they operate. For instance, women begin to play a more active role outside of the home and may earn more than their partners. Or, their occupational roles may include higher status or greater decision-making responsibility. Power balances are affected in the parental subsystem;

children and adolescents may be given more autonomy in part because parents cannot monitor or supervise them as closely. While familism is known to protect the mental health of the individuals (Gonzales et al., 2002), those Mexicans who are born in the United States may view their familism as eroding on account of the adaptation to mainstream life and see their cohesion weakened (Cuéllar et al., 1997; Gonzales et al., 2000). In Chapter Four, we hear Mexican-American mothers in El Centro, California, tell us in heartfelt words how preserving the positive qualities of their culture in their children is sometimes exhausting, but always challenging.

Emotional Vulnerability

We recognize that it is not simply adolescence, family functioning, or cultural features that raise the risk for suicide attempts. Ultimately, the suicide attempt is an individual action, and in order to discuss suicide attempts among teen Latinas, we must consider a girl's emotional vulnerability as a key determinant in the suicide attempt. By emotional vulnerability, I mean the propensity to experience distress or conflict as imminently threatening the integrity of the self. In other words, emotional vulnerability or sensitivity to a perceived or real threat shapes the way a girl engages with the world and is engaged by it, her perception of tensions and conflicts in her social milieu, and her response to stress and difficulty (including how she handles critical family situations). In this way, emotional vulnerability is closely related to psychosocial functioning but differs from it. Emotional vulnerability refers to the emotional tone through which a girl experiences and responds to her world, particularly the family crisis related to the suicide attempt. Psychosocial functioning refers more to the mastery of socially acceptable coping strategies.

Literature abounds regarding problems in psychological and social functioning associated with suicide attempts, and these concepts seem to be the same as or similar to those we have seen clinically. The common risk factors include major depression and dysthymic disorders, histories of physical and sexual abuse, low self-esteem, poor coping strategies, hopelessness, impulse control problems, deficient anger management, substance abuse, personality disorders, schizophrenia, and conduct disorders (Zayas et al., 2005). We see many of them in our research of young Latinas who have acted in a suicidal manner. They often use social withdrawal, wishful thinking, and blaming others as key coping strategies, unlike nonsuicidal adolescents who are more likely to use social support and cognitive restructuring (Spirito, Francis, Overholser, & Frank, 1996; Turner et al., 2002). Active coping buffers the effects of family stress among urban minority girls (Gonzales, Tein, Sandler, & Friedman, 2001). The suicide attempt may be an act of withdrawal from the intense interpersonal crisis. The vulnerability that the girls show toward suicidal behavior is often a convergence of many factors that have to do with parenting, family functioning, trauma, temperament, quality of the mentoring they received, and the sense of security they feel.

* * *

I have elaborated on research, concepts, and theories that formed my thinking about Latina suicide attempts. From clinical experience and the literature, it seems to me that conflicts with parents that strain the autonomy-relatedness process play important roles in the suicide attempts. These conflicts can come from parental opposition to a boyfriend, parental discovery of the adolescent's sexual involvement with a boyfriend, or other autonomy-related issues. And this is not exclusively a problem of the adolescent; instead, it involves the maladaptive interactions of parents and adolescents that intensify the conflict. As noted in other studies, accumulated stress in the family is generally a factor in suicide attempts (Moscicki, 1999; Moscicki & Crosby, 2003; Wagner, 1997). Studies show that precipitating events for suicide attempts typically occur in the month prior to the suicide attempt, that Latinas had planned their attempt for less than a day, they had largely attempted it via ingestion of medications, and that 75% of Latinas attribute their suicide attempt to conflicts with their mother or a boyfriend (Berne, 1983; Marttunen et al., 1993; Ng, 1996).

Acculturation levels may also be one of those cultural or transcultural issues that influence the suicide attempt. Since acculturative discrepancies between teenagers and parents often exist among Hispanics, this does not explain why other adolescent Hispanic girls matched for acculturation and generational status do not attempt suicide even when dealing with similar mental health issues. We should not think of acculturation and discrepancies in acculturation levels as acting alone in the family in bringing about a suicide attempt; instead, it can be thought of as part of a cocktail of family dysfunctions.

Often, the struggle for more autonomy is expressed in conflict over romantic or sexual issues, such as dating. This disruption in the family over the girl's developing sexuality and greater autonomy is expressed as a prolonged and intense family struggle with management of the girl's body (where she goes and with whom, what she wears, frequency of her menstruation, etc.) at center stage. When the girl is faced with a sense of unremitting parental and familial disapproval, a struggle may ensue between her autonomous self, who is making developmental strides, and her related self, which is part of a family unit.

In this situation, the emotionally vulnerable girl comes to experience the family conflict as an existential threat to herself and her family's unity (Zimmerman, 1991). As this conflict increasingly endangers the family's wholeness, the girl comes to feel that the willful extinguishing of this struggle through a suicide attempt is the only reasonable response.

We know well that human life is much more varied and complex than any depiction I could possibly render. Each girl I have treated or studied brings to her attempt some personal, unique idiosyncrasy or experience. Girls in foster care, girls with minor physical impediments or medical needs, girls psychologically tortured by trauma, loss, or shame, girls without any notable distinguishing characteristics from their peers, and girls with other particularities fall victim to the suicide attempt drama. Of the ideas I advance in this book, the most salient is the apparent disruption in the girls' lives. Something has gone awry in the family's functioning and the normal course of the girl's development. Suicide attempts are a major signal that the communication lines in these families are faltering. The attempts reflect a systemic family matter, a situation not caused simply by parents, siblings, and extended families, but contributed to by the girl.

4

Daughters, Familism, and Adulthood

Any time we study what appears to be a human anomaly, whether behavioral or biological, we have to keep in mind what the typical situation is, the norm. It is the question, "Abnormal compared to what?" In looking at suicidal behavior in young Latinas, we need to know something about the norm, what they are like most of the time. Therefore, to understand Latina teens and the forces that converge in the suicide attempts, we have to appreciate their upbringing, how they traverse childhood and adolescence into adulthood in the normal course of life. We need to take into account the social, economic, and cultural circumstances in which their development and maturation occurs. It is helpful to take a glimpse at what many Hispanic women say is their experience growing up in the United States and what Hispanic mothers say about raising daughters. By learning about the conditions under which they grow and develop, we can better appreciate why some girls go off course to suicidal acts, and why others do not.

Developmental sciences have lagged in addressing the normal or average progression of most minority children and teenagers in the United States, certainly leaving Latinas outside of the studies on how young women mature. Our scientific knowledge base has a long way to go to adequately inform us about what it is like to grow up female in a typical U.S. Hispanic family, especially first- and second-generation daughters. Lamentably, we know more about the many ills besetting Latina teenagers—things like adolescent pregnancy, dropping out of school, substance abuse, addiction,

HIV infection, physical and sexual trauma—than we do about the average Latina girl in the average Hispanic home growing up successfully in ordinary circumstances. The social problems just listed have dominated the developmental psychopathology literature and the popular media. It can be safely said that we have learned more about the problems of Latino youth, the deviations from the norm, than we have about their typical developmental process.

This chapter is about young Latinas and their families in ordinary circumstances. But it is impossible to provide in a single chapter or even in one book an exhaustive description of growing up Latina in the United States. I do not try here to deal with the many facets of normal Latina development, nor do I repeat what is already known about the social problems facing Latinas. Instead, I cover only a small part of their lives, those aspects of growing up within the family. It is, after all, the family context that is the basis for looking at the Hispanic daughter in the United States, a girl with a foot in each of two cultures. It is she who navigates a world in which "one must always walk alone, at one's own pace, and only after burying a part of one's soul" (Ojito, 2005, p. 221).

There are many inherent limitations to what an interested, sympathetic male writer can say, and what insights he can provide on being a Latina. No one but Latinas themselves in different stages of life can tell us their stories—there is no richer source, no fuller resonance than their own words. For this reason, I rely on the personal accounts given by Latina girls and women, whether their words appear in discussion groups, research interviews, or even fictional accounts. The memoirs, novels, and short stories by U.S. Latino writers, especially the group of Latina authors who have captured the essence and the trials of growing up in two cultures—writers such as Esmeralda Santiago (1993, 1999), Julia Alvarez (1991, 1998, 2007), Sandra Cisneros (1987, 1988), and Helena Maria Viramontes (1995)—are enormously instructive. What follows are snapshots of Hispanic women: lives colored by culture, gender, and the pressures to accommodate family, men, and society.

Cultural Values to Grow by

One place to start a partial story of a Latina life course is by understanding the cultural values that women are taught. Values in all cultures have many layers, nuanced and interconnected. In Hispanic cultures the closeness of the family and its openness to embracing others, as described in Chapter One, reflect the feature known as *familism*. A cultural construct, Hispanic familism places the family at the center of one's life: members put the family ahead of their individual interests and are expected to be dedicated to each other, especially to parents and elders.

Familism is an attitude, in which the person holds the family uppermost (Coohey, 2001; Valenzuela & Dornbusch, 1994). The obligations to the family are forged in heartfelt emotional *compromisos* (commitments) and loyalty. It is a cultural value that enjoins family members to provide emotional sustenance and material support for each other. Moreover, they depend and rely on family members *first*, and they are responsible to and be prepared to sacrifice for the benefit of the family (e.g., Agudelo et al., 2001; Heller et al., 2004; Kao et al., 2007; Nolle et al., 2010). Frequent and intense contact among members is part of the familistic beliefs of Hispanic cultures. Structurally, familism encourages family members to live near each other, as we saw in the quarrel between Papá and Uncle Luis in the opening pages of this book. We hear it again when young Latinas talk about the expectation of staying close to home when they go to college, never straying too far from family, even in marriage.

While familism is arguably a critical aspect in understanding the Latina girl, there are other values that add dimensionality. For example, the principal value of *respeto* (respect) plays an elemental role in familism and in the girl's development. *Respeto* honors the common humanity of people and their status in life, such as parents and grandparents. To respect the family is to abide by its integrity and its values. And *respeto*, as we hear young Latinas say, is the observance of one's own dignity and that of others; it includes respect for adults by children, respect by adults to children, respect within traditional gender roles, and interpersonal harmony (Unger et al., 2006).

Another value that overlaps with the interpersonal expression of *respeto* is the value of *personalismo*. This cultural value guides the person in establishing and maintaining warm, friendly, and respectful relationships (Cuéllar, Arnold, & González, 1995; Unger et al., 2006). The harmony that is implied in *personalismo* comes about through *simpatía*, a cultural script that connotes sociability, agreeableness, politeness, and affection (Flores et al., 1998; Griffith et al., 1998; Shapiro & Simonsen, 1994; Varela et al., 2004). Children and adults are judged on their *modales* (manners), for a well-mannered person is *bien educado* (well mannered), always comporting herself in a courteous and dignified manner. We see later in this chapter how Latinas embody these cultural values and how these scripts are played out in the interactions with their families.

Gender Roles

When it comes to gender roles commonly associated with Hispanic culture, *machismo* is the one most widely known. It is important to understand machismo in a book about Hispanic women. Machismo has become synonymous with womanizing, sexual prowess, dominance, authoritarianism, and aggression. This description of machismo brings with it a rigidity in the man's definition of his sex roles and those of women (Alvarez, 2007; Quintero & Estrada, 1998). There is some truth to this nearly caricatured description of machismo. It is a term that gained popularity during the advent of the women's movement of the 1960s and 1970s in North America. Machismo has become a popular slur in English, a situation from which it may never recover. Seeing it as one-dimensional, however, leaves out other aspects that were historically included in the definition.

Left out of most definitions of machismo is the male's sense of responsibility for protecting and providing for his family. A fuller picture includes loyalty to family inspired by honor. A *macho* can be an *hombre serio* (serious man), a man of his word, respectful, dignified, wise, and hardworking. A macho is also a *caballero* (gentleman) in the traditional sense of chivalry (Alvarez, 2007; Arciniega, Anderson, Tovar-Blank, & Terence, 2008; Torres et al., 2002). Manuel Peña (1991), in a paper based on research with immigrant Mexican working men who harvested fruits and nuts outside of Fresno, California, illustrates how a more complex picture of machismo is lived out by these men. Peña observes that

> The men who delighted in the performance of *charritas* [assorted, mostly off-color jokes, riddles, and rhymes] and other types of macho humor also evinced the other side of machismo—the typically Mexican sense of *respeto* that idealizes women. Like Mexican men everywhere, these workers bestowed an inordinate share of courtesy, protectiveness, and even reverence upon their mothers, sisters, wives, and "significant others," as long as their male supremacy was not challenged.
>
> In particular, the older married men who had families in Mexico expressed their concerns about making enough money to send back home, being away from their growing children for long periods, and burdening their wives with added domestic responsibilities while they were absent. (p. 37)

The degree to which a man leans toward one pole or the other on machismo is learned from peers and family, and especially older men in his life. This is true in all cultures. Childrearing practices and beliefs that give sons (and daughters) more room to experiment in the world with respect to self-assertion, sexuality, and protecting his family and their common dignity may be seen as preparatory to male adulthood. Machismo may never lose its negative connotations as a social label, but it is worth recognizing that there is a historical backdrop that may still be present in fathers' and mothers' minds as they raise their young men.

Marianismo—the much less known gender value for women—balances the relationships of men and women, wives and husbands, sisters and brothers. Marianismo connotes women's spiritual superiority, yet they remain submissive, suffering, and maternal. The origins of the term are found in the socioreligious histories and cultures of Latin America under the occupation of Spain. The worship of the Virgin Mary (Virgen Maria) in the heavily Roman Catholic Southern Europe and then the New World set the ideal for women's socialization. The feminine ideal in the conservative Catholicism that held for so long in the countries of the Caribbean, Mexico, and Central and South America included the qualities of self-sacrifice, chastity, virginity, virtue, and dedication. In The Maria Paradox: How Latinas Can Merge Old World Traditions With New World Self-Esteem (1997), Rosa M. Gil and Carmen Inoa Vazquez state that even in today's world, cultural traditions in Hispanic families retain a socialization process that puts an accent on being passive and demure. The role continues to encourage the young Latina's sense of hyperresponsibility for family obligations, unity, and harmony.

In today's world, however, the adherence to marianismo has given way to contemporary interpretations of femininity and women's roles that offer more flexible definitions. Nevertheless, some "marianistic" remnants may be found in the upbringing of U.S.- and foreign-born Latinas. We see this in the descriptions given by young Latinas. For example, to learn about the lives and the challenges Latinas face, Jill Taylor, Carmen Veloria, and Martina Verba (2007) held a series of meetings with six 10-grade girls, mostly Dominican. The girls told of negotiating the culture at home with the one outside. At home, life revolved around Dominican dialects, customs, views, and values that included submissiveness toward husbands or partners. The girls told of learning indirectly from their mothers, aunts, and other women that it was their responsibility as women to manage men's sexuality. In homes where there was a stepfather or mother's boyfriend, girls had to watch what they wore around the house, avoiding anything too tight, revealing, or provocative. Some girls were critical of their mothers for showing preferential treatment to the men in their lives, primarily husbands and boyfriends. The girls saw that the women around them glorified men's achievements outside the family but only sanctified women's roles when they took care of the family's needs. What women accomplished outside of the home seemed to be of lesser value, evoking less pride.

While they were Latinas at home following many cultural prescriptions, outside the home the girls had to negotiate a very different culture. That outside culture was one based on middle-class American attitudes and behaviors,

things they had to master for their upward mobility. Those girls with less acculturated mothers, whether in well-functioning families or not, often felt that
their mothers did not understand the problems and challenges they faced in
school, especially when it involved sexuality. The relationships with mothers,
fathers, and brothers occurred "against a backdrop of protectiveness and
restricted freedom" (Taylor, Veloria, & Verba, 2007, p. 162). This frustrated the
vocal young women in the group; they felt that they were not allowed to learn
from their mistakes. It hampered their ability to talk to their mothers openly
and honestly. While their mothers may have said to their daughters that they
should aspire, to *superarse* (improve themselves), to succeed in the world outside their culture, the girls felt an underlying resistance.

This tension between what the mothers said and what they did, according
to the girls, resembles the observations that Deborah Tannen (2006) makes
about mother–daughter communication. Tannen writes that mothers may feel
some regret or ambivalence when their daughters succeed. Mothers may be
motivated to protect and connect with their daughters, but daughters only see
limitations to their freedom and invasion of their privacy. Because of the closeness that mothers and daughters share as women—emotionally, physically,
and psychologically—their communication patterns create, as Tannen so aptly
puts it, a "constant negotiation of intimacy, closeness, power, and distance"
(p. 4). Tannen concludes that mothers may want to see their daughters succeed,
to soar, but it is a wish that is full of ambivalence. In words that gave weight to
Tannen's conclusions, the six Latinas in Taylor et al.'s (2007) group said that,
while their mothers told them to *superarse*, the mothers were just as quick to
require their daughters to do many chores in the house and care for younger
siblings, thus effectively clipping their wings. Their daughters may soar, but in
so doing they may well soar away from their mothers.

In his Pulitzer Prize–winning novel, *The Brief Wondrous Life of Oscar Wao*,
Junot Díaz (2007) conveys the experience of the young Latina and her mother
through the words of Lola, the protagonist's older sister:

> She was my Old World Dominican mother and I was her only daughter,
> the one she had raised up herself with the help of nobody, which meant it
> was her duty to keep me crushed under her heel. I was fourteen and
> desperate for my own patch of the world that had nothing to do with her.
> I wanted the life that I used to see when I watched *Big Blue Marble* as a
> kid, the life that drove me to make pen pals and to take atlases home
> from school. The life that existed beyond Paterson, beyond my family,
> beyond Spanish. And as soon as she became sick I saw my chance, and
> I'm not going to pretend or apologize; I saw my chance and eventually

I took it. If you didn't grow up like I did then you don't know and if you don't know it's probably better you don't judge. You don't know the hold our mothers have on us, even the ones that are never around—*especially* the ones that are never around. What it's like to be the perfect Dominican daughter, which is just a nice way of saying a perfect Dominican slave. (pp. 55–56)

Lola, Oscar Wao's sister, says that she took to heart her mother's lessons, the importance of chores, family obligations, and the expectation that she bring home good grades. Lola recalls her mother's very words:

From ages two to thirteen I believed her and because I believed her I was the perfect hija. I was the one cooking, cleaning, doing the wash, buying groceries, writing letters to the bank to explain why a house payment was going to be late, translating. I had the best grades in my class. I never caused trouble, even when the morenas use to come after me with scissors because of my straight-straight hair. I stayed at home and made sure Oscar was fed and that everything ran right while she was at work. I raised him and I raised me. I was the one. You're my hija, she said, that's what you're supposed to be doing. (p. 56)

Lola may not have been as forgiving of her mother as the girls in the discussion group were of their mothers (Taylor et al., 2007). Those girls understood and empathized with their mothers. We don't hear that in Lola's words. Despite barriers to being able to speak to their mothers about serious matters, the girls understood the often painful experiences that their mothers had to endure as women growing up in much more repressive conditions. They could appreciate the strengths that were revealed by their mothers, their abilities to survive and even thrive after childhood hardships, immigration-related traumas, and insensitive, sometimes abusive, men. The girls took away lessons, too, from knowing their mothers' experiences. They learned what could be attained in life even with barriers and setbacks. This motivated the girls.

Adriana: Love is the Key
BY ALLYSON P. NOLLE

Adriana, at age 17, describes her family as "a three-people family," consisting of herself, her mother, and her 14-year-old sister. Adriana's father left them when her mother was pregnant with her sister, and they have only seen him a few times since then. They think of him as dead because of the tremendous pain—both emotional and financial—that he inflicted upon the family. He is no longer around, thankfully. The family does not have extended family in New York, but both mother and daughter emphasize the significance of their network of neighbors:

> Like 'cause I don't have a family so like everybody in my neighborhood we're all like a family . . . the grown-ups will do a cook-in, and then the teenagers will go to the pool and play around, you know, a family thing.

Adriana's mother takes care of the income for the house and Adriana is responsible for the housework. She says, "My mother used to work 7 days a week and I'm the one that takes care of my little sister. I'm the one that's in charge of cooking and cleaning the house and washing clothes." Adriana feels protective of her sister, keeping an eye on her and making sure that she behaves. They have small quarrels about clothes, but these issues are usually resolved quickly.

The mother's family history is a sad one. Raised by her grandmother in the Dominican Republic, she was neglected as a child. No one remembered her birthday, celebrated when she got good grades, or gave her much attention. She was very depressed throughout adolescence and attempted suicide multiple times. She says that she keeps these things in mind in raising her girls. She tries to shower them with affection, celebrates their achievements, and is lenient about rules. She says, *"Toda la clave está en el amor."* ["Love is the key to everything."]

Abundant as love is in this family, there is financial hardship. Adriana understands the financial strain her mother is under, and she is trying to complete lifeguard training to get a job so she can help contribute to their expenses. Her mother says that she never asked Adriana to work, but that Adriana insists. Adriana's desire to work to alleviate the burden on her mother reflects some of the typical features of *familism*. In Adriana's words,

> It hurts me to see her stressed out because that's like the most valuable thing. I have my mother, my little sister, so for me to see her down kinda affects me a lot.

Adriana has not always been a well-behaved child. She says that she used to cut school a lot, "for really, really dumb reasons." And she became very aggressive, wanting to fight everybody. Her mother feels that Adriana's behavioral problems were directly linked to her [mother's] working too much and not being home to supervise. She did her best to be in contact with Adriana and her sister by phone, checking up on them to make sure they were home when they were supposed to be, and she asked her neighbors to watch out for the two girls as well. When her mother cut back on her work schedule and was able to be home more, Adriana's behavior improved greatly. She regrets that her absence fueled Adriana's problems, but she had no choice.

Adriana became more motivated about school when she started to realize that "it's not really taking me nowhere," but also because she started to realize the strain on her mother. "You don't want to see your mother falling apart," Adriana added, "And that's what I can really say that's changed me." She confides in her mother, because she feels that friends can come and go, but in the end, her mother and sister are going to be the ones that stand by her.

Adriana now attends a trade school, aspiring to work on airplanes. In another example of *familism*, Adriana wants to be able to get a good job in the future so that her mother will not have to work hard. Her mother is proud of her daughter and Adriana is dedicated to her mother:

> I decided I didn't want my mother to be disappointed about me. I don't want her to feel like, "My whole life I worked and my kids didn't even turn out . . ." I don't want her to feel like a failure, 'cause she's not a failure. So that's why I'm doing my side of the job.

Dating, Family, and *Respeto:* Conversations with Latinas

From learning at the feet of my mother and aunts as a young boy, watching my sisters grow up, conducting hundreds of hours of psychotherapy with Latinas of every age, race, and social class, and reveling in the countless conversations with women of all ages, I saw consistencies across Latinas from different Hispanic groups. The remarkable similarities in their descriptions of familism, *respeto*, dating, marriage, and motherhood left me with the impression that, save for some cultural variations and unique geographic and social circumstances, they can almost always speak for one another about their upbringing and particularly about their adolescence. Indeed, when I address audiences on growing up Latina and the forces that lead to suicide attempts, it is Hispanic women, regardless of their cultural origins, who express their agreement with "Amens" and trenchant nods of their heads on many of the issues in their lives, beliefs, and upbringing, and the messages that they were given by parents and society. Boys, and what parents warned them about, is the one issue that Latinas seem to agree easily on as the topic they heard most about from their parents and where the restrictions were sharpest. The writer, Julia A. Alvarez (1998), describes an adolescence like that of many Latinas, one in which she used her command of English to both circumvent her Spanish-speaking parents and debate the logic of their arguments. In Alvarez's case, she could win her father's consent to get what she wanted by quoting Shakespeare. But there were things she "couldn't touch even with a Shakespearean ten-foot pole: the area of boys and permission to go places where there might be boys, American boys, with their mouths full of bubblegum and their minds full of the devil" (p. 63). Alvarez conveys the experiences of many Latinas I have met over the years, women who describe the memories of their homes, families, and parents with great fondness but also memories colored with the sometimes unresolved pain of growing up under these very same constraints.

In the sections that follow, you will hear from Hispanic women directly. I selected excerpts from conversations held in the fall of 2009 with three sets of Mexican-American women in the El Centro and Calexico areas of California, just miles from Mexicali, Mexico. Their conversations provided lively, dramatic, poignant, and sometimes humorous insights into growing up in Hispanic families. These excerpts are the words of a small sample of Hispanic women, but their words also provide a frame for the voices of many others. I present segments of their verbatim interactions, translating most of the words but retaining their spontaneous, colorful idiomatic expressions from Spanish.

The first conversation went fluidly between Spanish and English with a group of four middle-class, professional women.[10] All had lived on the U.S.–Mexico border most of their lives and one was born in Mexico. All but one were married and had children. They ranged in ages from 27 to 45. They were well-educated women who had grown up in modest circumstances. Their parents had worked hard to provide them with the best lives they could, full of love and teachings that have stayed with them. We sat comfortably around a kitchen table chatting while husbands shot pool nearby. The digital recorder I placed on the table quickly seemed forgotten.

We first talked about dating. The women told of the tradition of being chaperoned when going out with a boy. It was customary, they said, to have the boy meet the girl's family, even if it was a minor date and there was no implicit romance in the friendship. In the first sequence of comments, the women described how gender roles, dating, family, and *respeto* are played out in the relationships with their boyfriends. With humor and insight, the women made it clear that the male must come to the girl's house if he is to expect to have a date with a young woman in traditional Mexican culture.

"To be a boyfriend," Araceli, the oldest member of the group, pointed out, "he had to come to the family's home. And if they were to go out, the boyfriend had to take [the girl's] sister and brother as chaperones."

Glenda, married and with children, added a fine point to Araceli's comment. "He cannot honk for you outside. No. He has to get out of his car, knock on the door, come inside, talk for a little bit, and *then* you are allowed to leave."

I asked if the young men they dated knew about this requirement and understood it in the same way that they did, especially if they were Mexican or if they had grown up around Mexicans. Glenda responded quickly.

"Yes. The nice thing about El Centro and Calexico is that even boys who are not Mexican but grew up in this area know about our culture. They know the rituals of having to go over to the parents' house and having to talk to the parents, and all that." A knowing laughter flowed among the women. "And if the boy doesn't go with that then, I'm sorry, he's 'out.'" The group laughed energetically.

"I dated a guy who was half-Irish, half-Dutch and grew up somewhere else," said Giovanna, the youngest and only single woman in the group. "It was very different for him when he came to the Valley and encountered our culture. It was hard for him to get used to. So where Glenda was saying that the guys here knew what to do, this guy didn't. I had to tell him 'When you pick me up you can't call me, that's like honking the horn.' I had to show him, and tell him and teach him."

I asked if the young men they dated ever balked at meeting the family so early in the dating relationship. I imagined that some found it peculiar and maybe even resisted. Giovana said that it depended on where the young man grew up.

"It's not weird to meet the parents early on in a relationship. What I have seen for those like us who were raised in the Mexican culture is that people whose parents did not raise them with the same values or who are not from our culture just don't understand this system of dating. I had an Anglo friend who said to me, 'You know, I'm dating this Latin guy and he wants me to meet his family.' And to her—and I've had boyfriends who thought the same—that meant 'He's going to ask me to marry him. Soon.' And she was very stressed out. I said to her, 'No. That's a good thing. He is just showing you respect and would like you to meet his family.' I said, 'In our culture, that doesn't mean he's going to marry you. He's just trying to get to know you and he wants you to get to know him.'"

Lilliana, a young married professional with a young child, expanded on Giovanna's point.

"To introduce the girlfriend or the boyfriend is very important so that the family knows whose company you're keeping. My mother always told me, '*Si es buen hijo, va a ser buen esposo. Y buen padre.*' [If he is a good son, he'll be a good husband. And a good father.] It's not a big deal to introduce you to the family. It's respect and nothing more."

Araceli elaborated that this did not imply anything more than simply showing respect to their families, so that the boy gets to know the girl and who she is. It is, at its essence, an invitation and nothing more.

"If we're having a birthday party," Araceli said, "we'll say to the guy, 'Come on over and meet everybody.' The guy who knows our ways, says 'Sure.'"

But the ritual of coming to the door and into the house to pick up his date signaled more than just observing *respeto* for her family. It was also an implicit statement from parents and family about their wish to protect their daughter, her chastity, and her reputation.

"We get lots of talks, too, from our parents, especially our mothers," Araceli joked, opening her eyes widely, eliciting agreement from the others. Like much of human experience, her words contained an implicit truth that the other women recognized.

"My mom would repeat a poem that was printed on a parchment at home," Liliana said, picking up on Araceli's statement. "I don't remember the full poem but the line I most remember said, 'Be woman but not a ragdoll.'"[11]

Giovanna's mother had a similar reminder for her when she said that "morals and values don't go out of style." Good morals and values endure even in times of change and cultural transitions.

At the point that a girl's relationship with a boy moved beyond more than simply meeting the parents on the first date, the stakes and requirements change. When a romantic or more intense friendship developed between the young couple, the brief encounter with parents when going out on dates gave way to more refined expectations of the girl and the boy.

"I remember my female cousins saying that to their home they didn't bring just any guy," Liliana recalled, "You don't just bring anybody to your home. You have to know that he is a guy that your parents will approve of."

"Even if it's not for marriage?" I asked.

"Yes. He has to be a good guy," Liliana answered. "And I remember that my aunt would say to us girls, '*No, no, mi hijita, aquí no me vas a traer a cualquiera.*' [No, no, my dear, you are not bringing just anybody here.] At parties and birthday celebrations you invite the boyfriend so that the family will approve of him. That is important."

"*Sí*, they can have many dates—they could be dinner dates, movie dates— *pero* the person you think you actually want to spend the rest of your life with, then he's a good person to meet your parents," Araceli said.

"The rule at our house," Glenda added, "was that they [parents] meet everybody. So if we did date, they met him. But if we were to bring them in and introduce them to the whole family, to the extended family, grandma, grandpa, cousins, then that was the person that you had thought would be the one to marry."

"That's if he didn't get scared and go away," Araceli joked. It was a humorous quip that caused them all to laugh. Their laughter not only conveyed the consensus of their experiences, but also served as recognition that it was a delicate dating and selection process fraught with challenges and special meanings.

"The standards are very marked for the family. Your family has to know that you are not going to associate with just anyone," Liliana said, as she told of learning about whom one could bring home and what values he had to reflect. "If you have a boyfriend, he had to share in your values and your parents' values, those your parents had taught you. He had to believe and live by them as well."

Viewed from the perspective of the young man, it seemed to me that he was not obligated to bring the girl to meet his parents as part of the dating ritual. As this group of women explained it, the young man would probably not introduce most of his dates or even girlfriends to his family. When he did, the act conveyed a very different message than when he was required to meet the girl's family. Liliana clarified this for me: "To me, the Mexican man is known for being *machista*; that he goes with lots of women. But when the man brings the girl to his family's home and introduces her to everyone in his family, he is saying 'I am with her' not with just anybody." The act of the formal introduction to the family signifies that the man is extending his respect to the woman and demonstrating the respect he has for his family.

Araceli explained that this act was a statement by young men that said, essentially, "I like and respect her enough to bring her home." In effect, this was not just another girl but a special one, one that his family would approve of. In turn, it was a sign of respect to his family that he would not just bring any girl to meet his family; he would introduce a girl into his home who met his family's values and criteria.

"Taking that one more step," Giovana went on to say, "it is an indication that they don't see you as an object for entertainment but as a possibility to marry and have a family with you. And that in itself is *respeto*. That they are going to respect you, that they are going to value the same culture, your same values. They are going to respect the standards you find acceptable."

The dating ritual or process had important effects on the woman as well as the man. Here is an exchange in the conversation that reveals how these women see it. It begins with my question about marriage and returns to dating and how that process informs marriage.

"When you marry, when a Mexican guy marries a Mexican woman, which of the two families do they gravitate to, his family or her family?"

"Hers!" they replied quickly, almost simultaneously, and very emphatically.

"You said that so quickly!" I pointed out, quite surprised by the swift and unanimous response, and the certainty with which it was conveyed. "Why is that?"

Liliana was first to answer. "I think, like we said at the beginning, the guy has to know that when he comes to pick me up, he won't whistle, he won't call. He will get out and come to the house. So the family has great expectations of the guy you are going to bring to the family. *Porque, verdaderamente, va a ser parte de la familia.* [Because, really, he will be part of the family.]"

Araceli interjected that the woman's family "takes him in right away." Parents, she reminded us, appreciate a young man's earnestness in following the cultural scripts for dating and courtship. The family, in turn, reflects its openness, embracing others and taking the young man in. He will, after all, be expected to protect their daughter.

"But why is it that you don't go to his family? And does the guy know that when he marries he will be with the wife's family?" I inquired. The tendency for a Mexican couple to be closer to the wife's family was not altogether surprising to me as I had seen it among other Hispanic families.

Liliana said, "Well, one really has to split time between the two families. But it is a curious thing that we tend to go toward the wife's family, maybe it is because we are a bit matriarchal."

Araceli agreed. "In the time that they are a romantic couple, the woman does not go to his house; he goes to her house. She is already bringing him into her family. And then that's when her family is with him.

"The same thing [happened] with my brother." Araceli continued. "When he started having girlfriends and then when he finally married, he was taken to her family. His priority is with her family." From the starting point of dating, the boy's family understands the girl's family's desire to protect and shelter her, just as they would their own daughter. The boy's family then adjusts to his increased involvement with the girl's family.

"One thing I think about is that in our culture," Liliana said, "the woman should leave her home dressed in white or married. Not so much in these times, but it's been like a law or a custom over hundreds of years, it's implicit, everywhere. And you don't leave your home to go study far away either. And you don't turn 18 and your parents say 'OK, my dear, you are now 18, we wish you the best, now go start your own life.' *No. En nuestra cultura pienso que lo más cercana que se pueda quedar a la familia, lo mejor.*

[No. In our culture I think that the closer one can stay to the family, the better.]"

A day after that kitchen table conversation, I sat in with a group of mothers at an after-school drop-in center. With us in the group was the youth worker who had invited the mothers to the conversation.[12] These were capable, successful parents facing challenging times, as their 12- and 13-year-old daughters, middle-schoolers, developed and matured physically and psychologically. Six mothers, mostly in their 30s, and one grandmother, much older than the others, gathered at the community center about 4 miles from the U.S.–Mexico border. All of them were born in Mexico and immigrated as teenagers or adults. The conversation, entirely in Spanish, was focused on the challenges and rewards of raising daughters in a different context than the one they grew up in. I wanted to know what they taught their daughters and why, and about the difficulties they faced. Knowing that I would hear later from their daughters, I wanted to collect information and impressions that I could raise with the girls when I met them. There was no reticence in this group of mothers; they were clearly there to talk and to teach me.

I asked about the values they wanted to teach their daughters, and what they saw as the proper demeanor for the woman. The first act among the women was one embodying *respeto*: they deferred to the eldest among them, Carmen, the grandmother in the group, to answer my initial questions about raising their daughters. Carmen began by describing a moment when she saw her granddaughter's unhappiness, her sadness about her absent her parents, and how life might be different if they were in her life.

"Look, my child," I said, "we are not all alike. I went through many things—I was a mother and now I am a grandmother. But you see, it was another adolescence, and nowadays it is harder than in those times. And you are traversing a very difficult period in your life. But you are not alone, you have many friends. When you are learning from those persons, grab the good, don't grab the bad." Carmen added that it is hard today, especially being Latina, for as she said, "we are Latinas and we live alongside other women in a life that is freer, more open [than we knew]. It is hard."

Layered over the challenges of their daughters' adolescence were the personal or family challenges. Lourdes, in the midst of a divorce, empathized with her daughter. Having tried to shelter her children from the pain of the divorce, it was inevitable that they would learn about it sooner or later.

"I was always careful to make sure that these aspects of life did not touch my kids," Lourdes said. "But the day came when we had to confront it and we did. And so, I think that the two things, the divorce and their adolescence, have affected them a bit, and I see my daughter as more serious about things, the way she looks. I tried to be patient when I saw the changes in her, but I was desperate because I wanted to get it out of her. Obviously, it was going to be little by little. It took a long time but we are now talking about it."

"We are the reflections of our parents," Mari stated. "I think about what I do very consciously because I know my daughter is watching and she will do what I do. If she sees that I get up from the dinner table and don't push my chair in or I say something, I know that she is going to imitate. Those girls who have lots of friends in the street learn more from them than in their own homes. The topic of values is a very hot topic because I can see that there are many differences in today's times than when I was growing up."

In their words and in their eyes, I could see that the values of their youth, the ones they wanted to instill, were being eroded no matter how hard they tried. Despite mere miles separating us that afternoon from the great land and culture of Mexico, it seemed like continents removed from us. Trying to uphold hallowed traditions was hard. Cynthia gave an example.

"I have a *comadre*," she said, "who had her daughter in a parochial school in Mexico. They brought her here last year and enrolled in her school. I saw such a difference between her and my daughter and her friends! When the girl entered the house she greeted everyone with, 'Hello. Good afternoon. Good morning.' *La educación* [upbringing] is so different. I ask myself, 'How is it that I have tried to inculcate the same things in my daughter but she doesn't do it?' It seems that here those manners are not as important but in Mexico they are. That's what I say. In Mexico the first thing my father would say to me was, 'How come you don't greet? What have they taught you in school?' It is that in school they don't teach them that! That girl who has lived all her life in Mexico has such good manners and values."

These were the *modales* or *la buena educación* that they wanted their children to retain from their original culture. It was difficult for them to get their children to observe these, like the girl from Mexico. The mothers speculated on why it is so hard for them to get their children to observe these social conventions. I have seen similar expectations of children in Puerto Rico and the Dominican Republic, that children must demonstrate good manners and respect when they enter a room of adults by greeting them. In they are kin or *padrinos* and *madrinas*, they may also be expected to ask the adult relative for their blessing (*la bendición*).

The first reason the women in this group on the U.S.–Mexico border gave as causing the erosion of these proud traditions was the way of life in the United States. Mirta felt that too much attention is given to money and to work in the United States. Cynthia agreed that life was very hurried here. Carmen spoke to the other mothers, describing her life as all work and having paid the price for her children having gone astray. Being the oldest in the group, she wanted to save other mothers from her travails. Carmen's tone was tinged with mild desperation, imploring the other mothers not to give up.

"Look," she said, "when I was a mother, it was pure work, work, work, money, money, money. And I learned now with my grandchildren that it can't be like that! We need to tell them what is going on and take more care of the children even more. We have to be telling them what they should do. When I was a mother, I could not run after them because I was always tired. Now as a grandmother, I cannot let myself get tired. But now I follow them, look after them, listen, and talk to them. Communication."

Another reason for the hardship of raising children with the traditional values and *modales* was that the way of life, of constant work and pursuit of money, seemed to the women to cause cultural changes that affected the family. Even elders who had spent more time in the United States, they said, were more lenient and less likely to teach, enforce, or model those values. In sentiments like those Cynthia expressed about the girl raised in Mexico with the good *modales*, Mari told of differences among two sets of grandparents.

"There's an important point to be made about this," she said. "In my family, we have the two grandmothers—the paternal and the maternal. The maternal grandmother, my mother, is in Mexico and the paternal one is here. And there is such a difference between them in the way they think. If my mother hears that, say, X happened with the kids, she will scream, 'But how could you let them? How could you permit them? I can't believe you let this happen.' And yet, over here, the paternal grandmother, well, it just slides off of her. She'll say, 'What? What's the problem?' as if it is not a big deal and the kids can get away with it."

"Even though we are so close to Mexico, it is very different, I think. The family is not as important here," Rosa, who had sat quietly, added. Others agreed that the conviviality of family life north of the border was not the same as it was in Mexico where one enjoys the company of one's family, where family unity is revered and jealously protected.

Lourdes, going through a divorce, yearned for the closeness of her mother and sisters living in Mexico. "I think that what happens in Mexico is that families get together more. For example, when I speak with my mother in Mexicali during the week, I ask 'Mamá, what are you doing?' And she says,

'Oh, your sister is here and your other sister and her boy and her daughter and the little nephew and they're all playing outside.' So they are living closer, together." Lourdes said this with a longing for that experience that was palpable, not just to be with her mothers, sisters, nieces, and nephews—but rather to celebrate the experience here. A fine point was made about how living across the border could have major consequential differences in children's *modales*. The border literally separated two countries, but more so, two cultures.

"How do you deal with these issues?" I asked. "How do you keep your daughters on the right path?"

Holding on to their values, fiercely, was one way. Rosa recounted telling her daughter that she must wait to use cosmetics until she is older. Others agreed that girls in their daughters' age group were too young for rouge, lipstick, mascara, and other makeup.

"My values, the ones I think served me well—*dignidad, respeto*—I teach them those," Rosa said emphatically. "They worked for me, for my brothers and sisters (there are seven of us) to this day. So I try to instill them in my daughter. I tell her, 'Look, *hija*, this is how I was taught and look at how these values served many other people. And I know they are going to help you.' Be sure, I motivate her to have those values of *dignidad, respeto*, and responsibility."

Mari followed Rosa, saying, "My husband and I say, '*Hija*, as long as I can, I will teach you good values as far as we can. When you go on in your own life, you will know what to do, right from wrong, and you will like yourself, what you are doing. This is how we can prepare you best for that world.'"

As the topic shifted to dating, I asked at what age most of them would allow their daughters to go out with boys on dates or have the boys come and visit their daughters at home. Most women said that the age of fifteen seemed reasonable. They used the tradition of the *quinceañera* as a milestone for dating. The *quinceañera* is a celebration, widely observed in Latin American cultures, of a girl's fifteenth birthday. The celebration may vary from one country to another, but it is steeped in tradition, pageantry, and festivities that bring family and community together. In her acclaimed book, *Once Upon a Quinceañera: Coming of Age in the USA* (2007), Julia A. Alvarez writes that the *quinceañera* like other cultural celebrations that immigrants bring with them is "about building community in a new land. Lifted out of our home cultures, traditions like the *quinceañera* ... become exquisite performances of our ethnicities within the larger host culture while at the same time reaffirming that we are not 'them' by connecting us if only in spirit to our root cultures" (p. 4).

Mirta, sister-in-law to Rosa, said that "After the *quinceañera* it seems to me that you can date but many mothers don't agree. They let their daughters go out at 12-years-old. I tell my daughter, 'Wait till your *quinceañera*, but if you have a boyfriend, there will be no *quinceañera*.' So my daughter lives with the illusion of the *quinceañera*, which may be something that's good for us!" The group laughed with Mirta.

"Let me give you an example," Rosa began. "In my home, I remember very well that my father told me, 'If you have a boyfriend before you turn 15, there will be no *quinceañera*. Forget it!'" The women laughed. "And I too told my child, 'No, you cannot have a boyfriend until you are fifteen.'"

The *quinceañera* had been very important to the women in their youth too. Mari made the point with her own experience: "In my home it was clear. I had some suitors, boys, you know? But I wanted my *quinceañera*! I couldn't risk my fifteenth birthday!" Again, the women laugh. "Even if I liked the boys, I waited until my fifteenth year."

While use of the chaperoning system was mentioned by the mothers in this group, most of them felt that in today's world they had to be more protective. Sending a young sibling along to chaperone did not seem to be enough, although it depended on where the daughter was going with the boy. If it was in the neighborhood for a walk, then a sibling was sufficient.

Lourdes introduced another detail about dating in her Mexican upbringing:

"You know something really important," she said. "I notice that my parents gave me, well, they didn't give me a lot of freedom. What they gave me was trust. You know what I mean?" The others understood and agreed with Lourdes.

"I think we should let them explore," Mari added, "to see that there is so much more, there is so much to choose from. They should meet people. In fact, I tell my daughter, *'porque no te vas a estudios 'foreign exchange?'* ["Why don't you go to a foreign exchange program?"] Yes, so that she can learn. Because I wasn't given the opportunity to know, to learn about the world. It was always like that."

Throughout the conversation, one mother, Dinora, sat quietly. The youth worker asked Dinora if she wanted so say anything. Born in Mexico but raised mostly in the United States, Dinora described some of what the women's daughters might feel, based on her own experience growing up with an immigrant mother.

"My mother is from Mexico and my father, also Mexican, was raised in the U.S. Growing up, it was a bit difficult because I wanted my mother to assimilate to the culture. But she wanted to impose all her traditions on me that had been put on her. And I would say to her, 'I am not from Mexico or anything. I don't live there.' She wanted to raise me like they raised her.

"I used to tell her that there were a lot of things, many things that happened and I wanted to be just like all the other kids. I think that over time she adjusted, she understood me and gave me a lot of trust. And now with my own daughters, I give them trust and I teach them the values that my mother taught me. All of the things she taught me and that I didn't want to follow, I am now teaching my daughters."

Dinora's story rounded off the discussion. Values endure, and even when the children resist, the women in El Centro understood the importance of teaching them to their daughters. These mothers were flexible in responding to their daughters' developmental needs and their individual personalities. But they were unyielding about how they wanted to prepare their daughters for adulthood.

A group of seven girls—effusive, amiable, introspective—capped my conversations in Imperial Valley, reinforcing much of what the women in the two earlier groups had said. They were the daughters and granddaughters of the women in the mothers' group; they were seventh and eighth graders, speaking mostly English but fluent in Spanish. They were Mexicans living among many other Mexicans. And except for one who had lived some years in San Francisco, they had known only Imperial Valley as their home. They were surrounded by reminders of their culture, not least of which was the access to Mexicali where they can get *tacos de borrego*, a delicious lamb-based taco.

I was interested in learning from this conversation about their socialization as girls. We began talking about the restrictions that their parents placed on them. Some of it, they said, came from the traditional concern with being a dignified woman, not one who hangs out in the street too much.

"And my mom says it looks bad for a girl to stay somewhere like really late," Anita said to open the discussion.

Paola agreed. "People will say, like, 'Oh, who's this girl? Where are her parents? She's always outside.'"

I asked how they dealt with their parents when told they could not do certain things, like date until a certain age. Mercedes was first to answer: "My mother will listen but she'll say I'm too young, 'you shouldn't see a boy.' Like they don't want to let us go yet. They're like afraid we're going to grow up."

"They worry that we're going to do something we're not supposed to do," Elena added.

Natalia spoke. "I feel like that and sometimes I ask, 'Why don't they let me?' And I think it's because sometimes boys trick girls to do stuff that they shouldn't. And I come to think, well, I'm just gonna have to wait. It's better if I grow up and my parents give me permission, and I can go without worrying that they're going to ground me or something."

I turned to the topic of the differences in how boys are raised and how girls are raised within the same family.

"Is there a difference in the way your brothers are allowed to do things . . ." I started to say but was interrupted by a spontaneous outcry from the girls.

"Omigod! Yes!" the girls said, nearly all at one time. They were emphatic and laughing.

"They get everything," Anita said. "Like when they go out to a party they get to stay out late. And they go like 'Mom, let me go and stay. Oh come on.'" She said this in a slightly whining manner, imitating her brother. "And my parents let them. That's why I like to be with my brother and go everywhere and get more stuff." The last statement revealed one of the benefits she derived from being a younger sister.

Nothing in the girls' words or in the way they spoke hinted at any serious resentment about their brothers' privileged position. They saw it as a status difference, something they seemed to understand and maybe even sympathize with. I asked whether they could articulate what lay beneath the differences in messages their brothers got from those that their parents had for them.

"But why do parent let boys stay out later than girls?" I asked.

Elena quickly answered, "'Cause they're guys. Guys are like more stronger and mature, and girls are more vulnerable."

"My brother," Melissa said, "he always uses his age, like 'Come on mom, I'm going to be 15 and you're not letting me do anything. I'm a guy. I need to do stuff.' And stuff like that. And we can't say that because we're girls. I try it but it doesn't work; he does it and she lets him go."

Julie was less accommodating to her brothers.

"I don't think that's fair. My brothers get to go out everywhere and stay out late with their friends, even on school nights. They get to go to parties, to the movies every week. They're almost the same age as me."

Anita, however, had a different perspective, "Our brothers get to do that because they are guys and guys are more tough and independent. 'Cause we're like girls and like we're treasures to our parents. And guys separate more from their parents than girls, and girls have more affection toward parents."

"I think it's because boys," Melissa began, adding specificity, "it's like they don't have that much affection towards . . . Well, they do but like they separate more when they grow up. Girls are more like 'Oh, mom. I like this boy. And mom this and mom that.' And boys like separate more."

"Not that they don't have affection for their parents. It's just . . ." Julia stated but was interrupted by Paola.

"That's right, it's not that they don't have affection for their moms and dads. It's just that boys don't go into details like girls do. They don't tell their moms everything like girls," Paola explained.

The topic turned from dating to marriage. I wanted to hear from them the perspectives they were establishing at their age, long before they began dating or even considering marriage.

"So when you get married . . ." I started to say.

"Someday," someone interjected quickly, followed by giggles and laughter. I was quickly clued in to the absurdity of a question about marriage with a group of adolescents who were not even allowed to date yet.

"Someday, someday," I deferred, laughing with the girls and recognizing the incongruity of my question to their lives.

"Okay. So when you marry, to whose family will you kind of be closer to, your family or your husband's family?"

"I think my family," Paola offered.

Most of the girls agreed that it would be their families to which they would be closer in marriage. Julie, however, balanced this point as the women in the earlier groups had.

"I think it will be equal. 'Cause you have to pay attention to both. You can't make one less than the other," she said.

Using words reminiscent of my conversation with the women at the kitchen table a day earlier, Melissa said, "I think that if my parents let me, I mean I'll take him to meet my parents and see how they agree with it [dating]. I wouldn't go hide it. I wouldn't date somebody that's all bad either. Oh, I like to go, like, 'Oh, this is my family.' And so they can get to know each other."

Finally, we talked about college and where they might go. Most said San Diego, a 2-hour drive, or nearby colleges. The general sentiment was the same: they would go to college somewhere near their families.

"I want to go somewhere distant, but I know I'm going to miss my family," Natalia said.

* * *

There was a great deal of consistency in the comments made by the three groups of Mexican women I met in El Centro and Imperial County. From their respective vantage points, the women shared the same kinds of concerns and ideas about dating, parents, *respeto*, affection, the roles of men and women, cultural rituals and customs, and familism. They added, like so many other Hispanic women had, to the knowledge I was collecting, and they verified some ideas that had long been questions in my studies.

One such lesson was related to child socialization. For a long time it had seemed to me that the socialization toward adulthood among more tradition- ally oriented Hispanics emphasized parenthood over other end points. That is, in many Latino families, the matter of growing up is couched often in terms that equate parenthood with adulthood. "When you become a parent" is treated the same as "When you grow up."[13] Adulthood was used synonymously with parenthood, rather than occupational roles. In our modern Western culture, we often define adulthood in terms of occupational roles. In fact, a question often posed to young children is "What are you going to be when you grow up?" Behind the question is the anticipation of an answer such as "a fireman" or "a teacher." Much less often we expect an answer that says, "I'm going to grow up to be a parent."

Viewing this through cross-cultural lenses, it is reasonably easy to see how different societies define adulthood. It is defined in highly nuanced ways, often depending on the histories and value orientations of each group. There is a view in mainstream American society that sees self-governance, emotional detachment, financial independence, separate residence, disengagement, graduation, and starting a family as the hallmarks of adulthood. Another view of adulthood is that of a person's movement into new roles and social positions, particularly the accession to adult family roles. Both views are quite familiar, normal to us.

The distinctions between these two points of view are very fine and quite subtle. But when we pause to consider how these nuances find their ways into the messages that a Latina receives every day, we can see that the results may be very pronounced, swaying the thinking and beliefs of the girl. We can say that traditional Hispanic socialization classifies adulthood as a change, an upgrade, in social and family roles and responsibilities, one for which women and men are prepared from childhood.

There isn't a great deal of empirical evidence, however, supporting my con- clusion. But a study by Carrie Saetermoe, Iris Beneli, and Robyn Busch (1999) offers some support to the observation about distinctions between Hispanic culture and mainstream American culture. In a study comparing the percep- tions of adulthood among parents of college students, Saetermoe, Beneli, and Busch start from the premise that social and familial expectations differ by what the cultural groups value most. In that study, Anglo parents in the study define adulthood in terms of independence, decision making, and problem solving more often than Latino parents. Latino parents defined adulthood more often than Anglo parents in terms of age, having children, and graduating from high school or college. In another contrast, Latino adulthood was defined in terms of helping family members, and Anglo adulthood was defined in terms of independence and moving away from home. Latino parents emphasized the importance of taking on different roles in the family (interdependence) as an indicator of adulthood. Latino parents believed that the qualities of adulthood are different for males and females, whereas the Anglo parents did not.

The words of the women in Imperial Valley add verity to the observation that parenthood is the crowning achievement of adulthood in Hispanic cultures. Not a bad definition, perhaps, for those of us who believe in the centrality of the family.

5

New Findings

After years of interest in the phenomenon of suicide attempts by adolescent Latinas, I was able to launch a large, well-funded study. My goal was not to count how many girls attempted; this had already been well documented in the scientific literature by 2005. Rather, I wanted to uncover the reasons that girls give for making suicide attempts in the first place and what the circumstances are that surround their attempts. It would be the first study of this size to embark on such a close examination of the lives of suicidal Latina teens and their families. It would be 5 years of many new challenges and discoveries. In this chapter, I give an overview of the objectives and design of the study and report our findings.

Study Objectives and Method

Our first research objective was to draw a portrait of the girls' psychological and social functioning, and their families' environments. We measured the girls' psychological and emotional functioning by focusing on the levels of internalizing and externalizing behaviors, as reported by the girls and their parents (Achenbach & Rescorla, 2001). We also measured their self-esteem (Rosenberg, Schooler, & Schoenbach, 1989). We derived information on the family through a questionnaire about the family's structure and history, dates and places of birth, when family members immigrated (if they had immigrated), the highest level of education the parents had attained, religious affiliation, family size, sibling order, parents' marital status, parental occupation, health insurance (as a proxy for income), and other information. We also measured families' levels of cohesion, expressiveness, conflict, organization, and control (Moos & Moos, 1981).

Given our theoretical premise that parents' relationships with their children have a powerful effect on children's outcomes, we assessed parent–adolescent relations. First, we measured the *mutuality* that exists between daughters and parents by adopting the definition and measure of mutuality developed by Nancy Genero (1992). Genero views mutuality as an interpersonal process of empathic engagement between two people, a relationship that is empowering and energy-releasing for both individuals. Second, we measured the quality of parents' mentorship of their daughters and defined mentoring narrowly as comprised of affection, communication, and support by parents. We selected items from other scales that would tap parents' nurturance, their demands for achievement and autonomy, companionship, consistency, and discipline, qualities that make for good mentors. Third, we measured the level of *conflict* that the adolescent girls reported having with their parents (not in the family as a whole) (Robin & Foster, 1989). We also measured the levels of acculturation to American society (Marín & Gamba, 1996) and of *familism* (Lugo-Steidel & Contreras, 2003) of both girls and parents. There were, of course, many other characteristics we could have measured, but we were concerned with those that in past research had been shown to be important.

Our second study objective was to explore the girls' experience—the phenomenology—of the suicide attempts. We wanted their reflections on the suicide attempt, and what meaning they made of it. To get at this, my team and I needed to draw out the girls' descriptions, even their analyses, of their subjective experiences, that is, what they felt, sensed, and thought, right up to the moment of the act—before, during, and after the suicide attempt. Our third objective was to place the girls within the context of family, social, and cultural systems by asking parents what they understood to be the reasons and meanings they attached to their daughters' suicide attempts. This information would amplify what the girls told us and permit us to contrast the reports of daughters, mothers, and fathers. We were particularly interested in the level of sensitivity that parents had about their developing teenage daughters.

Whereas we would achieve our first objective through questionnaires and quantitative scales and measures, we would achieve the last two objectives through detailed, in-depth interviews of girls and parents. The adolescent interviews explored specifically the suicide attempt from the girl's perspective. The interviews also delved into the family sociocultural environment with questions about the cultural beliefs and traditions that the family observed.

We learned quickly that with some girls we could ask the questions about the suicidal incident within minutes after starting the interview while others required more time to build rapport before broaching the topic. The interview guide and the experience of the trained interviewers aided us in making these decisions minute by minute in the conversations. Parents also provided a narrative of the events leading up to their daughters' suicide attempts. As in the girls' interviews, we focused on events and incidents that had preceded or influenced the suicide attempt. We inquired about the meanings parents ascribed to their daughter's suicide attempt or other behavior that they deemed relevant to the event. Nonattempters and their parents also completed detailed interviews similar to the attempters' except that there was no suicide attempt to refer to. Instead, with nonattempters and parents, we asked about a major conflict or crisis that had occurred between them and how it was resolved, probing for details that would give us clues as to the differences between attempters and nonattempters and their families. The crises, the girls' subjective experiences, and their parents' perceptions were to serve as comparison conflict resolution experiences in their families.

From hospitals and clinics, we recruited adolescent Latinas who had attempted suicide within the previous 6 months. The comparison group of nonattempters had to "look" demographically like the suicide attempters (i.e., similar ages, schools, social class). Therefore, we recruited the two groups from the same communities except that nonattempters came to us through social agencies, after-school programs, youth development projects, and word of mouth. We confirmed with the use of zip codes that the families lived in areas of New York City characterized as "inner city." That is, they were areas of high poverty and crime, crowded neighborhoods, densely occupied public housing projects, and suboptimal private housing.

We followed all human subject protections required by the Human Research Protections Office of Washington University in St. Louis and the institutional research boards of the participating agencies, clinics, and hospitals. We also followed the professional codes of ethics for social workers and psychologists. Therapists and research interviewers made sure that the Latinas with a suicide attempt in the previous 6 months met all criteria for inclusion in the study. Our efforts went into insuring the safety of our participants, particularly to protect the potentially fragile emotional states of the girls who had a history of suicide attempts. Parents of girls in both groups were invited to complete both the questionnaires and the qualitative interview.

Our interviewers were female, Hispanic, bicultural, bilingual, professional clinicians with experience interviewing teenagers and adults. By requiring that the interviewers be skilled clinicians, we would be assured that they could detect any emotional or psychiatric problems during the interviews and could probe into unspoken areas that might arise. But our study approach called for our interviewers to suspend their clinical know-how (to an extent, of course, since they did have to watch for any sign of trouble); we did not want them to act as therapists. It wasn't easy at first to recruit people with excellent clinical acumen and then ask them to suspend their natural therapeutic impulses during interviews. We insisted that the interviewers avoid any tendencies to make interventions, dynamic or even supportive interpretations, or to soothe the girls or their parents, or even make suggestions—all the things that clinicians do day in and day out. Rather, we wanted them to be curious and naïve about the girls (Dyche & Zayas, 1995), using the questionnaire and interview guides as maps of the terrain but with no prescribed routes. Each interview would find its own path in the interview guide. As the interviewers gained experience, they were less tied to the guide.

The Girls, Their Parents, and Families

In 2005, we took our study into the field—New York City—to explore what was behind the high rate of suicide attempts among young Latinas. Our data collection effort was spread throughout four boroughs (The Bronx, Brooklyn, Manhattan, and Queens) and continued until the summer of 2009. During that period, we faced many challenges in our recruitment of participants, which ranged from girls who were misidentified as attempters, to missed appointments, and to uncooperative staff in some recruitment sites. But we persevered and solved many of the problems (Zayas, Hausmann-Stabile, & Pilat, 2009).

Altogether, we enrolled 232 Latina teenagers. There were 122 girls who had made at least one suicide attempt within 6 months prior to the time that we met them and 110 who had no history of suicide attempts.[14] Seventy-eight percent of the girls were recruited in the Bronx, where we had our longest standing institutional relationships. Eleven percent of the girls were interviewed in Queens and 11% in Brooklyn. Table 5.1 shows how the two groups of girls compared. The only difference between them was that nonattempters were further along in school. Otherwise, they were very similar. The average age for all girls who entered the study was 15.45 (with a standard deviation of 2.02 years). The youngest girl in our study was 11, and the oldest at the time of recruitment was 19. They were in grades 5 through 12, and most were in the ninth grade. About 71% of all girls identified themselves as Catholic. Most of the girls were born in the United States ($n = 168$, 72%). The largest group of girls we interviewed was second generation ($n = 140$, 60.3%). Most mothers

(76%) and fathers (81%) were born outside of the United States, that is, they were first generation. For those girls who had attempted suicide, the average number of attempts over their lifetime was three, with 71 of the girls reporting one or two lifetime attempts (4 of who did not say how many attempts they had made beyond the one that brought them into our study), 18 reporting three attempts, and 33 recounting four or more attempts.

As shown in Table 5.2, over 60% of the girls identified themselves as either Dominican (28%) and Puerto Rican (35%). It did not come as a surprise to us that two thirds of the participants were Dominicans and Puerto Ricans; after all, they are the two largest Hispanic groups in New York City. Mexican girls comprised about 12% of the sample. Colombian, Ecuadoran, or Guatemalan girls represented 10%, 4%, and 1% of the sample, respectively. Some girls (7%) identified with multiple Hispanic subgroups or identified as being both American and part of a Hispanic subgroup (i.e., Mexican American, Ecuadoran American, etc.).

Over 60% of families reported having public health insurance (primarily Medicaid), 30% had private insurance, and about 10% either had no insurance or were unsure what kind of insurance they had. Many of the girls lived in households headed by one parent and had on average two siblings living with them at home. Forty-three percent of the girls interviewed came from homes headed by single mothers, and 3% were headed by single fathers. About 30% of the sample lived with biological parents, 17% with their mothers and a step-father or mother's boyfriend, 5% with another custodial adult, and 8% with at least one grandparent. The average household size including the presence of other blood relatives and other people such as friends was between three and four people. Most girls had siblings (82%), but some were only children (18%). Families typically had three children, although some of these children

TABLE 5.1. Demographic Characteristics of Latina Adolescent Suicide Attempters ($n = 122$) and Nonattempters ($n = 110$)

	Attempters				Nonattempters				
	n	%	M	SD	n	%	M	SD	t/χ^2 values
Age			15.34	1.79			15.58	2.25	$t(230) = .89$
Grade			8.39	1.69			8.88	2.35	$t(230) = 1.83^*$
U.S.-born	85	69.67			83	75.45			$\chi^2(1) = .97$
U.S. citizen	95	77.87			87	86.36			$\chi^2(1) = 2.98$
Catholic	93	71.31			72	70.00			$\chi^2(1) = .03$

Note: n = number; M = mean; SD = standard deviation.
$^*p < .05$.

TABLE 5.2. Countries of Origin or Heritage of All Girls (*N* = 232)

Country	Number of girls	Percent of sample
Colombia	23	9.91
Cuba	1	0.43
Dominican Republic	66	28.45
Ecuador	10	4.31
El Salvador	2	0.86
Guatemala	3	1.29
Honduras	1	0.43
Mexico	27	11.64
Peru	1	0.43
Puerto Rico	82	35.34
Venezuela	1	0.43
USA	3	1.29
Other	12	5.17

were stepsiblings of girls in our sample. Three attempters and one nonattempter reported that they had a child. Attempters and nonattempters did not differ on most household characteristics. However, significantly more nonattempter girls (42 of 110, or 38%) lived in homes with both biological parents than did suicide attempters (29 of 122, or 24%).

From our entire sample of 232 girls, 169 mothers (73% of the 232 families) and 36 fathers (16% of the 232 families) participated in the study. These levels of parental participation in research are fairly representative of other studies of adolescents. Mothers are typically more likely to participate than are fathers. Of the 122 Latinas who were in our attempters' group and completed the questionnaires, 73 of them also participated in in-depth interviews. Among their parents, 86 mothers completed the questionnaires, and only 46 of them also sat down for in-depth interviews; 19 fathers participated and 16 of them were interviewed in depth. Of the 110 girls with no suicide attempts who completed the questionnaires, we interviewed in depth 68 of them. Of the 83 mothers and 17 fathers of nonattempter Latinas who participated, 48 mothers and 14 fathers were interviewed in depth.

Like the adolescents in our study, parents of both attempters and nonattempters did not differ in their demographic characteristics. Fathers tended to be slightly older (average age 47) than mothers (average age 42). Most parents had a 10th grade education, although mothers of nonattempters had an 11th grade education on average. Over 60% of mothers and 70% of fathers worked full-time. Fifteen percent of all the parents who were interviewed were unemployed, over half of those people were unemployed for health reasons. Significantly more mothers of attempters were full-time homemakers than mothers of nonattempters.

At a glance, we see two points emerging from these statistics. *The first point is that having a mother who works outside of the home does not seem to raise the likelihood that a girl will be identified as an attempter. The second is that Latinas who never registered a suicide attempt in their lives were more likely to live in homes with both biological parents.* These results dispel the myth of the harmful effects on youth of having mothers in the labor force. Indeed, it is possible to conclude that mothers in the labor force may be better equipped to deal with their daughters' lives. Through employment and involvement with coworkers, mothers establish their own social identities and provide useful modeling for their daughters. Employment may also enhance a mother's acculturation and provide her with coworkers and a wider, more diverse social world from which she can learn about the challenges of adolescence and different parenting approaches. The findings also reinforce the value of having two parents at home on youth's behavior and development.

Contrasting Suicide Attempters and Nonattempters

A point of clarification is in order before presenting our comparisons of girls and parents. When I present findings that compare the two groups of Latinas, they are based on the two full samples of girls, 122 who attempted and 110 who did not attempt. When comparing parents, however, the comparisons are only for those parents who participated, that is 86 mothers and 19 fathers of attempters and 83 mothers and 17 fathers of nonattempters. When the comparisons are between girls and their parents, I report on only the 86 mother–daughter dyads in the attempt group and 83 mother–daughter dyads in the nonattempter group. The same occurs with the 19 father–daughter pairs in the suicide attempts group and 17 father–daughter pairs in the nonattempts group, although these are fewer.

The two groups of adolescent girls and their parents did not differ from one another substantially in their demographic characteristics. Their similarities bolster our confidence in comparing the two groups of families on the many variables that interested us in this project. There are a lot of findings to present, and for the sake of simplicity I provide a quick depiction of the differences between attempters and nonattempters and their parents.

Latinas and Parents on Acculturation and Familism

As we anticipated in recruiting young Latinas from similar communities, the attempter and nonattempter girls did not differ from each other in their levels of acculturation. Both sets of Latinas met the criteria for being "bicultural;" that is, they had scores on the measure of acculturation that were above the threshold scores for both Hispanic and non-Hispanic cultural domains (Marín & Gamba, 1996). As shown on Table 5.3, their average scores were very close, and the differences were so small as to be statistically insignificant. What is important about this information is that it reinforces the idea that accultura-tion does not mean a gain in one direction and a loss in the other. *The young Latinas in our study felt equally comfortable with the two orientations; they are*

TABLE 5.3. Comparison of Latina Adolescent Suicide Attempters ($n = 122$) and Nonattempters ($n = 110$) on Cultural and Family Variables

	Attempters		Nonattempters		
	M	SD	M	SD	t values (df)
Acculturation					
Hispanic	2.86	.72	2.90	.62	$t(229) = 0.52$
Non-Hispanic	3.53	.54	3.0	.44	$t(230) = 1.04$
Familism	7.35	1.32	7.51	1.04	$t(228) = 1.07$
Support	7.89	1.23	7.91	1.13	$t(228) = 0.10$
Interconnectedness	7.90	1.58	8.26	1.13	$t(228) = 1.98^*$
Honor	6.35	1.62	6.47	1.37	$t(227) = 0.58$
Subjugation	7.71	1.36	7.86	1.23	$t(227) = 1.07$
Family environment					
Cohesion	5.39	2.28	6.53	1.93	$t(221) = 4.03^{***}$
Conflict	4.50	2.20	3.55	2.22	$t(224) = -3.25^{**}$
Organization	5.65	2.14	6.25	2.05	$t(216) = 2.11^*$
Mutuality					
With mother	4.04	.90	4.53	.76	$t(225) = 4.38^{***}$
With father	3.91	1.12	4.34	.93	$t(146) = 2.58^*$
Mothers'					
Affection	17.18	5.55	20.10	4.62	$t(221) = 4.27^{**}$
Communication	16.18	5.26	18.88	4.72	$t(222) = 3.92^{**}$
Support	25.32	5.69	27.48	4.67	$t(220) = 3.08^{**}$
Fathers'					
Affection	16.62	6.24	18.56	5.25	$t(147) = 2.05^*$
Communication	15.25	5.92	16.92	5.66	$t(147) = 1.76^*$
Support	22.92	7.36	25.62	5.90	$t(135) = 2.45^*$

M = mean; SD = standard deviation.
*p <.05. **p <.01. ***p <.001.

effectively bicultural. Although the girls described themselves as bicultural, we must keep in mind that their higher endorsement of norms associated with mainstream American culture can generate tensions with their parents' more conservative adoption of those norms.

The pattern of acculturation for parents of the two groups of girls was also very similar, except that in their case, parents were less bicultural and more Hispanic oriented than their daughters. You can see in Tables 5.4 and 5.5 that mothers and fathers of nonattempters had slightly higher non-Hispanic scores than the parents of attempters. We have to read this cautiously because the differences between the two groups were too small to be statistically significant.

TABLE 5.4. Comparisons of Mothers of Adolescent Suicide Attempters ($n = 86$) and Mothers of Nonattempters ($n = 83$) on Cultural and Family Variables and Daughter's Behavior

	Mothers of attempters		Mothers of nonattempters		
	M	SD	M	SD	t values (df)
Acculturation					
Hispanic	3.34	.60	3.40	.47	$t(167) = 0.81$
Non-Hispanic	2.37	1.01	2.46	.85	$t(167) = 0.64$
Familism (Total Score)	7.93	1.01	8.05	1.05	$t(155) = 0.80$
Support	7.98	1.23	8.04	1.29	$t(166) = 0.34$
Interconnectedness	9.21	.76	9.31	1.00	$t(166) = .73$
Honor	6.68	1.61	6.80	1.54	$t(166) = .50$
Subjugation	8.12	1.20	8.15	1.21	$t(166) = 0.15$
Family environment					
Cohesion	6.64	1.85	7.14	1.65	$t(153) = 1.79^*$
Conflict	3.41	1.98	3.03	1.67	$t(161) = -1.34$
Organization	6.44	2.38	6.80	2.06	$t(164) = 1.06$
Mutuality	4.23	.88	4.78	.73	$t(163) = 4.37^{***}$
Affection	21.44	2.70	21.75	3.02	$t(163) = .70$
Communication	20.36	3.08	21.38	2.64	$t(163) = 2.28^*$
Support	29.58	3.58	30.35	3.30	$t(163) = 1.42$
Externalizing behaviors	18.03	11.24	9.11	7.36	$t(140) = -5.65^{***}$
Aggressive	11.5	7.34	5.70	4.95	$t(153) = -5.79^{***}$
Rule-breaking	5.40	4.39	2.62	2.43	$t(142) = -4.78^{***}$
Internalizing Behaviors	20.12	11.16	11.75	8.27	$t(144) = -5.20^{***}$
Anxious depression	8.45	5.32	4.71	3.65	$t(146) = -5.04^{***}$
Withdrawn depression	6.19	4.06	3.18	3.08	$t(150) = -5.18^{***}$
Somatic	5.41	3.57	3.42	2.87	$t(157) = -3.88^{***}$

M = mean; SD = standard deviation.
$^*p < .05.$ $^{**}p < .01.$ $^{***}p < .001.$

TABLE 5.5. Comparisons of Fathers of Adolescent Suicide Attempters ($n = 17$) and Fathers of Nonattempters ($n = 19$) on Cultural and Family Variables and Daughters' Behavior

	Fathers of attempters		Fathers of nonattempters		
	M	SD	M	SD	t values (df)
Acculturation					
Hispanic	3.15	.93	3.31	.68	t(34) = 0.62
Non-Hispanic	2.30	1.07	2.71	.74	t(34) = 1.32
Familism (Total Score)	8.57	.83	8.43	1.28	t(34) = −0.39
Support	8.90	1.00	8.56	1.65	t(34) = −0.74
Interconnectedness	9.23	9.27	.76	.92	t(34) = 0.14
Honor	7.82	1.39	7.58	1.59	t(34) = −0.49
Subjugation	8.68	.92	8.51	1.59	t(34) = −0.39
Family environment					
Cohesion	7.28	1.71	8.06	.83	t(33) = 3.25**
Conflict	2.58	1.71	2.59	1.42	t(34) = .02
Organization	7.05	1.43	7.65	1.50	t(34) = 1.22
Mutuality	4.48	.93	5.16	.66	t(33) = 2.66*
Affection	21.67	3.29	22.38	2.55	t(32) = .70
Communication	20.74	3.40	21.29	2.31	t(34) = 0.57
Support	28.00	3.57	29.25	5.21	t(33) = 0.84
Externalizing behaviors	18.29	9.21	8.35	4.94	t(29) = −3.84***
Aggressive	11.11	5.49	5.94	3.93	t(33) = −3.19**
Rule-breaking	6.29	3.12	1.76	1.30	t(29) = −5.79***
Internalizing behaviors	21.82	10.47	9.82	6.82	t(32) = −4.04***
Anxious depression	9.94	4.53	4.76	3.49	t(32) = −3.73***
Withdrawn depression	6.22	3.78	2.83	2.07	t(33) = −3.88***
Somatic	5.72	4.00	1.88	2.12	t(33) = −3.52**

M = mean; SD = standard deviation.
*p <.05. **p <.01. ***p <.001.

However, it does raise interesting questions of whether parents' higher non-Hispanic acculturation reduces their daughters' potential to attempt suicide. In a study of how cultural risk factors and assets affect Latino adolescents' mental health, Paul Smokowski, Rachel Buchanan, and Martica Bacallao (2009) also found that parents' U.S. cultural involvement was inversely related to anxiety for foreign-born females, and to social problems for foreign-born males and females.

Both sets of girls were more acculturated than their parents, significantly more non-Hispanic oriented than their mothers and fathers. Similar patterns have been reported on Hispanic youth in past research on acculturation. What is interesting is that, in general, greater adolescent acculturation in comparison to parents is often associated with negative youth behaviors, but this was not the case with our sample of Latinas, as both attempters and nonattempters were highly acculturated.

On familism, we found that attempters and nonattempters reported similar feelings of familism. Mothers and fathers of the two sets of girls did not differ from each other in familism. Not unexpectedly, mothers and fathers tended to endorse higher levels of familism than their daughters. Comparing girls and their parents on familism revealed that both groups of girls are less familistic than their parents and that they differ from their parents in familism at the same levels (i.e., the differences were similar for attempters and nonattempters). This finding does not mean that the Latinas in our study were not familistic in their attitudes. Rather it indicates that they were less familistic in comparison to their parents.

On the several measures of family functioning and the parent–daughter relationship, we uncovered some interesting differences. The teen Latinas in our two groups differed significantly from one another on how they viewed their families' environments. Attempters rated their families as lower on organization than was reported by nonattempters. Attempters also reported less cohesion and higher family conflict than did the nonattempters. Based on our past experience, this finding did not surprise us.

Differences between the girls were evident in other measures of relational qualities. In their sense of mutuality with mothers, Latinas with no attempt histories rated this relational quality as significantly higher (i.e., more mutuality) than did the Latinas with attempts. The same pattern is reflected in the girls' reports about the mutuality with their fathers. The two sets of girls differed significantly on their perceptions of their mothers' affection, communication, and support (i.e., mentoring). Suicide attempters generally reported significantly lower levels in these three qualities than did those who had not made a suicide attempt. The same pattern emerged with the fathers to a significant degree as well (but with so few fathers, we need to be cautious in interpreting these results).

In summary, Latinas with a suicide attempt history tended to report much lower levels of emotional attunement (i.e., mutuality) with their parents than did nonattempters. The attempters felt that they were not receiving affection or support at the level of other girls and that communication with their parents was poorer than girls without a history of attempts. The attempters reported that their parents were not inspiring mentors while nonattempters felt that their parents did a reasonably good job as mentors to them. These findings fit with our clinical experiences and past research, but they represent only one informant's point of view, that of the young Latina. The picture is sharpened by turning to parents' reports.

Parents' Perceptions of Their Daughters and Families

With respect to the family environments of cohesion, organization, and conflict, mothers of attempters and mothers of nonattempters did not differ from each other in their reports. Despite this lack of differences, mothers' scores suggest that they perceive more organization and cohesion and less conflict than their daughters. We found a significant difference between mothers of attempters and mothers of nonattempters on mutuality. Mothers of nonattempters, like their daughters, endorsed statements that the mutuality that exists between them was strong. Mothers of attempters rated their relationships with daughters as much less mutual and reciprocal. In terms of affection, communication, and support, mothers of both groups of girls described themselves as demonstrating affection and support to their daughters at about equal levels (Table 5.4). However, nonattempters' mothers reported higher levels of communication than attempters' mothers but this was not statistically significant.

We found a significant difference in the cohesion scores of fathers of nonattempters overall. These fathers saw more cohesion in their families than did the fathers of attempters. Otherwise, the two groups of fathers were not dissimilar with regard to familial organization and conflict. The two small groups of participating fathers also differed significantly from each other: fathers of nonattempters reported more mutuality than fathers of suicide attempters. Fathers did not differ at all from one another in their reports of affection, communication, or support. Parents of attempters and nonattempters did not differ from each other significantly on variables that described the family environment, including family conflict and organization, except for family cohesion. The difference here was that both mothers and fathers of nonattempters reported that their families showed significantly more cohesion than mothers and fathers of suicide attempters.

In summary, it appears that the parents of adolescent Latina suicide attempters and nonattempters perceive their families in pretty much the same ways. As seen earlier in this chapter, the two groups of daughters differed significantly from one another on all family relational variables—attempters painting a grimmer picture of their families than nonattempters. Mothers of the two groups of girls also differed from each other but not as radically.

Questions linger, however. How different from one another are these families or, rather, how much do the daughters and parents agree or disagree with one another on their relationships and functioning? To what extent are the differences between attempters and their parents and between nonattempters and their parents significant? What can be understood about suicide attempters and their parents when we examine them in juxtaposition to nonattempters and parents?

To answer these questions, we undertook analyses that compared the differences in mean scores on the various family and relational measures between the girls and their parents. In arithmetic terms, we took the parents' mean scores and subtracted the daughters' mean scores. The result of this subtraction yielded a "gap" or difference score. In other words, parents' mean score minus daughter's mean score equals "gap score." If the gap score had a *positive* value, this indicated that parents reported a higher value than their daughters. If the gap score had a *negative* value, this meant that the daughters had scores higher than their parents. Then the two gap scores between attempter parent–daughter dyads and nonattempter parent–daughter dyads were compared to determine if the differences were significant. Table 5.6 shows the mother–daughter differences, and Table 5.7 shows the father–daughter differences.

Beginning with mothers' and daughters' scores on family organization, cohesion, and conflict, we found that only in the measurement of conflict did the differences reach statistical significance. That is, the gap between attempters and their mothers was wider than the gap between nonattempters and their mothers (Table 5.6). Put another way, adolescent Latinas in both groups said that they saw more conflict in their families than their mothers did. This may not be at all surprising since adolescents in general report more conflict with their parents, especially in the early adolescent period (14 to 15 years), partly due to the natural developmental process. But attempters had a larger gap score between them and their mothers than between nonattempters and their mothers in how much conflict they reported. The gap scores for fathers did not reveal any significant differences (Table 5.7). On mutuality, the gap between girls and their mothers, and between girls and their fathers, was not significant.

Where significant differences in the gaps between mothers and daughters only (not fathers) appeared was in the mentoring variables, namely, affection, communication, and support. In all cases, attempters' gap scores from their mothers were significantly greater than those of nonattempters from their mothers. The gap in affection scores, for example, was twice as large in the attempter–mother dyads as in nonattempter–mother dyads. The same held for

TABLE 5.6. Comparison of Differences between Adolescent Suicide Attempters and Their Mothers (n = 86) and between Nonattempters and Their Mothers (n = 83) on Cultural and Family Variation[1]

	Mothers and attempters		Mothers and nonattempters		
	M	SD	M	SD	t values (df)
Acculturation					
Hispanic	.48	.61	.51	.62	$t(167) = 0.29$
Non-Hispanic	−1.19	.95	−1.14	−1.34	$t(167) = 0.34$
Familism	.66	1.58	.55	1.44	$t(166) = -0.44$
Support	.16	1.68	.16	1.61	$t(166) = -0.001$
Interconnectedness	1.39	1.71	1.09	1.50	$t(166) = -1.23$
Honor	.38	2.15	.32	2.11	$t(165) = -0.17$
Subjugation	.48	1.71	.26	1.71	$t(165) = -0.84$
Family environment					
Cohesion	1.35	2.83	1.12	2.26	$t(146) = -1.68$
Conflict	−1.24	2.60	−.33	2.20	$t(158) = 2.39^*$
Organization	.94	2.62	.44	2.37	$t(157) = -1.27$
Mutuality	.23	1.01	.25	.83	$t(163) = 0.14$
Affection	3.70	5.28	1.40	4.16	$t(160) = -3.07^{**}$
Communication	4.36	6.03	2.31	4.17	$t(161) = -2.51^*$
Support	4.53	5.78	2.79	5.22	$t(160) = -2.01^*$

*p <.05. **p <.01. ***p<.001

[1] A negative value for the mean score indicates that daughters reported higher scores than their mothers on the variable. A positive value for the mean score indicates that the mothers reported a higher score on the variable than the daughters.

communication and support but to a lesser extent (that is, the gap was not wide, but significant nonetheless).

That the gap scores between attempters and their mothers in conflict, affection, communication, and support were large probably does not come as a surprise to the intuitive reader. We know that conflict occurs in all families, it's a natural part of a dynamic family life irrespective of culture, race, ethnicity, social class, or national origin. And we know too that adolescents in general complain more than other age groups that their parents don't understand, listen, or support them as much as the teenager would like. But when that conflict is large and family members perceive its magnitude differently, we can easily conclude that it can be the basis for more family disruption and individual distress and acting out. Similarly, misjudging the level of affection, communication, support, and mutuality that exists in a family and between adolescent and parent can generate a situation of further mistrust and acrimony.

TABLE 5.7. Comparison of Differences between Adolescent Suicide Attempters and Their Fathers (n = 19) and between Nonattempters and Their Fathers (n = 17) on Cultural and Family Variables[1]

	Fathers and attempters		Fathers and nonattempters		
	M	SD	M	SD	t values (df)
Acculturation					
Hispanic	.22	.73	.44	.69	t(34) = 0.96
Non-Hispanic	−1.27	1.04	−.86	.79	t(34) = 1.30
Familism	.74	1.36	.98	1.67	t(33) = −0.46
Support	.70	1.56	.73	1.99	t(33) = 0.04
Interconnectedness	.74	1.49	.85	1.30	t(33) = 0.22
Honor	.99	1.92	1.45	2.31	t(32) = .64
Subjugation	.56	1.57	.72	2.22	t(32) = 0.25
Family environment					
Cohesion	1.35	2.83	1.12	2.26	t(32) = −0.27
Conflict	−1.71	2.11	−.82	2.07	t(32) = 1.23
Organization	1.16	2.63	1.87	1.73	t(32) = .90
Mutuality	.33	.98	.81	1.00	t(31) = 1.37
Affection	4.41	6.62	1.50	2.90	t(31) = −1.62
Communication	5.12	5.94	3.59	5.83	t(32) = −0.76
Support	2.88	6.98	2.44	5.92	t(30) = −.19

*p <.05. **p <.01. ***p <.001.

Latinas' Psychosocial Profiles

On the measures of psychological and behavioral functioning, the two groups of girls differed significantly from one another (Table 5.8). On conflict between the teenagers and their parents—not the family conflict discussed earlier—our analyses revealed that attempters reported significantly higher levels of conflict with their parents than nonattempters (Kuhlberg, Peña, & Zayas, 2010). (Parents were not asked about parent–adolescent conflicts.)

When we turn to other psychological and behavioral measures, we find some clues as to how parents might have answered questions about their daughters' level of conflict with them. These can be glimpsed through the externalizing behavior (e.g., aggression, rule-breaking) scales that the girls and parents reported (Achenbach & Rescorla, 2001). Externalizing behaviors in adolescents represent those negative actions and activities that are outwardly

TABLE 5.8. Comparison of Latina Adolescent Suicide Attempters (n = 122) and Nonattempters (n = 110) on Psychosocial Variables

	Attempters		Nonattempters		
	M	SD	M	SD	t values (df)
Parent–Adolescent conflict	6.62	4.83	3.68	3.86	t(211) = −4.90***
Externalizing Behaviors	19.95	10.82	11.42	6.86	t(217) = −6.93***
Aggressive	12.76	6.70	7.76	5.03	t(219) = −6.25***
Rule-breaking	7.15	5.01	3.79	2.77	t(218) = −6.10***
Internalizing behaviors	25.79	10.85	14.92	8.61	t(218) = −8.21***
Anxious depression	10.65	5.63	5.66	4.25	t(219) = −7.41***
Withdrawn/depressed	7.38	3.14	4.38	2.99	t(222) = −7.31***
Somatic	7.67	4.14	4.88	3.32	t(221) = −5.53***
Self-Esteem	26.88	5.28	31.88	4.98	t(215) = 7.16***

M = mean; SD = standard deviation.
*p <.05. **p <.01. ***p <.001.

directed, such as when the adolescent displays a persistent pattern of aggression toward others and to the property of others; breaking social, school, or legal rules; and problems in functioning socially with others due to antisocial or volatile behaviors. The externalizing disorders include oppositional-defiant behaviors and conduct problems. Latinas who were attempters were higher on aggression and rule breaking than Latinas who were not attempters. Mothers and fathers of suicide attempters also reported higher levels of externalizing behaviors among their daughters than did parents of nonattempters (see Tables 5.4 and 5.5).

Internalizing behaviors are characterized by anxiety, depression, withdrawal from family and peers, bodily (i.e., somatic) complaints, and discomfort. These problems may not be visible to parents or teachers and may not rise to the level of "problematic" because the adolescent's conduct does not create problems for others. Girls with suicide attempts reported significantly higher levels of internalized distress than nonattempters. Girls with a suicidal history reported significantly more anxiety, withdrawal, depression, and somatic complaints than nonattempters. When we look at only the parents' reports about their daughters (Table 5.4 and 5.5), the results are similar. Parents of the Latinas who attempted suicide saw more depression and somatization in their daughters than parents of Latinas without attempts. Unfortunately, though, our other data suggest that parents of attempters were not sufficiently attentive, tuned-in, or communicative with their daughters despite recognizing the signs of internalizing behaviors. Perhaps, too, they were aware but the communication in the family had broken down, or was never adequate, to encourage a healthy exchange.

An interesting pattern emerged, however, in the levels of internalizing and externalizing behavior problems reported by the suicidal girls and their parents. Young Latinas with suicide attempts assessed themselves to be *worse* in both externalizing and internalizing conditions by their own estimation than by their parents' estimation. The differences were not statistically significant, but they do show that the girls are sensitive to their behaviors. Often, we expect that teenagers play down the severity of their behaviors, but in the case of the Latina suicide attempters in our study, they were less inclined to deny or minimize their problem behaviors.

Other Findings

Beyond simply comparing the groups to each other on the specific variables that interested us, we wanted to examine the relationship of different cultural, familial, and individual-level variables with each other. For instance, does lower self-esteem lead to more conflict and possibly to higher odds of suicide attempts? Or, does self-esteem mediate the pathway of family conflict to suicide attempts? To answer questions like this one, we conducted several types of analyses. I will present only those analyses that showed significant results.

Jill Kuhlberg, Juan Peña, and I (2010) found significant relationships among various cultural, family, and individual-level variables. Using a path model approach that is able to measure both direct and indirect effects that variables have on each other simultaneously (i.e., how parent–adolescent conflict is related to internalizing behaviors and how, in turn, they are related to suicide attempts), we found that familism had a negative relationship with parent–adolescent conflict and a positive relationship with internalizing behaviors and self-esteem. That is, higher familism seems to act as a protective cultural factor against parent–adolescent conflict. But only to an extent. As attitudes toward familism increased, so did the girls' reports of internalizing behaviors, indicating that the girls in our sample with higher familism scores tended to have less conflict with their parents but internalized their problems more. It is conceivable that higher levels of familism in a restrictive family system may only act to silence the girl from speaking up against seemingly unfair constraints and emphasis on cohesion. This may have served to throttle her sense of the right and freedom to argue against what she perceived as unjust. Girls with lower familistic beliefs might deal with the stressful situations they face within their families by fighting with their parents; that is, they may be more verbally expressive or defiant which may have been allowed by parents and given the girl a sense of freedom to discharge her stress.

Our finding of the link between high familism and the concomitant family cohesiveness that it requires of family members points to need to consider that too much familism can also be detrimental. When familism becomes a means of psychological control of the person by more powerful family members, usually parents and other elders, it can have very negative effects. Parents' psychological control leaves children and adolescents vulnerable to many adjustment problems including, as shown in our research, internalizing symptoms (Barber, 1996; Silk, Morris, Kanaya, & Steinberg, 2003). And psychological control can have more deleterious effects during adolescence, a time when the search for autonomy, identity, and self-expression is at its apogee. This limits the development of the adolescent's social interaction skills that are needed to negotiate interpersonal stresses. At the same time, psychological control suppresses the self-expression that is part of the exploration of one's identity. It can lead to heightened guilt, worry, and physiological arousal, and low sense of competence and self-worth (Barber & Harmon, 2002). In this same model, parent–adolescent conflict was also negatively related to self-esteem and positively related to internalizing behaviors. As one might expect, girls who report more conflict with their parents also report lower self esteem and higher levels of depression, anxiety, and withdrawal (i.e., internalizing behaviors) than those girls who reported less conflict with their parents. In turn, both self-esteem and internalizing behaviors were significantly related to suicide attempts. *Jill, Juan, and I (2010) found that a 1-point increase in the measure of self-esteem significantly decreased the odds of being a suicide attempter. A 1-point increase in the measure of internalizing behavior was associated with a significant increase in the odds of attempting suicide.*

In addition to the direct relationships just detailed, several variables in this model had indirect effects on suicide attempts; that is, their relationship to suicide attempts mediated other variables. For example, although parent–adolescent conflict did not have a significant direct relationship to suicide attempts in this model, it did have a significant indirect relationship through its effects on internalizing behaviors and self-esteem. In other words, parent–adolescent conflict was related significantly to internalizing behaviors and self-esteem, which in turn, were significant predictors of suicide attempts. Similarly, suicide attempters and nonattempters did not differ significantly in their levels of reported familism, yet familism had indirect effects on suicide attempts through its mediation of internalizing behaviors.

In another publication (Zayas, Bright, Alvarez-Sanchez, & Cabassa, 2009), we reported several other interesting findings on girls' age and their perceived mutuality with mothers. On age alone (controlling for mutuality), a 1-year increase in the young Latina's age was associated with a 21% decrease in odds of being an attempter. Thus, the maturational process during adolescence may help mitigate the potential for a suicide attempt. More startling in its clinical implications is that when we controlled for the girls' age at the time of the interview, *we found that a 1-point increase on the girls' scores on the instrument that we used to measure mutuality was associated with a 57% decrease in the probability of being an attempter.*

Other analyses we have performed show that the adolescent girl's feelings of familism are related to how she views her family and the degree to which she presents externalizing behaviors. Using latent class analysis, a statistical modeling technique that classifies respondents into different classes or groups based on their questionnaire response patterns across multiple measures, we were able to group the adolescent girls as belonging to one of three types of families based on their reports of family-level conflict and cohesion. About half of the sample of adolescents reported high cohesion within the family and low conflict. One quarter of the girls reported having moderate cohesion and moderate conflict, and the remaining quarter of the sample described their families as having high conflict and low cohesion. When we examined how familism related to these family types, we found that girls who reported higher levels of familism were more likely to be in the high-cohesion and low-conflict families than the low-cohesion and high-conflict families. We also found that girls with low conflict and high cohesion were less likely to attempt suicide. In addition to familism's relationship to family type, it was shown to have a negative relationship to externalizing behaviors. That is, the more familism a girl reported to have, the fewer externalizing behaviors she reported.

* * *

Many of these findings easily match an intuitive observer's conclusion that families and girls with problems such as conflict, low communication and support, and other psychosocial problems would, more likely than not, be found in a group of suicide attempters. Adolescent suicide attempters in this sample look very similar to nonattempters in terms of acculturation and familism. Although familism was not related to suicide attempts, the importance lies in its association with other factors, including family conflict, internalizing, behaviors, and family types.

It is not surprising that adolescent Latinas are more acculturated and less familistic than their parents. And it is also not surprising that a group of teenagers would see the world and themselves in that world differently from the way their parents see their daughters. The two groups of Latinas in our study differ on their relationships with their mothers, their self-esteem, and their behavior within and outside the family setting. Attempters' mothers and fathers report similar parenting capacity but more strained relationships with their daughters than do nonattempters' parents, and they describe their daughters as more dysfunctional in terms of behavior. On all study measures where attempters and nonattempters differ, attempters appear more distressed.

Some very interesting relationships were uncovered. For instance, our inferential statistical analyses showed that with an increase of a sense of mutuality with her mother, there is a drop-off of over 50% in the odds that the girl would attempt suicide. That communication is healthy for relationships is not a remarkable discovery. What is more useful to my argument for clinical interventions and prevention programs is the finding that a small dose of improved sense of emotional attunement between mother and daughter, which commonly comes as a result of improved communication, affection, and experience of support, can possibly prevent a suicide attempt.

6

Anatomy of the Suicide Attempt

The instruments that the girls completed for our study tell only a part of their stories: attempters had lower self-esteem, and less organized family environments, and relationships with parents filled with conflict. Latinas with no history of suicidality reported conflicts with parents, just not as severe or protracted as those of suicidal girls. Parents of the two groups were similar in their sociodemographic profiles but differed significantly in their emotional attunement to daughters, and in communication, support, and affection. As girls' and parents' mutuality rose, their chances of attempting suicide dropped by half. Just as we would expect developmental and family systems theories to predict, those Latinas who attempt suicide often live in and react to toxic family environments and maladaptive parent-daughter interactions. In sum, the results of our questionnaires provide us with numerical profiles of over 230 young Latinas, many of their mothers, and a handful of fathers. We understand now a little more about what being a teenage Latina in the United States is like, and what leads some to manage life's challenges without resorting to self-injurious acts and what leads others to act on suicidal impulses.

What the numbers from our questionnaire cannot tell us about the interiors of their lives and minds especially following suicide attempts, the girls' own words do. We learn that the suicide attempts communicate much of the anguish that the girls feel, the chaos around them, the hurtful words and experiences they faced, and the sense that they are not listened to or understood. A 17-year-old Ecuadoran girl who made a suicide attempt by cutting herself with a razor blade said, "I've seen things that I shouldn't have seen. And like, when I was a child, when I was *supposed* to be a child, I was more of an adult, trying to, like, protect my brother and sister. And now, sometimes, when I'm supposed to be an adult and mature, I act like a child." Her words carry a desperate plea for the protection that she needed and should have gotten from the adults around her, a plea that went unheard by them. Where she needed adults to act responsibly, she was left to take care of herself and others.

The words of Margarita, a 17-year-old girl born of a Nicaraguan mother and a Mexican father, also embody the urgent, full-to-bursting need to communicate that was felt by so many girls. Of her suicide attempt, Margarita said,

> It's like I have so much pain inside, it's kinda like I cry inside. It's kind of hard to explain. But like, I guess when I cut myself, I feel like I'm letting out endless words. I'm taking out my pain.

Most adolescents in our study wanted to have their stories heard and understood. Indeed, many of the girls—attempters and nonattempters alike—kept diaries, wrote poetry, and did artwork to release their thoughts and emotions. The words from their interviews paint the best pictures of the sensations, thoughts, emotions, and interactions with fathers and mothers, the families' prevailing moods, and the intimate family experiences. Describing their suffering to others helped them make sense of this episode in their lives.

Recalling Trautman

In-depth interviews with 73 of our adolescent research participants pointed to the many similarities in their suicide attempts to those of the women studied by Trautman in 1961. The attempts by girls in our study were sudden, impulsive acts of escape, usually in the home with others nearby or in another room of the home. The girls who attempted suicide acted impulsively, had few ways of expressing their feelings, and had trouble regulating their emotions. As in Trautman's sample, prior to the suicidal act there was acute emotional excitation with a period of mounting anger and frustration. Our girls felt a need to escape the charged emotions or to try to control them. Lacking useful coping skills that can open new ways of solving dilemmas, the girls turned their actions against themselves. As we learned from a 16-year-old U.S.-born Colombian girl:

Yo me corté; no me acuerdo porqué pero sé que mi mamá me estaba peleando. Entonces me llené de rabia. No podía hacer nada. So, pa' desahogarme, me comencé a cortar. [I cut myself; I don't remember why, but I know that my mother was fighting with me. Then I became full of rage. I couldn't do anything. So, to unburden myself, I began to cut myself.]

Nearly all the attempts occurred after an intense interpersonal conflict, usually with someone in the family, a pattern reminiscent of Trautman's Puerto Rican women. There were altercations with fathers, mothers, or siblings. In the case of 14-year-old, Colombian-born Marietta, the argument was with her father just after he had struck her for lying to him.

Él me dio y me dijo un montón de cosas. Entonces él se fue para el cuarto y yo después vine y hablé con él. Le pedí disculpas por todo y entonces él se quedó callado. Me dijo que bueno, que estaba bien, que siempre yo hacía lo mismo pero que nada. Entonces después de eso yo vine y me tomé las pastillas. [He hit me and he said a bunch of things to me. Then he went to his room and then I came and I talked to him. I asked for his pardon for everything and he stayed quiet. He told me "it's okay," that it was okay, that I always did the same thing but nothing ever changes. After that I went and took the pills.]

The means of the suicide attempts—the ingestion of a prescription or over-the counter medication or a household detergent—were similar to those reported by Trautman. Where our sample diverged from Trautman's sample was in the higher incidence of cutting among our young Latinas.

The adolescents' thoughts at the time of the suicide attempt showed no signs that the girls wanted to die, and often the girls were not fully aware of their thoughts. That we saw no psychotic symptoms among our sample was primarily due to the selection process that we used, one that eliminated seriously mentally ill girls. However, in a few cases the girls' descriptions gave us reason to consider the possibility of an underlying mental disturbance that might have been transient or subclinical. When asked about what they were thinking during the incident, many reported their minds being blocked or going blank and not knowing what they were doing, as if they were in another world. An 18-year-old born in Puerto Rico described it as a mental block:

Como que se me bloqueaba la mente, como que no sabía lo que hacía. [As if my mind was blocked, like I didn't know what I was doing.]

A 16-year-old, Mexican-born girl described it as the absence of any thoughts:

I was just feeling bad. I wasn't thinking about my parents. I wasn't thinking about anything. I was just thinking about how to take the pain away because I was not feeling good.

A deadened or numb state was also part of the suicide attempt of many girls. Feeling like she was in an anesthetized state was the way a 13-year-old, foreign-born Ecuadoran described her experience:

Parecía como si estuviera bajo anestesia, como si me hubieran puesto algo. Sentía como si no me doliera nada. Mi mente estaba en blanco. [It was like I was under anesthesia, like they had put something in me. I felt like nothing hurt me. My mind was blank.]

Some of the young Latinas conceded that they wanted to die; others saw it as a way of managing their emotions. Still, others were ambivalent about the act. Those who wanted death were driven by the emotions they felt at the time of the attempt—often sadness, loneliness, guilt, and worthlessness. The underlying depression brought about a sense of despair and hopelessness. Those who wanted to manage their emotions really did not want to kill themselves. These girls might feel frustration, sadness, stress, or even confusion, but they predominantly felt anger. Most of the girls simply wanted to cope with the stress and pain. The following exchange between Selma, a 15-year-old U.S.-born Mexican participant, and our interviewer, exemplifies how some girls explained their intention.

Interviewer: What was your plan when you were cutting? To hurt yourself? To commit suicide?
Selma: No. To numb the pain.

Escalating Tension and a Trigger

The young Latinas' descriptions of the building anger had the quality of a pressure cooker; their heated anger could not escape or find expression. The girls described frustration and anger building to a crescendo, a point at which they knew no other way of managing than through the suicide attempt. As I discussed in Chapter Three on the flexibility that is seen in healthy family interactions, the family systems of many attempters appeared inflexible, often systems in which parents were unbending in their expectations of their daughters. Some other families had such porous, overly flexible boundaries that the needs of others (often a father, mother, or mothers' boyfriend) were more important than those of the young attempter. In a paper examining the patterns of distress and how the suicide attempts came about, Lauren Gulbas, Nicole Fedoravicius, Leo Cabassa, and I (Zayas, Gulbas, Fedoravicius, & Cabassa, 2010) analyzed 27 interviews closely to locate the circumstances leading up to the suicide attempt. From this subset of interviews, we found a persistent family ambience in which repeated incidents occurred, one of which would become the trigger at the point of the attempt. The trigger activates an overwhelming rush of emotions, often from a fight with a parent, usually the mother. But the trigger and subsequent suicide attempt can also come about as the result of a fight or conflict with siblings, other family members, or peers. We found that the presence of the trigger, however, is not what explains the suicide attempt. The trigger does not exist by itself, nor is it a separate element that brings about the suicide attempt. In fact, the trigger is actually embedded in a situation of continuous conflict and tension in the family between the teenager and her parents and siblings. Compounding this are family situations that are unstable: people coming and going, separations and divorces, death and losses.

The suicidal conditions are set over time. We learned in our study that the trigger represents a unique moment—or the culmination of a series of related moments—that takes place in the girl's life, a time when she might feel vulnerable, unprotected, or violated. The repercussions of this vulnerability endure, and the trigger causes the girl to relive the moment, or the emotion of those moments, again. She may feel misunderstood, not taken seriously, or bereft of support and protection from others, and she, too, might feel violated physically, psychologically, and emotionally. It is at this moment, after the girl has been primed by a pattern of emotional turmoil, that the trigger event causes her anguish and awakens painful reminders past experiences that she no longer wants to feel. Like combustion, "kindling" conditions have accumulated and a mere spark ignites the attempt.

Fathers Present and Absent

Before turning to the family environments that foster the tension-escalating and trigger conditions, a note about fathers is necessary. All too often fathers escape our scrutiny, yet they form part of the environments and the problems that adolescent Latinas face. Because mothers generally spend so much more time caring for their children, they are more likely to participate in research with their children, often because they have to give approval for the child to participate in the research or bring the child to the research appointment. While having mothers engage in research on their children helps researchers generate more knowledge that can be used to improve lives, their participation makes mothers vulnerable to being misunderstood or worse, blamed for their children's problems. Too often mothers bear the brunt of blame unjustifiably. This is not only unfortunate but unfair, and it is something I do not wish to perpetuate in this book. From the many clinical and research observations, there is no way to acquit fathers from the significant, maybe culpable, roles they play in creating or promoting the conditions that set off the suicide attempts.

Many single mothers—raising children *contra viento y marea* (against wind and tide), against all odds—participated in our study, and many of them were mothers of girls who had never attempted suicide or engaged in self-harm of any kind. There were single mothers of healthy children and well-functioning homes. There were mothers whose marriages were in turmoil or even crumbling, whose husbands were of little help, yet they managed to provide emotionally balanced conditions at home that did not push their daughters to despair. Elizabeth, a U.S.-born 14-year-old of Dominican descent, was among our group of girls who had not attempted suicide and whose family illustrates strength even in the face of adversity. As their lives quaked, mother and daughter held on to each other.

Elizabeth's parents had a tense marriage since early in their 15-year union, and the problems had reached a point where their communication was acrimonious and distant. In fact, her father left for a visit to the Dominican Republic without planning with or telling his family. Elizabeth began acting out, partially in response to the family stresses and partly from her budding attempts at independence. Her mother worked long hours and attended college. In spite of these family circumstances, Elizabeth's mother was sensitive to her daughter and her daughter to her. Elizabeth understood why her mother would "go off" in a tirade whenever she reprimanded her and recognized that her mother would stop fussing when "she realized that she went overboard." When asked about getting along with her parents, Elizabeth replied,

> That bond is always there, I guess. It's like I can't get mad at them, whatever; I have to get along with them. I live with them. [Interviewer: And is it difficult to get along with them?] Not really. Just if you do what they say. If you don't, you get in trouble and you get yelled at. And then you feel horrible.

As a result of some truancy that was discovered by her mother, Elizabeth was grounded and stripped of a few luxuries. The interviewer asked Elizabeth how she got the punishment lifted:

'Cause I'm not bad anymore. I changed. Don't cut school anymore. I go to school. We turned a new leaf, we started over, started fresh, going to the new school. [Interviewer: And who decided that?] I did. Me and my mother. We decided: start school, start fresh. We decided together.

Elizabeth's mother corroborated much of this information, recognizing that she does yell too much when she's annoyed with her two children. In a recent conflict about Elizabeth making some decisions without her mother's permission, Elizabeth's mother realized that "*ya yo estaba frustrada y lo que hice fue dejarla tranquila. Porque si seguía entonces le iba a pegar y yo no le quería pegar.*" [I was just frustrated, and what I did was leave her alone. If I continued, I would hit her and I didn't want to do that.] Instead, they took a car ride to together, though Elizabeth remained silent throughout the trip.

In spite of her husband's recent distancing in the marriage, Elizabeth's mother never maligned him in his children's presence. It was evident from her narrative that her husband had been a good father and had been able to instill good qualities in his children. Hers was a good example of mothers who made the best of a difficult family situation for herself and her children, with mostly positive results although not without conflict and stress. It illustrates too the impact of fathers even when they are offstage.

In our studies, the few fathers who participated played powerful parts in the lives of their daughters, for both those girls who attempted suicide and those who did not. Whether the men were present or absent physically or emotionally, they played a role. For instance, we saw fathers of nonattempters who were strong, caring, and involved and had a critical presence in helping raise their daughters, including fathers separated or divorced from the girls' mothers. Even among fathers who did not participate in our study, we heard from their nonsuicidal daughters and the girls' mothers of the affirming parts they played in the family and in the adolescents' lives.

Most fathers of attempters did not participate in our study. Their daughters and wives or ex-wives spoke explicitly or implicitly about the toxic influences the fathers had on their families. Sometimes, however, the scores on the measure of mutuality that attempters gave their fathers were higher than the ones they assigned to their mothers. That is, these girls reported that their fathers were more attuned to them than their mothers. I found these to be illusory most of the time. Girls separated from their fathers sometimes had weekly telephone conversations with or visited them on weekends or during summer vacation. Many of these fathers lived outside the home or outside of the country, some in prison, with irregular exposure and limited interactions with their daughters. It was as easy for the girls to see their fathers favorably as it was for the fathers to present a façade of compassion and thoughtfulness. In short conversations, the men could counsel their daughters, offer considered advice, make statements of understanding and empathy, or offer promises of a brighter time together. It was easy to see how girls might then idealize their fathers and report high levels of mutuality, communication, affection, and support. These fathers, however, did not have day-to-day responsibilities of taking care of their daughters or dealing with schools, boyfriends, peers, loneliness, desperation, household chores, petty mischief, major defiance, sibling quarrels, and all the mundane but challenging elements in the life of a household with an adolescent. Mothers faced these tests all the time.

In describing the family environments of suicide attempters, it may appear that mothers played a greater role than fathers in some of the problems at home. This is not at all what I mean to convey; it should not be construed as only a matter of mothers and their daughters. Instead, we have to see that the men's influence, indeed the patriarchy that they personify, was always present, a hovering influential presence in the women's and children's lives. From family systems theory we know that even those family members who have died or are not physically present may still exert a great deal of influence on how family members think and act.

Environments of Chaos and Failed Communication

The escalating tension and the trigger occurred in environments with many difficulties, a context that took many different forms. Girls described conflicts and turmoil that did not get resolved, poor communication between parents and with their daughters, and evidence of skewed family systems where roles were reversed or altered from what is typically expected. There were boundary violations of psychological or physical intrusions in some families. Some girls had mentally or physically ill parents. There were families in which teenagers had experienced profound losses or had felt abandoned physically and emotionally. Outright psychological, verbal, physical, or sexual abuse was described in some families. There was sexual abuse that had been hidden by girls because they feared their parents would not believe them or feared their parents' reactions. And in other families, there was no hint of such trauma.

Not all families had the same relational problems or manifested them in the same way, and the magnitude or severity differed as well, but there were problems that persisted. In essence, there was no one kind of family environment that easily distinguished the girls who attempted suicide. The following descriptions of different family environments that were given by girls and parents do not represent all the possible family environments that one could find in the lives of suicidal Latinas. In fact, typically most families did not reflect just one of these family scenarios. Often a family might have two or more scenarios that overlapped.

At their core, most families had patterns of communication that were broken and what often ensued were misunderstandings, insensitivities, mistrust, defiance, and conflict. Conflicts often reflected girls' ongoing frustration with their parents and the lack of communication among family members. Amparo, a 16-year-old U.S.-born girl of mixed Dominican and Puerto Rican parentage, described the interactions in her family that contributed to her suicide attempt as "I felt anger in my family, because we don't know how to speak to each other."

The interviews also highlighted girls' strained relationships with their parents, most often manifested in their interaction with mothers but not without the complicity of the father, whether present in the home or not. Many young Latinas felt misunderstood by their mothers and described a sense of alienation and distance from them. Two girls described their unique experiences. Jacinta, a 16-year-old foreign-born Mexican girl said,

> I am tired of my mother trying to change me and my mother trying to make me be something that I am not. I am tired of her stuff. I really do want to get up and leave sometimes, but I just solve it by not even talking to her. I walk into the house, and it will be like we are strangers. It's a hi and bye. That's about it.

Jocelyn, a U.S.-born 15-year-old of Dominican heritage, described her experience in a slightly different way:

> [My mother said] that I don't do nothing around the house, that I never help her or anything. That I never listen to her, that I don't respect the house, that I don't respect her. That I always do what I want. All that stuff. And then, I wanted to like, I didn't want to be there, 'cause she was like screaming or whatever. I was getting impatient, I wanted to leave.

The case of 15-year-old Sofia who attempted suicide adds detail to how family environments affect the girls.[15] Sofia had grown up with a violent father, but since his deportation to the Dominican Republic, Sofia has lived with her mother and two brothers. They have extended family support nearby.

We learned that Sofia's mother is having difficulty with her daughter's development. Both Sofia and her mother describe the relationship as growing increasingly distant. Yet, Sofia undersands that this separateness is simply a natural outcome of growing older. She says, "We can't be close to our mother. Come on, we're older." However, Sofia's mother interprets this distance as Sofia's loss of love for her, putting Sofia in the position of having to assure her mother that this is not the case—telling her mother she loves her, hugging her, and saying, "Mother, come on, I'm getting older. I don't have to talk to you about everything." Her mother often tells Sofia that she misses her, although they live together. Her mother thinks that her daughter's pulling away from her is due to her strict and old-fashioned ways. Sofia and her mother have different understandings of their growing detachment. The girl views it as a normal developmental movement complicated by a highly dependent mother, whereas the mother perceives their distance from a singular, self-referential perspective, rather than with more understanding.

Prior to her attempt, Sofia had exhibited signs of depression and frequently felt that "life was pointless." Her mother noticed Sofia's apparent depression when Sofia told her mother that she wanted to see a psychologist 2 weeks prior to the attempt. The mother did not think much of Sofia's request to see a therapist—expressing much regret later for not taking action. But when her daughter told her that "life has no meaning," the mother took Sofia to her pediatrician the following day for a mental health referral. This mother tried to help her daughter, but unfortunately, the only available opening was weeks away. Sofia couldn't hold on: her suicide attempt occurred almost a month before she could be seen by a psychiatric clinician.

As for many attempters, the suicide attempt came after an argument between Sofia and her mother. Sofia was very stressed about a school project that was supposed to be done as a group with other students but put the project off until late on a Sunday night. Sofia says the mother screamed and yelled at her. After the fight, Sofia realized she "didn't want to wake up to my future." She felt she was working hard enough and that she would become "another piece of scum on earth. I don't wanna be that so I'd just rather die." Sofia's mother feels that her maternal instincts failed her at the time of Sofia's desperation.

Hurtful Words and Missing Affection

The schoolyard rhyme of "sticks and stones may break my bones but words will never hurt me" is a good lesson when we want our children to ignore the taunts of classmates and others. But a children's rhyme is grossly ineffective in the context of a family: Words do hurt, more so when they come from the very people who are supposed to be there to make us feel secure, to whom we turn for comfort and affirmation. There were cases of girls among our attempters who were subject to verbal and emotional abuse, sometimes called "stupid," "worthless," or "whore" by their parents and siblings. Some girls described being repeatedly degraded by their parents, causing them to feel unloved or angry. A 13-year-old Ecuadoran girl who had cut herself with a knife described her relationship with her mother this way:

> Mi mamá cuando se enoja me dice "no te quiero ver, te odio, te odio, no te quiero, lárgate. No te quiero ver aquí en mi vida." Mi mamá dijo "no hubieras existido en mi vida." [My mother when she gets angry tells me, "I don't want to see you, I hate you, I hate you, I don't love you, get lost. I don't want to see you here in my life." My mother said, "You should never have existed in my life."]

Amparo, who described her family as never speaking properly or sensitively to one another, made the suicide attempt after one of many fights with her rebellious older sister.

> I said, "Why are you arguing with Mother?" She started yelling at me, "Get the hell out; shut the fuck up; why don't you mind your business?" Because ever since she turned 18, she went terrible, worse than what she was. She thinks she can do whatever she wants, that she can tell anything to anyone, anytime, or whatever. And it hurt me.

No doubt there were instances in which parents or siblings, even in the families of nonattempters, said hurtful things to each other. However, in the life of the suicide attempters the verbal and emotional abuse was omnipresent and part of the functioning of its members. Imelda, the 14-year old U.S.-born daughter of a Peruvian father who was a naturalized U.S. citizen and Mexican mother who was an undocumented immigrant, describes a family environment that was chaotic to the extent that they spent time in a shelter for the homeless. Some of the problematic environment was a direct result of ongoing, relentless, and damaging paternal verbal abuse. Imelda attempted suicide with an overdose of 30 analgesic tablets. Imelda describes her father's unremitting behavior that spanned many years in the following way:

> With me, he would see every little thing wrong. Like since I was little, if I broke a page out of my notebook, or if I didn't pick up my toys after

I played, he would just like come up and beat me. He was like, "Why are you doing this?" Like he'd start like cursing at me and he'd beat me, and then after that he would make me feel bad. He would make me feel like I deserved it. And sometimes even if it didn't even involve me, he would just pick on me. . . . Like, he knew my boyfriend, and he said, "I'm tired of her and her boyfriend. I don't want them together. She's a slut. She's this and she's that." And one day I remember, I was washing the dishes and my dad was sitting there and my mother was sewing. So my dad was seeing a movie, and my mother commented to my dad, "Oh, have you heard the news about this girl that was helping her parents 'cause they got deported? And she's in charge of her younger siblings." And my dad was like, "Oh see? They have a good daughter. Those parents should be proud of their daughter. Unlike us. We have a daughter that's worthless and she's only getting us in trouble." He's like, "She's nothing. She's worthless. She's this, she's that. She's never gonna prosper. Look what we've raised. She's trash. You raised trash."

Other examples of hurtful words appear in the trigger event of Anabel's suicide attempt. A retaliatory comment by her half-sister was intended to remind a vulnerable Anabel of how she was abandoned by her father. and her sense that even her mother was not protecting her. This 13-year-old daughter of a Puerto Rican mother and Dominican father reports the incident this way:

I was mad at my sister, and I went into the kitchen and took a bottle of pills and swallowed the bottle of pills in the bathroom. We were arguing the whole day, and then my mother kept defending her so I got mad. 'Cause at first we started off arguing about the computer, and then she said something about my father: that he's never there for me or something like that. I got mad. That's when I went into the kitchen and took a bottle of the pills, and then I went into the bathroom and took, swallowed them.

As we saw in other girls, Anabel felt bereft of the presence of a person or people who could provide emotional anchors. Anabel told her mother what she had done as a suicide attempt, "I wanted to go rub it in my mother's face. Like to taunt her about what I did, to make her feel bad, to make her feel like it was her fault."

The absence of supportive, loving words was sometimes as painful to the girls as the harsh words of their family members. Jacinta, the 16-year-old undocumented Mexican immigrant who complained that her mother wanted her to be what she wasn't, expressed the cruel effects of not receiving affection:

> Basically I was always more afraid of my mother than my own father. My father and I always got along with. Then as years passed it just got worse. I noticed that my mother never hugged me or gave me a kiss or never said she loved me. She never expressed feelings towards my sisters or me. I noticed that my father did, so I became tighter with my father than with my own mother. My mother always backed away, and every time I would try to tell her about something that happened at school she would always blame me, like I was the one who started it or something.

Zuleika: Actions and Words That Hurt
BY ANA A. BAUMANN

Communication between family members is a mix of words and actions. In Zuleika's family people speak mostly through actions and much less so through words. Oftentimes, words are used to inflict pain. Zuleika is a 15-year-old born in the U.S. of Dominican parents who now lives with her mother, four siblings, and an aunt who has two young children. Her father is in prison for drug dealing.

Zuleika's mother supports all eight people in the house financially, as her sister is not working at the moment. To help at home, Zuleika babysits her cousins and does other house chores. She is trying to balance her obligations at home and at school.

> School is stressful just because I feel like there's things that I should know for my age that I don't know. Because when I was in middle school, I looked at school like it's playtime. And I do regret that 'cause I go to school now and there's things I should know for my age and I don't know. So it's stressful and I just sit there and feel stupid. So that's stressful. Maintain grades, stressful. Coming home to take care of two kids, very stressful. And knowing that, like me personally at my age, I think that kids don't think about bills to pay and stuff like that. I think about it every minute, so that's stressful.

Zuleika's mother had a difficult childhood, raised by an aunt and grandmother who punished her with violence. The mother reports that "*no le importaba a nadie lo que yo sentía . . . si estaba enojada o no estaba enojada. No le importaba a nadie*" [Nobody cared what I felt . . . if I was mad or not. Nobody cared].

Both Zuleika and her mother say that their relationship was not always bad, but when Zuleika was 12, she told her mother of being raped:

I was raped by my uncle at 8, and then it stopped – like it was 3 years that it went on. At 12 years old, I told my mother. I expected her to do something; she didn't. And I felt like she, maybe she didn't do it 'cause she was like in denial. I don't know what it was. I was frustrated that she didn't do anything, so I saw that she didn't care. That's why I like lost my respect for her, or started treating her differently. So that's why we don't get along now.

Her uncle went unpunished. Zuleika says that she does not allow herself to get close to others and admits to reacting physically, fighting with her sister, schoolmates, and even punching the school principal.

Zuleika's violence seems to have been modeled at home, which is presented in her mother's interview in a very graphic manner. When she gets angry at Zuleika, her mother says:

Yo lo que quiero es agarrarla y desbaratarla. La agarro y si la tengo que ahorcar, la ahorco. Yo le digo a ella que estoy pidiendo a Dios que me ayude a calmarme para no agarrarla y matarla. Yo te di la vida y yo te la quito. [What I want to do is to grab and tear her apart. I grab her and if I need to strangle her, I will. I tell her that I am asking God to help me calm myself so as not to grab her and kill her. I gave you life, I will take it away.]

Yet, she states that she has never hit Zuleika and she tries to control herself:

Me tranco en mi habitación y no salgo de ahí hasta que no me calme. O me entro al baño y agarro . . y me empiezo a echar agua por la cabeza hasta calmarme.
[I lock myself in my room and do not come out until I calm down. Or I go in the bathroom and I splash water on my head until I am calmed down.]

Her mother's description of Zuleika follows a similar pattern of ambivalence. She describes Zuleika as

Un fosforito, una dinamita que está esperando un fósforo para explotar inmediatamente. Pero también ella es una niña buena, con buenos sentimientos.
[A little match, a dynamite that is waiting for a match to explode immediately. But she is also a good girl, with good intentions.]

Zuleika became pregnant by her 20-year-old boyfriend. During the pregnancy, she says that her communication with her mother improved. It was not, however, a smooth period. Her boyfriend was absent because he lived in another state. As a mandated reporter, her counselor notified the child protection service about the pregnancy and that it was caused by the adult boyfriend five years her senior. Zuleika was very hurt and upset.

Zuleika miscarried at 3 months. Both daughter and mother believe the miscarriage was the result of a vaccine to prevent cervical cancer that Zuleika was given at the beginning of the pregnancy. After the miscarriage, the communication with her mother broke down again. She says that no one cared about her and felt that her mother's actions were saying, "Since there's no baby, I don't have to, like, be there for you as much anymore."

Zuleika made a suicide attempt, triggered by a fight with her sister, who accused her of taking money from her aunt. Zuleika admits stealing the money, but she did not want her family to know. As for the attempt, she says that she did not want to kill herself but she wanted to stop feeling pain:

> I was frustrated. And then after I did it, like I stopped crying 'cause I didn't feel, I was like numb when the blood was coming out. So after that I felt fine. You don't think. Like me, personally, I didn't think anything, I was just, like nothing was going through my mind. I was just calm, looking at it. Nothing. You don't think about anything, like everything's fine.

It was 2 months before anyone in her family noticed the scars.

Although Zuleika's house is full of people, loneliness is a pervasive feeling. To communicate, this family acts rather than talks, hurts rather than heals.

Disappointed and Unprotected

Since words and deeds help the adolescent feel secure and loved, their combined absence deeply affected some of the girls who attempted suicide. In the case of sexual abuse, the girls rarely reported the event to their mothers for fear of not being believed or of causing a rift in the family. For example, a 13-year-old, U.S.-born girl of Dominican and Puerto Rican parents told her mother about being sexually molested by a male relative of the mother's new husband. However, she felt that her cries for help were left ignored. The young teenager conveys her disappointment and lack of affirmation.

> I was telling her because he started touching me around my chest area and I was telling her "I want to go home, I wanna go home." My mother started yelling at me. She was like "You're not coming home, you're not

coming home." She wanted to start her summer with her husband or whatever. She was only worrying about herself. She didn't let me go home.

Two nights later the girl attempted suicide with a large overdose of acetaminophen mixed with codeine.

On the whole, girls who experienced abuse developed patterns of aggressive behavior toward their parents, expressing their anger for not having been protected. This anger was often unleashed through suicide attempts. In other cases, girls' responded to the abuse with guilt, either because they interpreted their actions as a cause of the abuse or because they failed to stop the abuse.

Lorena: "All that happened was my fault"
BY CAROLINA HAUSMANN-STABILE

The guilt that many abused girls felt is illustrated by the case of Lorena. This 13-year-old, U.S.-born girl of Mexican descent, lives with her mother, stepfather, and three half siblings, ages 7, 5, and 5 months. Lorena spends some weekends a year at her father's home, where she joins a stepmother and two other half-siblings. We met Lorena shortly after her suicide attempt, an event that was preceded by a long story of sexual abuse and emotional neglect.

The abuse began when she was 9, at the hands of the brother of her mother's boyfriend at the time. Left alone to care for her younger brother while mother worked, Lorena made an easy target for this man who forced the girl to perform fellatio on him. Lorena took to eating pumice:

> *Yo me salía (del cuarto del abusador). Entonces yo iba con mi hermanito.*
> *El estaba chiquito y yo le decía lo que había pasado. Pero yo sabía que no iba a*
> *entender, pero nomás me lo quería sacar. Yo luego iba al baño y encontraba la*
> *esponja y me la empezaba a poner en mi boca para limpiarme. Al hacer eso, lo*
> *comí.* [I would leave (the abuser's room). Then I would go with my little
> brother. He was young, and I would tell him what had happened. But I knew
> he would not understand, but I just wanted to get it out. Later I would go
> into the bathroom and find the pumice, and I started to put it inside my
> mouth to clean myself. By doing that, I ended up eating it.]

When the abuse was discovered, her parents chose not to report it to the authorities. The perpetrator moved out of the house and the family resumed its life. Within a few months, Lorena was being victimized again, this time by her mother's boyfriend. There was no safe place for Lorena at home. She was abused even while her mother cooked just a few feet away or while she and her siblings watched cartoons. After 2 years, her mother finally took notice.

The abuse was not reported and Lorena continued living with her abuser. Her mother's sole reaction was to put a lock on the children's room door and lock them inside when the boyfriend was in the house. This measure did not last long, and the sexual abuse started again. On the night preceding her last suicide attempt, Lorena awoke to find the man molesting her. She told a friend at school who then approached a school counselor, and the case was reported to child protective services and the police. No charges were filed, leaving Lorena baffled and aware that her mother could not be trusted to protect or seek justice for her.

It is understandable that Lorena sees her mother as complicit in the abuse: her mother explains away her daughter's suicide attempts with "*Cada vez que ella tiene anemia, ella le da por comer, querer comer cosas.*" [Every time she has anemia, she takes to eating, she wants to eat things]. Her mother's disregard for Lorena's needs and emotional state made the abuse possible, and reinforced Lorena's sense of hopelessness and guilt.

As seen in cases like those of Lorena, girls often felt that they lacked the parental mentoring and modeling that would provide them with solace during times of upheaval and times of quiescence, mentoring that would help them develop the capacities to deal with stress. But many lived in family environments characterized by instability. Their words and actions were suffused with a deep sense of disappointment. The girls could not count on a reliable person to "show them the ropes" in life and provide good advice that was buttressed by behavior that the girls could model. The girls had to learn on their own by trying not to do what their mothers and fathers did. But trying not to repeat their behaviors was not enough. The girls may try to avoid doing what they have seen but without healthy alternative examples of what they *could* or *should do* they were susceptible to repeating what they knew.

Jacinta, a 16-year-old Mexican immigrant, was bitterly disappointed when her father left home for another woman, after his many displays of being a "good guy." This was compounded by the disappointment in her mother for her reaction to the husband's leaving:

Since my father left, she is like trying to get him back. I see her like she is a little girl, like she is trying to get him back no matter what. I always say to myself: "Guys don't rule me." I rule myself. It is like, basically, I don't throw myself on the floor for a guy.

Imelda, too, the Mexican-Peruvian girl whose father was verbally abusive, experienced her mother's vulnerability and ineffectiveness in managing her life. Her mother did not know how to negotiate social service systems, indelibly marking the impression of her mother's ineffectualness. It was fed by the vulnerability that her father bred in her mother:

And I told [child welfare] how my mother was scared 'cause she didn't have her papers, 'cause she was an immigrant. She didn't have her green card or nothing, and she was scared to call the police on my dad, 'cause my dad was a citizen. He has his citizenship. And my dad would always like tell my mother, "If you leave, or if you call the cops on me, I'll call the cops on you and say you're an immigrant and you will get deported. And I'll take my children with me. You're an immigrant, and you can't take care of the children. They'll take them away from you. I have papers. They'll give them to me." And I would never want to be with my dad.

In the suicide attempt moment, Imelda said, "I felt like nobody understood how I felt and they wouldn't help me. So I just decided to take the pills and cut myself." Imelda had not learned how to cope on her own. While she didn't want to be as vulnerable as her mother, Imelda's repertory of coping skills was limited.

In the case of Maritza, an 18-year-old Puerto Rican attempter, a series of significant losses—her parents' divorce, her brother's suicide, and her father's death—left her without an anchor or the emotional and cognitive means to deal with her solitude.

Me sentía muy sola, muy sola. Mi papá falleció antes de venir yo para acá. Además yo era la nena linda de mi papá. Que me dolió mucho su partida y en verdad lo que me hizo que me cortara. Creo que es, en verdad, que me sentía muy sola. [I felt very along, very alone. . . . My father died before I came here (to the United States). I guess I was my father's darling baby girl. His death really hurt me. Really, it made me cut myself. I think I really just felt very alone.]

Yvonne and Linda: Contrasting Two Lives

Yvonne and Linda, two girls about the same age, lived under difficult home circumstances, both girls acting as caregivers to their ailing mothers.[16] As we see, their outcomes look very different. How effectively they managed their stressful lives seem to be a function of the nature and quality of family interactions and parent–daughter relations, and each girl's own emotional and psychological strengths.

Seventeen-year-old Yvonne, who alternated between Spanish and English in her interview, lives with her mother and younger sister. She has never known her father as he was incarcerated before she was born. Yvonne has a strong relationship with a maternal aunt who lives in Puerto Rico, where both of her parents and she were born. Her aunt is the only person, she feels, with whom she can talk and feel understood. Her mother suffers from cirrhosis of the liver and leg ulcers, with multiple hospitalizations and is now bedridden. Despite the help of a home attendant assigned to her mother, Yvonne feels responsible for her mother's care in the evenings and weekends.

Although she had problems attending school when she was enrolled in school, she dropped out because she felt she needed to be home with her mother. Her mother said in the interview that she was upset that her daughter was skipping school but did not express much disappointment at the fact that she was staying out of school to help her. Yvonne talked about how much she worries that her mother will have a heart attack or fall at home when Yvonne is not there to help. Yvonne's mother does not speak English well, so her daughter must translate and act as a cultural broker for her mother.

Yvonne and her sister take responsibility for many of the household duties: "At home I'm the one who cooks for my mother 'cause like she is supposed to be in bed, she can't get up." When asked who takes care of her, Yvonne said, "*Bueno, puedo decir que yo misma, porque ella se la pasa acostada.*" [Well, I can say that I do, 'cause she's always lying down.] Yvonne accepts her role as the caretaker for her mother, but she says that at times she gets tired of having to be at home for her mother:

Está bien, yo sé que soy la única que la tiene que atender a ella, y hacerle a ella sus cosas. Pero ella tiene que entenderle a uno también. I mean, *uno es joven. Uno por lo menos quiere salir, divertirse, no estar metido adentro de una casa viendo televisión o haciendo cosas.* [It's okay, I know that I'm the only one who has to attend to her, and do things for her. But she has to understand me too. I mean, I am young. I want to at least go out, enjoy myself, not be stuck inside a house watching television or doing chores.]

Yvonne faces a conundrum even though she understands that her mother needs her. On the one hand, Yvonne's mother expects adult-like behavior from Yvonne in caring for her and in taking care of the home. On the other hand, her mother wants to have a say in or have control over Yvonne's friendships and social life. This places Yvonne in a position of being treated like an adult in many matters but then being restricted in other, age-appropriate matters. The signals are inconsistent.

The trigger event for Yvonne's suicide attempt came during a series of agitated telephone calls with her boyfriend, who had acted jealously and insulted her in front of her younger sister. Her mother knew of the insult, having heard it from the younger daughter. Yvonne tried to cope with her anger and frustration by cooking, watching a movie, and calling her aunt, all in an effort to get her mind off of the situation. Still, Yvonne felt she had no one to comfort her and provide solace. Her mother's only offer was to try to talk to Yvonne and to call the boyfriend on Sofia's behalf to help resolve things. This was of little use to Yvonne, a girl accustomed to dealing with her hardships independently. Her mother's offer was not only too little too late, but it was also a rather inept attempt to help her daughter. In her emotional spiral, Yvonne drank rubbing alcohol and some of her mother's painkillers.

When asked about her impressions of her daughter's attempt, Yvonne's mother seemed surprised by the attempt, and surprised to learn that Yvonne was depressed. She had not noticed Yvonne's complaints of trouble eating and sleeping, and not socializing. Instead, the mother attributed the attempt to the conflict with the girl's boyfriend.

Like Yvonne, the other girl in this story, Linda, had to be a primary caregiver to her mother, who had suffered a serious spinal injury. This 18-year-old girl of Colombian descent lives with her mother. An older brother lives outside the home. Her parents separated when she was about 12 after her father's infidelity. Both the mother and daughter say that family is very important, and that they value their relationships with the mother's siblings who are all in Colombia. Linda speaks of family reunions and trips to Colombia. They do not have relatives nearby, except her father, who lives in another state.

Linda's father had been absent for several years but was now back be in their lives again. He visited every weekend and stayed with Linda and her mother, providing some financial assistance as well. For the mother, the reappearance of her ex-husband is a source of stress. In addition to her depression, she harbors anger toward him for the infidelity and abandonment. Linda feels a better connection with her father than her mother and looks to him for guidance but does not discuss other details of her life, such as dating. She feels that she is more like her dad than her mother in the way they view problems:

He doesn't stress things, so that's why me and my mother have more problems, because she likes to be on top of everything, and she says if

this goes wrong, everything goes wrong. It's a matter of life o1
her, and I don't think, I don't think anything is like that.

Because of her mother's debilitating injury and other ailments, ⎩
compelled to drop out of school at age 15 in order to work and sup₊ ₋. ner
mother. She got a job at a fast-food restaurant and later at a supermarket, giving
the money to her mother for the bills. She recalls that she did not like telling
people that she had dropped out of school. Linda views her teenage years as
abnormal:

> I feel kind of disappointed also 'cause I should be in school, you know?
> I was 15 years old and I was working. Why was I working? I'm not
> supposed to be working, you know. I mean, I could be working if I
> wanted to have money in my pocket. But for supporting a home? It's kind
> of hard, and I feel that's the worst period of my teenage years. I don't
> have a regular teenage life, I think.

Linda is very responsible and motivated, making decisions and thinking
things through. She felt responsible for her mother because she cannot speak
English and is easily overwhelmed by problems: "It's just that I think my
mother is a child basically." Linda accompanies her mother to medical appointments and does all the talking for her. Her mother depends on Linda, even
deferring major financial responsibilities to her. Speaking of her worries about
paying the rent, Linda's mother places the responsibility on Linda: "*Ahí que ella
vaya a ver como soluciona.*" [There, let's see how she solves it.]

Since Linda's father's reintegration in her life, she has gone back to school,
taking business classes and working on a high school equivalency diploma.
Linda is very resourceful, finding scholarships for books and locating people to
help her get into college and other academic programs. She says that her father
is supportive of her career aspirations. Her mother seems very pleased that her
daughter is back in school but expresses feeling lonely if Linda takes too long
to come home after school. Linda says that she would like to go to college, but
she does not feel capable of leaving her mother alone.

Hope is a major theme for Linda. She looks forward to her future. When she
gets stressed or frustrated, she talks to her best friend. She also keeps a journal:

> I write a lot: what's good for me, what do you want for your future, and
> you just have to go . . . do whatever you have to do, but go for it.

* * *

For many of the young Hispanic women in our study—whether they attempted suicide or not—the age-old generation gap is overlaid by an acculturation gap. That is, that girls differ with their parents around the typical issues of adolescence (e.g., independence, values, argot, attire) that are part of the generational gap. But the acculturation gap complicates the relationship even more. Girls are moving into the mainstream society more rapidly than their parents wish. This is seen in women's roles they want to adopt and the family interactions that are evident in the mainstream culture. Clashes in the values of their parents' traditional culture and the modern mainstream culture are evident in both groups of girls in our study. These two gaps—generational and acculturational—makes the adjustment in adolescence to new self-definitions as women so difficult for many Latinas, particularly those whose parents may resists strongly. Those girls who attempted suicide reported that their parents were not in synch with their emotional or developmental needs. The suicide attempts were forms of communication about the failed communication and the inadequacies in the family and parent–daughter relationships. The failed communication and attunement were partially the result of generational and acculturational differences but also due to family environments that where chaotic or inflexible.

The attempts are emotional, psychological, visceral experiences, and they derive from an accumulation of stress, trauma, and upheavals in the young Latinas' lives. We can see how cultural differences between girls and parents, in familism, acculturation, and changing cultural values and mores, can create stresses that potentially add fuel to an attempt. There is also economic hardship in families, neighborhood conditions that strike fear in parents and cause them to be restrictive with their children, and often crowded living circumstances. Congested, underperforming public schools and other social factors have their unique contributions. But to sociologize the suicide attempts omits the important part played by psychological factors. At the family and individual level, many dynamics are unconscious, among them the full implications of the cultural differences among family members. We see at times family dysfunction that primes the conditions for suicide attempts by leaving them emotionally vulnerable, without the psychosocial capacities (e.g., adequate coping skills; capacities to modulate or regulate their emotions; frustration tolerance and impulse control) to deal effectively with the strife in their lives. The absence of caring, consistent mentors is often a feature in the lives of Latinas who attempt, in contrast to those who do not.

7

Explanations

No study, including the one described in this book, has yet fully answered the question of why Latinas attempt suicide more often than adolescent girls from other ethnic and racial groups in the same age range. We have, however, a better understanding of the suicide attempt phenomenon than we did previously. But it will take much more behavioral and anthropological research and insights garnered from clinical practice before we can confidently say that we have a reasonably solid grasp of this complex phenomenon.

As I pointed out in the opening pages of this book, the evidence has accumulated over the years, and it points to an interaction of factors. These factors converge, maybe even clash, at a critical moment in the girl's life with such force that it triggers the suicide attempt. And the conditions of the suicide attempt are set over time for the attempt to be made. We found that the trigger event is not an isolated event; rather it is spread across in a series of incidents that weaken the girl's coping capacity or overwhelms her. In the case of many girls in our study and those seen by other clinicians, there is often a pre-existing vulnerability, such as difficulty regulating their emotions or a history of trauma from abuse, neglect, or long separations from parents at critical ages.

Triggers among our study participants occurred when the situation felt intolerable and girls were emotionally vulnerable, when after long periods of conflict and tension during which they felt unsupported, their meager coping skills simply could no longer help them. Still shrouded in mystery and uncertainty are the reasons that Hispanic girls are more prone to attempting suicide than Asian, Black, White, and American Indian girls. If what distinguish these girls from one another are their cultures, then what are the features of U.S. Hispanic cultures and growing up in the United States that are so unique as to compel the adolescent Latina to attempt? Our findings appear to confirm that psychological and social factors, cultural traditions and transitions, and acculturational differences between the girls and their parents, along with aspects of family functioning, are mixed with the natural forces of development, maturation, and the individual characteristics of the teenage Latina to create the circumstances for a suicide attempt.

Walking in Two Cultures

"Whatever the ultimate trajectory," states a Pew Hispanic Center (2009) report on a national survey of Latino youth, "it is clear that many of today's Latino youths, be they first or second generation, are straddling two worlds as they adapt to the new homeland" (p. 3). The Pew Hispanic Center report goes on to say that many young Hispanics are socialized by families to emphasize their Latin American heritage; many say their parents speak with pride about their countries of origin, and the youth share this pride. These kinds of messages from their parents and families are apt to influence the young Latina to refer to herself by her family's country of origin. I return now to what managing, not just walking, in two cultures means to the Latina.

In the context of the suicide attempts of young Latinas, the idea of two cultures is fundamental to helping explain the phenomenon. We know that their suicide attempts derive from a complex mix of individual psychology, social and family factors, and other powerful cultural forces. Straddling two cultures only begins to explain the experience of growing up Latina. A more apt description might be that of an intricate dance that she must learn to bring together in her heart and mind the many cultures and identities that she encounters while the ground on which she dances is shifting between the traditional and the modern. It is a transitional process, but not one in which she is simply going from one culture to another. Rather, it is an integration process, a transitional challenge of bringing two or more cultures together in forging her identity (Zayas, Gulbas, Fedoravicius, & Cabassa, 2010).

Latinas have often "grown up between two cultures, belonging to both and to neither of them" (Itzigsohn & Dore-Cabral, 2001, p. 319). The two worlds that the young Latina must negotiate as she grows are played out in the environments she inhabits: her family and the world outside. What are the cultures and cultural times that Latinas are straddling? There is the traditional Hispanic culture, the one that emphasizes very strongly familism and the importance of sacrificing her needs in order to fulfill the obligations, indeed expectations, to the family collective (Kao et al., 2007; Nolle et al., 2011). And this emphasis stands in contrast to traditional Western values that prioritize individualism and independence (Lester, 2007). The contradictions of two competing cultural socialization systems that define selfhood and womanhood in different ways become apparent. Despite the diminished authority of *machismo* in the lives of Hispanic women that has been brought about by cultural and socio-political changes in modern times, it remains alive and continues to influence gender roles in Latino families and their cultures (Ascensio, 1999; Chant, 2003; Nencel, 2001). In a world of changing norms, women's traditional gender roles are changing from those of passivity and dependence to those that value power, assertiveness, and strength. In this way, being a Latina daughter of immigrant parents represents a cultural-developmental point where she is neither a traditional Hispanic woman nor a modern mainstream woman, neither a child nor an adult—she is "betwixt and between assigned cultural positions" (Gutmann, 1996, p. 31). The young Latina has to negotiate loyalty to family and gendered traditions and the call of the mainstream society. Listening to the latter, which encourages a psychological, emotional, and behavioral independence, can put her at odds with the family's traditional ways. These are the two worlds that the young girls in the case studies from our research and the girls that we met in El Centro, California, will face and for which their mothers are working hard to get them ready.

The discontinuity between these two worlds can create a lonely, anomic place for her to occupy. It reflects the wider cultural discontinuity in coming from the culture of her parents and ancestors to engaging in the broader culture into which she is inserted. Like others around her, the young Latina views these two worlds as in flux, feeling ambivalence about each and both. Moving from the culture she knew at home as a little girl and entering a new, very appealing one, trying to blend them, can shake her sense of stability and security. Suicide attempts among young Latinas may be a response to the "the unmaking of time-honored value systems" (Biehl, Good, & Kleinman, 2007, p. 3).

The young Latinas of my research and my clinical practice seem to understand the infringement of Western cultural ideals on the traditional cultural values of their parents. The complexity and anguish in bridging this cultural discontinuity, the two often contradictory value systems, may be among their biggest challenges. It can fracture the girls' sense of connection to their families, leaving traditional roles and adopting new ones, and it also complicates the sense of her identity, particularly in the early adolescent years. Pushing toward the autonomy presented by the mainstream culture that comes with development and the preparation to accede to adult roles (Erikson, 1950) that imply an adoption of a different definition of self and womanhood can be at once appealing and frightening—frightening because she may feel at times that she has to "go it alone." The young Latina and her parents see the possible distance that her independence will mean for them, threatening or weakening the familism that has such emotional meaning. We saw this in the words of Ramona's parents (Chapter Three), who understand that their daughter will someday move away from them; all they can do is get her prepared for that day. Latinas in families that functional well, families that have the capacity to adapt while remaining psychologically cohesive, can bridge the two worlds. In families without these same resources, the young Latina tries to cope with the fragmentation that the dilemma poses, possibly leading her to resort to self-destructive acts.

Individual Psychopathology

Cultural strains may be part of the background to suicide attempts of young Latinas but we have to guard against seeing it all through cultural lenses for, in fact, there are individual psychological and psychopathology evident in the suicide attempters. As I discussed in Chapter Five, there are deficits in the self-esteem of suicide attempters. While the girls in our study who had never attempted had similar scores as past studies of non-Hispanic White and Black youth in the general population, the attempters suffered from low or poor self-esteem. Using coping skills that were immature or ineffective (e.g., withdrawal, wishful thinking) was evident in the many transcripts of interviews with suicide attempters that we coded. Few of the girls in our study had major depressive episodes but most suffered from depressions that were of long duration (what we often call dysthymic disorders [American Psychiatric Association, 2000]) or reactive depressions to recurrent family or interpersonal stresses.

One characteristic that was seen often in our suicide attempters were those who had difficulty regulating their emotions in socially appropriate ways. Emotional regulation is a complex psychological and neurochemical process but for this discussion I focus on the psychological process. The process begins, essentially, when the adolescent girl detects or perceives a threat to her sense of safety and stability. The perception can be accurate, due to positive experiences in her development, or inaccurate, perhaps due to past experiences that prime her to be especially sensitive to slights or insults (Ornduff, Kelsey, & O'Leary,

2001). The slight, the insult, or the threat generate an emotional response, one that might brush-off the perceived attack or one that reacts viscerally to it (Dickstein & Leibenluft, 2006). It is at this point—a situation that may have occurred in an instant—that the aroused emotions are regulated well or poorly.

Mature emotional regulation will lead the girl to judicious decisions. She reacts or, better, *responds* to the situation with an intensity that matches the insult or attack. However, for the girl with poor emotional regulation, the process goes astray because she cannot adequately control or manage the feelings that are activated within her. She may lash out at others (externalize) or turn her reaction inward against herself (internalize). Emotional regulation brings together cognitive abilities and the recognition and categorization of the emotions, a process that comes from having been assisted in her development to deal with conflict and in witnessing how important models in her life managed conflict. Emotional regulation is a learned behavior, one that is acquired within an interpersonal framework of parent and child, teacher and student, sibling and sibling, and so on. As a result, it can also be unlearned through psychotherapy. Without models from whom to learn emotional regulation, the child either mimics the inadequate models or has to construct ways of managing her emotions. Left alone, she may not be able to develop the best means of controlling emotion. Loss of parents or separation from parents for extended periods during critical times of psychosocial developmental can have deleterious effects. We see some of the possible results of separation as we look at what happens to some Latinas who have been left behind in their birth countries when their parents emigrated in search of better lives for themselves and their children.

Attachment, Separation, and Trauma

The human need to maintain a bond—an attachment to a secure, loving figure—is universal. From the very earliest years we seek the warmth and security of primary caregivers, typically the mother but also the father and other familiar adults. By coming close to and staying with the attachment figure (and receiving the right amount of love, nurturance, protection, sensitivity, and sense of safety), the child grows in her sense of security. It is, as John Bowlby (1969, 1973, 1980, 1988) set forth in his landmark writings, an innate emotion-regulation system that helps the vulnerable child learn how to manage the distress that come from the psychological and physical threats. Without disruptions in the attachment, the child experiences the parent or other caregiver as available in good and bad times, and can anticipate the parents' return and their comfort during separations that cause stress in the child. It is understood that when parents provide a secure base for the young child, the child develops a secure attachment, that is, she can regulate her emotions and feel that the world is a "safe place, that one can rely on protective others, and that one can therefore confidently explore the environment and engage effectively with other people" (Mikulincer, Shaver, & Pereg, 2003, p. 78).

Although attachment is a process established primarily during the first two years of life, it has consequences for many years, including adolescence (Brumariu & Kerns, 2010; Hankin, Kassel, & Abela, 2005). Left without adequate caregivers, the child experiences insecurity about the caregivers and is constantly worrying if they will protect and take care of her. Research has shown that the level of security in our attachment figures influences how we develop and mature, and how we handle stress when it befalls us. Insecure attachment, for example, can lead to the kinds of emotional dysregulation, depression and anxiety that we see in some of the adolescent suicide attempters.

Byron Egeland and Elizabeth A. Carlson (2004) make a compelling connection between insecure attachment and depression, and it is probably safe to say other problems, like anxiety and conduct problems. When the infant experiences the parents as unable to provide a secure base, she develops an ambivalent attachment. This is the child who shows excessive fear and anxiety, has intense attachment needs, and who is very dependent on the caregiver as a way to receive the parent's closeness. As she grows, she views difficulties and stresses in adolescence with a sense of helplessness.

Those children who show avoidant attachment mask their negative affects toward the mother or father by acting indifferently toward them. It is a premature need to be self-reliant in times of stress by rejecting the caregiver to avoid the caregiver's rejection) feel unloved and unlovable, leading to a sense of inadequacy. The world becomes an unsupportive place where others hurt you. As adolescents, they may feel alienated and powerless, seeing little hope. Disorganized attachment (i.e., the child with no coherent, effective coping strategies, who sometimes shows bizarre, sometimes hostile behaviors when distressed, and views the caregiver as someone to turn to in distress but is apprehensive of them) is often seen in those children who have suffered unspeakable trauma in their lives. They may grow into adolescence easily overwhelmed by their emotions and by what they perceive others as doing to them. They develop a self that feels incapable of dealing with challenges, have poor coping skills, are unable to regulate their emotions, and tend to be susceptible to depression and other disorders.

Separation from secure, loving caregivers has profound effects, especially when we don't understand why we lost or are separated from them. This ambiguity about the loss and the insecurity of knowing when we will be reunited with our attachment figure has a corrosive effect on the human being, weakening our capacity to engage in the world with equanimity. Pauline Boss (2004) observes that ambiguous loss, is a situation in which the loss of the beloved person is not clear because the person does not know if the person is dead or alive, returning, or permanently gone. When loss is gradual, known, or understood, we grieve and mourn, and there are many social rituals that we can engage in to make sense of it. But when that loss is ambiguous—sudden, inexplicable, uncertain if there will ever be a reunion—it is much more painful and debilitating. Unlike unambiguous loss in which we can rely on rituals to comfort us (e.g., funerals, memorials), in ambiguous loss there are no easily available rites; we may have to construct them.

When there is a rupture from an attachment figure, as happens among the children of immigrant parents who must leave their children in their home countries for months if not years while they find employment and start a new life for their children, the effects can be considerable, even traumatic for the children. The younger the age of the child at the time of the separation, the more difficulty that may ensue since the older child may have already had time to establish a secure attachment to the parent, a stable, internalized memory of the loving parent. In clinical practice, we may see a *reactive attachment disorder* (American Psychiatric Association, 2000) among children of immigrants who have had to make the painful choice of separating from them for lengthy periods of time (Zayas, 1995). The reactive attachment behavior may be seen in inappropriate social relatedness to the parents and others: they may attach themselves indiscriminately to others, or be aggressive, or excessively dependent and fearful.

The effects of this type of separation were evident in the young Latinas we studied and in those I treated (with or without suicide attempts). We see what can happen in the two cases that follow. Beatriz and Marietta had been left in their home countries in the care of others while their parents sought a better future for them and their siblings. But the separations lasted years and weakened the parent-child ties. The effects on the girls' attachment and bonding, and their capacities to manage their emotions, were complicated by other environmental factors. The problems became manifest when reunions took place years later. Beatriz arrived to live with a mother she had really never known and a stepfather. Neither the girl nor her parents knew how to manage the reunions. In Marietta's case of separation through immigration, it was not solely the absence of connection to parents—the attachment figures—that intensely affected her behaviors and emotions. Compounding the long separation was her family dysfunction and her mother's mental illness. The psychopathology of parents in the form of personality or psychotic disorders, or just sociopathic characteristics, can also have devastating effects that confuse the adolescent. In the case of Marietta, a mother's vindictiveness and manipulation were wrapped into the process leading to a suicide attempt.

Beatriz: "I didn't know them, they didn't know me"
BY CAROLINA HAUSMANN-STABILE

Beatriz is a 16-year-old Ecuadoran girl we interviewed following a recent suicide attempt. She lives with her mother, a 20-year-old sister, 13-year-old brother, 5-year-old nephew, and stepfather. Her parents separated when she was 3. They are now divorced and have emigrated to the United States separately. Beatriz and her siblings were left in Ecuador with kin for 7 years, a period marked by instability, neglect, violence, and sexual abuse. When abuse was discovered in one home, Beatriz and her siblings would be relocated, only to be victimized again:

> Mi mamá decidió por nosotros; mi mamá hablaba con las hermanas de ella a ver quién nos va a cuidar. Vivimos unos años con la madrina de mi hermano pero ella nos maltrataba. Nos pegaba con mangueras, con cables. Nunca le dijimos a mi mamá de eso porque nos tenían amenazados. Solo cuando mi mamá se dio cuenta (le dijimos) y viajamos de ahí a otro lugar a vivir con otras tías. Y mis otras tías ya se vinieron para acá [U.S.] así que teníamos que mudarnos a otras tías. [My mom decided for us; she would talk to her sisters to see who would take care of us. We lived for a couple of years with a godmother who abused us. She would hit us with hoses, with cords. We never told my mother about it because they had threatened us. Only when my mother realized [what was happening] (we told her) and we traveled from there to another place to live with some aunts. And my other aunts had already come here [U.S.], so we had to move to live in another place with some other aunts].

Their mother's contact was limited to phone calls and occasional visits to her children in Ecuador. Her visits were followed by dangerous desert crossings back to the United States. Beatriz's father, who was documented and could have traveled without risk, never visited his children. At the age of 11, Beatriz was reunited with her parents in the United States:

Llegué aquí a Nueva York y yo no le conocía a mi papá. Cuando me bajé del
avión y caminé hacia fuera donde todos están, no sabía a dónde irme. Me sentía
como una extraña; yo no le conocía a mi familia ni ellos me conocían a mí.
[I arrived here in New York, and I did not know my father. When I got off
the plane, I walked toward [the area] where the people are [waiting], I did not
know where to go. I felt like a stranger; I did not know my family and they
did not know me.]

The family's reunification, like all such processes in immigrant families, was challenging, particularly because there were adolescent and preadolescent children
involved. On the day of her arrival, Beatriz's father asked her to choose which
parent she wanted to live with. The children chose their mother. Beatriz reflects on
the past and the present:

Yo era una niña. Yo no sabía nada, nada de la vida. Acá como que ya vine a
crecer. Allá era una niña, no veía ni problemas; ni los veía a mis papas ahí
peleando ni nada de eso. Acá es cuando realmente vi todo lo que un día me faltó.
[I was a little girl. I did not know anything, anything about life. Like here I
grew up. There I was a child, I did not see problems; I didn't even see my
parents fighting or anything like that. Here is where I really saw everything
that I had missed.]

Although the mother understands that her children have suffered, she sees
the root of their adjustment problems as due to their modest living conditions
rather than as the absence of affection and empathic interactions. She says of her
children:

Me acuerdo tan claro que ellos llegaron y ellos dijeron, "Mami, donde
está mi cuarto?" Yo no tenía donde recibirlos. A ellos les afecto muchísimo, venir
de donde lo tenían todo para ellos solos y acá estar en un cuarto durmiendo en el
piso. [I remember so clearly when they arrived and
they said, "Mom, where is my room?" I didn't have anywhere to
receive them. This affected them a lot, to come from a place where they
had everything for themselves and here be in a room sleeping on the
floor.]

Beatriz's mother initially engaged professional help to ease their transition, as she
says, *"Para que se adapten ellos a mí y yo a ellos."* [So they could get used to me and
me to them.] Her parenting capacity is limited, and she assumes that adjusting to
each other is like a toggle switch:

Ahora viniendo a este país ya tienen una madre. Ya tienen una persona que les diga esto está mal, esto está bien. [Now coming to this country, they have a mother. They have a person who can tell them this is wrong, this is right.]

But Beatriz questions her mother's perspective, recognizing that it is not so simple and that the family lacks communication, support, and the critical affection that can enhance their cohesiveness. In fact, Beatriz has an entirely different perspective on whether they are learning what is right and what is wrong:

En mi casa cada uno vive con sus problemas, vive en su propio mundo y no se dan cuenta de los problemas que realmente tenemos todos. Todos hacemos lo que se nos da la gana, porque aquí no hay nadie que nos diga, "Eso está mal." [At home everybody lives with their own problems, lives in their own world, and they don't see the problems that we all have. We all do whatever we want, because there is no one to tell us, "That is wrong."]

Despite her insightful words, Beatriz continues to feel the abandonment. The results are notable in her self-worth and her suicide attempt. When asked what she was thinking when she made the attempts, Beatriz replies,

Que realmente no lo importaba a nadie. Así como mi mamá y mi papá me dejaron en Ecuador, me dejaron cuando tenía 4 años. No les importé nunca. Todo el mundo me odia, nadie me quiere. ¿Por qué estoy aquí en este mundo? A nadie le importo. [That really I was not important to anybody. Just like the way my mother and my father left me in Ecuador, they left me when I was 4 years old. I was never important to them. Everybody hates me, nobody loves me. Why am I in this world? I am not important to anyone.]

Her sentiments are confirmed by her parents' words and actions: Her father claims not to be her biological father and refuses to offer financial support. Beatriz's relationship with him is full of resentment—*"El tiene la culpa de todo esto."* ["He is guilty for all this."] Her mother blames Beatriz for her father's rejection: *"Yo pienso que ella le está faltando el respeto."* ["I think that she is disrespecting him."]

Beatriz cuts classes and has attempted suicide repeatedly. Abuse allegations have prompted the involvement of child protective services. Financial problems loom over them constantly. Her 13-year-old brother has impregnated a girlfriend. The older sister, a single mother, has relegated the baby's care to Beatriz. Freedoms, rewards, punishments, chores, all are chaotically handled by the children who feel cheated and misunderstood. Arguments are the soundtrack of their shared time. Without intervention, crises that offer opportunities for growth will only continue to mire this family in disappointment and animosity.

Marietta: A Story of Transnational Trauma
BY ALLYSON P. NOLLE

In her 14 years, Marietta has received more than her share of mixed messages from her parents. Unlike other children of divorced parents who are shuffled between parents' homes for weekends, this teen traveled between two countries to live with her divorced parents, dealing with often contentious family relationships. During the 2 years that she has lived in the United States with her father and stepmother, the effects of this trauma have been compounded by conflict at home, stress of acculturation and learning English, problems with a boyfriend, and depression.

Marietta was born in Colombia, where her parents separated when she was 4 years old. Her father moved to the United States and remarried. She was raised by her mother in Colombia, where she experienced her mother's inconsistent, violent, and unpredictable parenting. When Marietta was 12, her father invited her to come live with him and his wife and her son in New York. Though it was Marietta's decision to immigrate to the United States, her mother (who still harbored ill feelings toward Marietta's father) seized the opportunity to use Marietta to get back at her ex-husband. Along with Marietta's paternal grandmother, who disliked her son's new wife, her mother told Marietta many terrible things about her stepmother. Marietta's mother instructed her to go live in New York and break up her father's new marriage. Marietta says, "*Ellas dos me llenaron la cabeza de puras cosas malas hacia ellos.*" ["The two of them filled my head with just bad things about them."] Marietta was manipulated by her mother and grandmother to believe that her stepmother was "*una bruja*" ["a witch"]. Marietta arrived in the United States ready to set in motion her mother's plans to spoil her father's marriage by creating as many problems as she could.

Shortly after she began living with her father and stepmother, Marietta realized that all the things that her mother had told her about her stepmother were untrue. She discovered that her stepmother was a very caring and supportive woman who wanted to help her. Struggling to learn English and trying to make friends, Marietta turned to her stepmother and found someone in whom she could confide. As she began to build a relationship with her stepmother, her connection with her mother in Colombia deteriorated. In anger, her mother called Marietta a traitor and told her that she did not love her, that she was a bad daughter. The calls from her mother in Colombia often left Marietta feeling guilty and conflicted. Marietta resorted to acting out and causing problems for her father and stepmother in an effort to regain her mother's trust and affection.

Marietta turned to her boyfriend for support as she struggled to sort out her relationships with the parents in her life. She says that for a time she wanted to be left alone, to create her own world, where her parents would not bother her. She began to sneak her boyfriend into her room and to sneak out to parties without permission. One day, her stepmother came home to discover that Marietta was in the shower with her boyfriend. Fuming, she called her husband who told her to intervene and make Marietta and her boyfriend wait for him to get home. Marietta reports that her father was furious when he arrived, grabbed her by her blouse and threw her onto a chair but did not hurt her. The young couple were forbidden to see each other for a period of time.

Sometime after the shower incident, Marietta learned from friends at school that her boyfriend had another girlfriend. She met up with him one day after school—against her parents' wishes—and the boyfriend hit her. When Marietta came home later, she told her stepmother that she had been out with friends and that a girl had hit her. The stepmother says that she did not believe Marietta entirely, because she did not look as if she had been in a fight. When she later disclosed that she had seen her boyfriend that day, her father spanked and yelled at her. After this fight, Marietta says that she went to the bathroom and took a bunch of pills, intending to end her life.

Marietta has tried to commit suicide three times, expressing that she felt very alone and did not want to cause more problems for her family. Overwhelmed by the mixed messages she was receiving from her parents, hurt by her boyfriend's actions, and frightened that her father would send her back to Colombia, she felt that she couldn't go on and that taking her life was the only solution. After one of her attempts, Marietta confided to her stepmother that her mother had been harassing her, sometimes calling her several times a week to tell her that she was a failure, that she was a bad daughter, that she didn't love her because she hadn't fulfilled what she had promised her.

Marietta now recognizes the inconsistency of her mother's love, the extent of her mother's lies, and the emotional trauma she inflicted on her. It is an insight gained as she sees her father through her own eyes:

Reconozco más las cosas de mi mamá mientras veo lo que mi papá hace por mí. Y mi papá siempre está conmigo, siempre me da lo que yo quiero, pero yo nunca reconocía eso. Yo siempre reconocía solo lo que mi mamá hace, y más que mi mamá siempre me hablaba mal de mi papá. So ahorita que yo vine a este país fue que vi que eso no era verdad. So por eso me ha quedado tan difícil venir y reconocer, pero ahorita que lo estoy viendo todavía me cuesta y todavía siento como una, como una rabia por eso, por todo lo que ella me ha dicho. [I recognize my mother's ways more as I see the things that my dad does for me. My dad is always with me, he always gives me what I need, but I never recognized that. Instead I always recognized what my mother does, and even that my mom always talks badly to me about my father. So now that I came here to this country, it was then that I saw that (what mother said) wasn't true. So because of that, it's been so hard for me to come and recognize it, but now I'm seeing that it's still hard for me and I feel like an anger because of that, because of all that she has told me.]

Marietta says that her father has "normal" house rules but gives her freedom if she shows him that she can be trusted. She also feels that her dad and stepmother have a good relationship—one built on respect and shared responsibilities. She observes that they communicate well and make decisions together. Conflict between Marietta's father and stepmother is uncommon, although the stepmother feels that she has not received enough support from her husband when it comes to reprimanding Marietta. Her husband does not want to do anything to anger Marietta or to jeopardize their fragile relationship. For a long time, he refused to believe the severity of her psychiatric problems.

It may take more time for this father to revise his approach to his daughter. In spite of the trauma and confusion she has had in her short life, Marietta may be more ready to move forward. She regrets her decision to try to take her life.

"Life is beautiful," she says.

A Cultural Idiom of Distress?

Many Latinas undergo this cultural transition, certainly, without resorting to suicide attempts. Why, of all the many reactions they could have, is it that some Latinas turn to a self-destructive form of expression? In resolving the dilemma of the traditional and the modern, why is it such a seemingly uniform expression of their distress? The answer may be that it is a means provided by the cultures of Latin America to demonstrate the pain they feel, what is known in cultural psychiatry as an *idiom of distress*. An idiom of distress refers to recurrent, locality-specific patterns of aberrant behavior, means for expression that are provided by the indigenous context of the group manifesting the idiom (APA, 2000; Guarnaccia & Rogler, 1999). The suicide attempt represents a means provided by culture through which the girls can communicate what is happening to them, in them, and around them.

As Lauren Gulbas and I (Zayas & Gulbas, 2011) see it in our analyses of interviews and synthesis of what is known, the term *idiom of distress* applies to the suicide attempts of young Latinas. Instead of conceiving of culture as a rather bounded, localized, and discrete system of shared meanings, beliefs, and behaviors (Rebhun, 2004; Ware & Kleinman, 1992), we subscribe to the idea that cultures are "temporary, ever-changing constructions that emerge from interactions between individuals, communities, and larger ideologies and institutional practices" (Kirmayer, 2001, p. 22). Because America's Latinas undergo an adolescent developmental process that is occurring in a rapidly changing world with technology accelerating their acculturation and changing the means for social relations, the cultures that they grow in are not stable and fixed, as they might be in a remote village where traditions and customs change slowly. The concept of an idiom of distress then offers a way of thinking of illness and symptomatology as linked with psychological, interpersonal, and cultural factors. Basically, it is a way of communicating our psychosomatic experiences (Kirmayer & Sartorius, 2007; Nichter, 1981). An idiom represents local *responses* to certain kinds of distress that surface as the result of various kinds of psychosocial problems (Nichter, 1981). By viewing Latinas' suicide attempts as an idiom of distress, we capture the elements that shape mental health and illness and see the possible meanings of it and what illness *communicates* about the broader sociocultural world order (Kirmayer & Sartorius, 2007). As Hollan (2004) points out,

> Although idioms of distress must be shared for us to call them "idioms" or "cultural," their effects are variable because the social, bodily, and psychological experiences of the people who use them are variable. However, despite this variability in usage, cultural differences in the availability of particular idioms do have an impact on how one both experiences, and in turn expresses suffering and psycho-bodily insult. (p. 68)

In this way, the concept of idioms of distress accounts for individual variation in the experience and enactment of distress, and therefore, illness. Hollan argues that this is precisely the reason why certain idioms persist across time: "they are flexible and ambiguous enough to be articulated with a variety of life experiences" (p. 76). By looking at other idioms of distress, we can understand the basis for thinking of suicide attempts in this way.

One such idiom of distress is that of *nervios* (translated literally as "nerves"). Recognized in many Latin American cultures, *nervios* represents an expression of a person's suffering and a sickness that is constructed socially to display the physical and emotional anguish. *Nervios* often comes out of family stress related to such stressors as finances, children's behaviors, or sudden emergencies (Guarnaccia & Farias, 1988). Nelly Salgado de Snyder, Maria de Jesus Diaz-Perez, and Victoria Ojeda (2000) report that *nervios* among the people they studied in rural Mexican communities is considered an illness process. It has a cognitive component, such as when an idea gets "stuck" in the mind; a physical component in the form of aches, pains, stomach problems, and other body experiences; and an emotional component that often includes affects of anger, sadness, or irritability, among others. *Nervios* does not necessarily imply a psychiatric disorder or some type of psychopathology, although it can co-occur with depression, anxiety, and other mental disorders. It is thought that the somatization that is often seen in people complaining of *nervios* is the individuals' attempts to rebalance themselves, to return to a state of equilibrium between the personal and the social (Koss, 1990).

Nervios is often the result of a sudden disruption in the person's familial, personal, or social network. It is more common in women than men, and more likely among poor, less educated populations. Salgado de Snyder and her colleagues (2000) note that *nervios* is more often seen among low-income women, especially among those from "traditional societies with a strict gender role differentiation, who additionally face many responsibilities and obligations in a context of poverty and scarcity" (p. 454). It derives from a context that includes social oppression and disadvantage, and few social means to express powerlessness, anger, and dysphoria (Guarnaccia & Farias, 1988). In fact, it is considered a process rather than an illness, a progressive deterioration that weakens the person's capacity to manage stress (Salgado de Snyder et al., 2000). The similarity of the suicide attempts of U.S. Latinas to *nervios* is that they both show a process of progressively weakening emotional capacities to manage intense and protracted family stress.

Closely associated to idioms of distress and culture-bound syndromes is "folk illness," syndromes that people in a particular group "claim to suffer and for which their culture provides an etiology, a diagnosis, preventive measures, and regimens for healing" (Rubell, 1964, p. 268). One such folk illness that is sometimes referred to as a culture-bound syndrome and well known among Mexican, Central, and South American people is *susto*. Arthur Rubell, Carl O'Nell, and Roland Collado-Ardón (1991) describe it as a separation of the spirit from the body, or the loss of the soul. Literally translated, the term *susto* means "fright," specifically a startle response to a sudden event. Rubell and colleagues note that

> *susto* will appear only in social situations that victims perceive to be stressful. . . . The social stresses in *susto* will be intracultural and intrasocietal in nature. Stresses occasioned by conflict between cultures or by an individual's cultural marginality or social mobility (in other words, the frustration or alienation that often result from relations with members of a social stratum distinct from that into which one has been socialized) will be symbolized by problems other than *susto*. . . . *Susto* will appear as a consequence of an episode in which an individual is unable to meet the expectations of his or her own society for a social role in which he or she has been socialized. (pp. 11–12).

In *susto* the sudden, frightening incident causes the individual's spirit to weaken and, thus, the soul is separated from the body (Greenway, 1998; Poss & Jezewski, 2002). Some of the symptoms of *susto* include problems in appetite, sleeping, sadness, and somatic complaints such as headaches, gastrointestinal disorders, and muscular aches and pains. Among Mayan refugees from Guatemala who entered Chiapas, Mexico, during a prolonged civil conflict in their country, a group of researchers (Smith, Sabin, Berlin, & Nackerud, 2009) found that nearly 60% of adults and 48% of children had experienced *susto*. Considering that an idiom of distress is intracultural in nature and in its expression, and that children were still in the early socialization process of learning how to experience and express *susto*, these figures make intuitive sense.

Another culture-bound syndrome known among Hispanics and related to the idioms just described is called *ataques de nervios*. The phenomenology of an *ataque* closely resembles the experience of Latina suicide attempts that Trautman (1961a, 1961b) and our research have reported. *Ataques* are dissociative experiences characterized by intense affect (Lewis-Fernandez, Guarnaccia et al., 2002). The *ataque* can include fainting, crying, trembling, screaming, becoming verbally or physically aggressive, feeling a sense of loss of control, and, sometimes, suicidal gestures (Guarnaccia, Lewis-Fernández, & Marano, 2003; Oquendo, 1994). *Ataques*, which share some overlap with panic disorders but are a more inclusive construct (Lewis-Fernandez, Garrido, et al., 2002; Liebowitz et al., 1994), "frequently occur as a direct result of a stressful event relating to the family" (APA, 2000, p. 899). Among a group of older Puerto Rican patients in a primary care clinic, 26% reported having had an *ataque*, and the *ataque* was most commonly brought about by an interpersonal conflict (Tolin, Robison, Gastambide, Horowitz, & Blank, 2007). Central to the experience of the *ataque*—and to the suicide attempt—is the threat to the integrity of the woman's social world, especially that of her family (Guarnaccia, 1993; Guarnaccia, Canino, Rubio-Stipec, & Bravo, 1993).

The suicide attempts of young Hispanic girls also appear to be linked to a family relational disruption, a tangible threat to familism. One difference between *ataques* and suicide attempts is the age of sufferers: *ataques* are more common among adult women whereas suicide attempts happen more often in adolescent girls. Other forms of disruption to family unity, such as divorce and separation, are correlated with suicidal ideation and attempts among Puerto Ricans, Mexican Americans, and Cubans, especially among younger women (Ungemack & Guarnaccia, 1998). Sometimes suicide attempts are part of the *ataque*.

The suicide attempts of Latinas meet the criterion of being recurrent and repetitive among primarily young females. The attempts are locally specific, another criterion, in that it is evident in a cultural subgroup. And they meet the criterion of being influenced by local cultural factors, in this case, the clash of cultures. Like many idioms, suicide attempts are a response to social and interpersonal turmoil, in which the person or her important social networks—family, marriage, children, friendships—are threatened.

The suicide attempt may have its history, its long cultural roots, in other idioms of distress that are seen in people, particularly women, from traditional societies. In these traditional cultures there are strict gender roles and obligations. Sufferers of idioms of distress or culture-bound syndromes occupy low social status, have little education or access to sources of power, and have limited opportunities for advancement (Guarnaccia & Farias, 1988; Salgado de Snyder et al., 2000). The suicide attempts of young Latinas, as we have seen, are also part of an emotionally deteriorating process that weakens the young Latina's ability to deal with the intense, protracted interpersonal stress that often comes from within the family (Zayas, Gulbas, Fedoravicius, & Cabassa, 2010). Moreover, *nervios, susto,* and *ataques de nervios* among women appears to be a coping strategy that frees them from the demands and expectations that family and spouses put on them (Finerman, 1989; Guarnaccia & Farias, 1988; Salgado de Snyder et al., 2000). These idioms have the unique function—maybe the benefit—of liberating the woman from these demands, whereby she withdraws, if temporarily, from the multiple pressures and expectations until she regains her psychological, emotional, and social equilibrium, and by doing so communicates to those around her the turmoil that she is experiencing (Finerman, 1989).

While many other idioms of distress tend to be seen in women, men too manifest these folk idioms, just not with the same frequency as women. In the suicidal ideation, planning, and acts of young Latinas as seen in the CDC surveys across the years, Latino males also have higher rates of suicidal behavior than other adolescent males. It is likely the case that in the suicide attempts, as the research on *nervios, susto,* and *ataques de nervios* shows, males may have more culturally acceptable means of expressions of distress, such as alcohol, violence, and other physical and behavior outlets. Men may consume alcohol to mask their distress, an outlet that in many traditional Latin American cultures is not readily available to women (Guarnaccia & Farias, 1988; Salgado de Snyder et al., 2000).

Refining a Conceptual Model

I began my research with a simple linear model, one that drew from developmental systems theory, family systems, and cultural psychology. The initial model, shown in Figure 7.1, considered the elements that my colleagues and I thought best explained and described the phenomenon of suicide attempts by adolescent Latinas (Zayas et al., 2000, 2005).

The model was based on developmental and family systems theory and incorporated the elements of adolescent development, culture, and cultural traditions of Hispanic families, all of the influences that appear in the microsystems and mesosystems that were described earlier. Growing up in family environments with their panoply of strengths and weaknesses, girls develop the heartiness or vulnerability to deal with stress, responding to it in their own inimitable way. We applied this model as much to the girl who has attempted as to the girl who has not attempted, for the crises they face are not always dissimilar. The difference between the attempters and nonattempters is the outcomes of their crisis.

The early model, however, depicted mostly the influences of the family and its immediate sociocultural milieu; it did not identify other elements in the

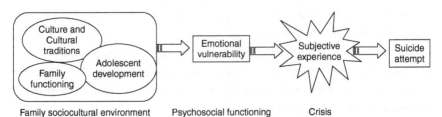

FIGURE 7.1. Initial conceptual model of Latina suicide attempts (adapted from Zayas et al., 2005).

life environments of the girls and their families. To leave it there would be misleading since we know that exosystems and macrosystems play background roles. Sociologists and economists have models and ideas about how these larger forces impinge on family life. But it is hard to account for how broad-scale systems affect the suicide attempts of young Latinas in a direct and meaningful way. Can we say, for example, that television images of young adolescents enjoying fewer restrictions on their behavior, more autonomy, or greater tolerance by parents of early sexual experimentation directly influence a suicide attempt? There is probably no doubt that it may establish a general climate in which adolescents' ideas and emotions are affected. However, it is less likely at the individual level that we can ascribe the suicide attempt to media images that the Latina sees. We can neither dismiss the impact of such images nor fit them neatly into a model. What we can account for in clinical research and practice are the circumstances in micro- and mesosystems that have a direct effect on the suicide attempt. The conceptual model that I started with and the one that has evolved to the present operate on the assumption that forces that are distant from the actual attempt play a supporting or background role but are not the specific trigger or the proximate factors for the attempt.

The original model in Figure 7.1 shows that there is a crisis that triggers the suicidal action, often an incident that occurs after an escalation of tensions in the family that is sustained over a period of time. The trigger happens at a point in which the factors in the family environment and the girl's vulnerability collide under sufficient stress to bring about the suicide attempt. The model in Figure 7.1 was first conceived about 10 years ago and does not include a deeper understanding of the trigger as one among many incidents that occurs within a specific moment. Figure 7.1 does not demonstrate how the adolescent's autonomy struggles interact with other influences.

With what we have learned in the past 5 years, I have expanded the conceptual model beyond its origins to encompass and represent many of the variables that research shows as contributing to the suicide attempt. The new model in Figure 7.2 shows the many factors, their pathways, interactions, and how they mediate or are mediated by other factors, in arriving at the ultimate outcome, a suicide attempt. It is fundamentally the same model, just more elaborate. It shows the context in which all of the interactions, influences, mediations, and outcomes that the findings of our research project point us to. It is framed by the cultural environments that the Latina faces, the competing cultural traditions and the swiftly changing norms of the prevailing cultures. It is difficult in a model to capture all of these currents. The variable labeled *social images* in Figure 7.2 represents only a part of the cultural environment in which the young Latina grows and finds her identity and self-expression.

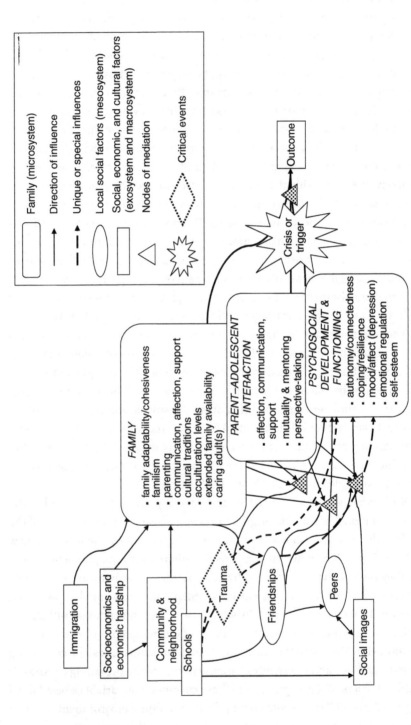

FIGURE 7.2. Conceptual model of suicide attempts among young Latinas.

Pathways are a common means to depict how different factors influence and affect one another in human development and family functioning. For this discussion we can think of pathways as any number of routes that are taken on your way to a destination. On a car trip, for example, we know that things like flooding, traffic jams, accidents, roadwork, and so on will affect the quality of your travel, how long it takes, your arrival time, and your emotional reactions to the detours and delay. As part of the use of pathways in the revised conceptual framework shown in Figure 7.2, I drew on *family stress models*. Family stress models often consist of any number of variables that are ordered in a manner that explains any one or more pathways. Family stress models capture the effects of pressures on the family's functioning and actions that take place later or "downstream" in the pathway. Economic pressures on couples and families, for example, have many possible pathways of impact, in a domino-like fashion that has significant effects on children's outcomes (Conger & Elder, 1994; Conger et al., 2002; Leinonen, Solantaus, & Punamäki, 2002; McLoyd, 1998). Take, for example, what happens when a family of limited means or low-income is confronted with unexpected but substantial negative financial events (e.g., breakdown of the family car, job loss, costly medical expenses). Such financial pressures have a definite effect on the primary caregivers of a family; it can frustrate parents, arouse anger (even shame in partners), shorten their emotional fuses, or cause physical or verbal reactions that are sometimes out of proportion to the situation. The pressures and alterations in parents' moods can impair the quality of their marriage, which can then affect their capacity to nurture and adequately parent their children, affecting children's behavioral, emotional, and academic outcomes. Like a series of dominoes in which the first one is tipped and creates a chain reaction, family stress has a similar set of actions.

What's more is that this pathway does not just apply to poor families; the effects are visible in families from all social classes and backgrounds. The pressures do not have to be financial. The death of a child or of a parent, losses that may not affect income or wealth, have devastating consequences on families that can set into motion the kinds of pathway effects just enumerated. It may not be financial pressure but the possible blaming or recriminations between parents when a child dies or the shifting of one parent's priorities after the loss of a spouse.

Figure 7.2 operates from similar assumptions that variables affect one another. Also present in pathway models are mediators that are known or even thought to blunt or magnify or direct the influence that one variable has on another. Our refined conceptual model operates on the assumption that it is individual psychology, social, and family supports that affect or mediate the management of traumas, crises, and stresses in families' lives. The arrows in Figure 7.2 represent the direction of influence.

Beginning at the far left of the model, we see what might be termed "distal" social, economic, political, and cultural factors (shown by rectangles). These are systems that have overarching influences on Hispanic and other families and their children but are not as close as microsystems. For many Hispanics, immigration in the present generation or recent generation has deep, long-lasting influences on people in the family systems. Whether the immigration occurred in the grandparents' generation or the parents,' or even the young Latina's, it is a profoundly transformative experience.

The socioeconomics of the family—things like education, employment, earnings, and assets—affect all members. In this model it is the economic hardships during the postimmigration period that have direct effects, although the preimmigration economic factors continue to have tangible and psychological or emotional effects, too. Remittances to children and siblings left behind in their countries of origin are one such tangible effect. Psychological or emotional effects may include the fear of financial instability, deprivation, or past political oppression. Parents' employment and the impact of the economic sectors in which their jobs are based (e.g., manufacturing, service, farming) are among the many systems that impinge on families. The economic conditions, of course, affect the kinds of communities and neighborhoods that families can reside in, and what schools their children attend.

In the conceptual model, schools are assumed to have two effects: direct and indirect. The direct one is the impact it has on the individual child. Indirect effects can come from, for example, how teachers interact with students and how supportive teachers are of students. Or, the indirect effects of school can come about by its social climate, how safe students feel, and how peer pressure and bullying are managed by faculty and staff. While schools have an interaction with the family, it cannot be said that they influence how a family functions, but the child's performance in school is influenced by the family.

Social images in the model include but are not limited to the media, celebrities, and/or even *telenovelas* (for those girls who watch them) that have an influence on things like body image, attire, argot, fashions, and fads, and trendy ways of interactiing with one another, generally distal factors to the management of a crisis. Family influences shown in the rounded rectangles are more directly related to the suicide attempt. There is no doubt that distant factors take a toll on people, but in this model I posit that they affect the family system and, through the family's stress and interactions, impinge on the adolescent.

The model distinguishes *peers* from *friendships* for purposes of making clear the distinct effects they have on youth. I elected to represent peers as other youths at school or in the neighborhood, communities, or organizations the young Latina is involved in. These are youths to whom she has direct exposure (in contrast to the social images of youth that are presented in the media although there is an overlap with peerlike individuals in the media). Peers and the pressure they apply on the adolescent have a strong social influence that can be growth inducing or hurtful. Friendships in the model represent close, intimate relationships, the "best friends" (*amigas intima*), whether males or females, who have earned the young Latina's confidence. By separating friends from peers I highlight the typically salutary effects of best friends, often peers with whom there is an emotional tie, who have relationships in which secrets are shared and held, and empathy is exchanged that are important to youth. Peers can influence a girl's self-esteem, how she copes with pressures, and other factors. Friendships have a similar effect, but they also serve to buffer against the peer group, they help protect against peer pressure. Whom she selects as her friends is influenced by her family and parents and the availability of such friends from within the peer group.

Shown by patterned triangles are *nodes*, critical points at which significant relationships among the many forces and factors in the adolescent's life can be altered, amplified, or muted for positive or negative effects. The node is tied primarily to one route of influence, such as those shown in the pathways from peers or trauma to psychosocial functioning, but is also subject to several influences that converge to mediate the effects of the primary route, shown by the solid lines. That is, the nodal point through which an influence runs is affected by the other important aspects of the Latina's social system. These arrows bring the influence from their point of origin to bear on the effects of the primary source. Depending upon the type and strength of the influences that enter the nodal point, the effects of the original source, say, peers or trauma, are mediated. The node is not opaque and is therefore not the inscrutable "black box" that is often used to describe a process that is known to exist but about which we know very little. The reason for the patterned texture of the nodes is that they are partially known but not fully elucidated, yet. For example, behavioral research has shown that the influence of friendships with youths engaged in deviant behaviors can be mediated based on the nature and intensity of parental supervision and parent–adolescent relationships. In the past few decades, as powerful and sophisticated statistical techniques have been developed, a growing body of research on adolescence has been able to show how mediators operate, how they are ordered, and what weight they bear, and what predictions we can make about the impact of many variables.

To illustrate this point, let's take the effects of friendships on psychosocial functioning. Friendships are defined by their intensity and intimacy; they often come out of the peer group and evolve from acquaintances to close relationships. Friendships are themselves influenced by family, directly as when parents encourage the bonds with particular friends (or when they do not support them) and indirectly by what they have taught their daughters. Recall, for instance, the women of El Centro who dated boys with shared values and of whom their families would approve. Or recall the girl whose parents had their daughter invite her boyfriend to visit the home rather than banning the relationship, knowing that in time it would end. The arrow in Figure 7.2 from the family to friendships demonstrates this type of influence.

Friendships also mediate the relationships that run from peers to psychosocial functioning by influencing the node and interacting with the influences of the peer group. Friendships can help reduce the negative effects of some peer interaction, but friendships do not act alone on the node. Rather, the adolescent Latina gains an ally through close friends who do not engage her in deviant behaviors, and she is strengthened by her relationship with parents. Together, these two influences mitigate the negative effects of peer pressure. Of course, their self-esteem and self-efficacy, and their coping abilities—important in leading to a sense of agency—play important roles in managing the emotional and social response to peer pressure.

Other routes, such as those from trauma and social images, have nodal points too that can be influenced by forces that originate elsewhere in her life's ecology. The social images node, for example, is hypothesized to be mediated by the parent–adolescent relationship and friendships, too. Thus, a girl concerned with being too fat or too thin, or not having the right hair to match the idealized beauty on television, can find solace in parents and others who remind her of her beauty, assure her of her worth, and thus strengthen or at least not weaken her coping abilities and psychosocial functioning.

At the center of the model is the family microsystem with three dimensions shown in rounded rectangles: the family system, the parent–adolescent relationship, and the young woman. The family's functioning is a critical linchpin in the path to suicide attempts. The three dimensions contain only a small number of variables and factors since they are too numerous to list in an illustration. The overlap of these three dimensions is intended to demonstrate that they exist in the microsystem of the family.

As we saw in the profiles of the girls and their families in our study and the studies of others, the tolerance for crises, or trigger events, and the adequacy of their management through the girls' coping abilities and capacity to regulate her emotions, comes out of the family environment. Distress and conflicts are a normal fact of life, and how the adolescent Latina handles them is a function of the immediate influences of the three family dimensions.

A separate and distinct spot is reserved for traumatic events in the model. Trauma may or may not be family related and thus is placed separately. As we have seen in our research and the case studies, girls who have suffered trauma do not necessarily attempt suicide. Thus, mediators that influence the node are the family's overall functioning and the relationship the adolescent has with her parents. Friends too can have an influence in mediating the effects of trauma, but they are not emphasized in the model, for their influences are more limited than is the family's capacity to affect the traumatized young woman. Trauma in the model can be of any type: sexual molestation, rape, physical abuse, community violence, major accidents, or an infinite number of possibilities. The path from traumatic experiences to a suicide attempt is usually, though unfortunately, related to the absence of caring, empathic adults who will listen, protect her, and provide her with the care (e.g., mental health and social services) and comfort (e.g., privacy, sensitivity, attentiveness) that she needs.

* * *

We have seen in the analysis of young Latinas the moves they must make as they cross and meld cultures. Whether foreign-born or native-born, the young women encounter vast and swiftly moving currents that require of them deep personal, familial, and cultural changes. The constant cultural changes brought to Latin America and the United States—indeed, the world—by globalization, technology, and modernity may make choices for some young Latinas easier, less fraught with challenges. For other Latinas the challenges may be too great, too troublesome, too overwhelming. But with more research and enhancements in clinical practice and prevention, there may come a time when suicide attempts among Hispanic youth are no different from those of other groups. Providing conceptual models and cultural perspectives on the suicide attempts that emerge from close scientific scrutiny can help researchers and clinicians better understand, prevent, and treat the suicide attempts.

8

Saving Young Latinas

Looking back at some of the girls we studied, and some that I treated, it was apparent that the counselling or therapy that the girls and their families received after their suicide attempts may have helped break the failed problem-solving patterns of their past. All of the girls in our study who had attempted suicide were recruited from mental health clinics where they and their families were receiving therapy and other services. We can view the comments and reflections that the girls and their parents shared with us about the sequelae of their suicide attempts and the changes in their lives as related to the positive impact of therapy. After the attempt and possibly through therapy, some girls realized that, as said by a 14-year-old Venezuelan girl who had attempted by an overdose of acetaminophen, "there are people who care, because a lot of people wanna help me."

Others felt that their crises had helped bring their families closer and opened channels of communication that previously did not exist or were shut down. Sometimes, the improvement in girls' psychological functioning and in their interaction with parents and siblings were felt immediately. For others, progress was slower and more tentative, in which the family's delicate equilibrium, a perilous one, was being reconsidered, possibly reset to a healthier mode of functioning in the aftermath. A 13-year-old Dominican–Puerto Rican girl, hospitalized for an overdose of acetaminophen with codeine, noted that the relationship with her mother was still "not beautiful, but it's getting better."

As with many of the insights that people have after a major episode in their lives that was a result of mistakes in judgment, there were regrets among the Latinas for their suicide attempts. Many of our young Latinas made discoveries about themselves that made them feel guilty and regretful. There was often a residual confusion or puzzlement about why they had attempted suicide in the first place, why they had acted so dramatically to hurt their bodies or remove themselves from their families and friends. Remorse and regrets were expressed by girls, sometimes articulated with a foreboding that they would be forever marked as "crazy" for their actions. As one 15-year-old Mexican multiple-attempter remarked, "I should have stopped the first time that I did that. I didn't want to go through what I went through. Like go to the hospital. Because it is for mental people, I felt like embarrassed." Other girls worried that their attempt or attempts will affect their future deeply, that they may not be able to get jobs or that it will impact their future children. One 15-year-old Ecuadoran girl who had cut herself severely with a broken glass worried that "When I grow up, my children are going to see the scar. They are going to ask me why, why is that there. And I'm going to end up having to tell them, and it's like setting a bad example." Had she appreciated what the consequences could have been and had she reasoned about what her actions meant, she may not have had to worry about what her children might see or think.

How can we prevent young Latinas from having to go through a painful process of attempting suicide? What do we need to do to treat those who have already attempted suicide? This chapter explores several modes through which we can treat Latinas and also prevent their suicidal actions. When the self-corrections that the girls and their parents should take cannot be done alone, we can use interventions to prevent problems, and treatments to change noxious individual and family patterns can be implemented. Even small redirections by caring and capable professionals can get a girl and her family on the path to improved relationships. Such is the case of Corina.

Corina: Learning to be a Family . . . with a Little Help
BY LAUREN E. GULBAS

Corina is 17 years old. Although both parents immigrated to New York from Puerto Rico, her mother and father are drastically different. Corina feels her mother is more "American" than her father. Her mother enjoys listening to American singers from the 1950s, whereas her father is "old-fashioned Puerto Rican, who just plays dominoes with his friends." This difference extends to the ways in which Corina interacts with her parents. Corina feels very close to her mother, explaining that her mom "really raised" her. She feels she does not know her father: "When it comes to communication, he doesn't really communicate. He's very ignorant. He doesn't communicate at all, and that's just the way his mind is."

Corina's parents separated about six months ago, a decision Corina feels was the right thing for her family. Her father abused drugs and beat her mother. As a child, she felt unable to protect her mother, but now that she is older, she states that "I'll hurt him if he touches my mom. I don't care if he's my father, I'll hurt him."

Her father's departure has placed an immense financial burden on her mother. They cannot afford their one-bedroom apartment and cannot find affordable housing. They are contemplating relocating to another state, but her mother does not want to ask Corina to move. She knows that Corina will follow her, but they find themselves in a quandary: either the mother must sacrifice for Corina and let her stay in New York, or Corina must sacrifice for her mother and move away. Any action will require forgoing individual needs for the sake of the family.

For Corina's mother, the outcome of this dilemma has left her alone and scared. She does not want to become too dependent upon Corina as she has done in the past. Her mother says,

> I get scared because I feel like I'm losing yet another family member. I feel like, after 19 years, I've lost my husband, and I might be at risk of losing my daughter. So I feel like I'm lost! It's very scary, feeling like, "Oh my God, I don't have anyone there." I just feel like, well, was it worth it, to try and raise her and then to turn around and be alone? I don't know.

Corina's mother feels that she has let her daughter down in the past. For example, her mother would work long days just to avoid coming home to the problems with her husband and his abuse. As a result, all of the household duties fell to Corina. As her mother notes, "Back in my subconscious, I knew that things weren't well between her father and me. So I used to rely heavily on her because I was trying to avoid the house." Sometimes, life was simply too much for Corina's mother. She would scream at Corina and sometimes hit her. Corina feels that her mother is too hard on herself. Of an incident in which her mother hit her with a glass plate, Corina reflects, "I said a nasty comment to my mom. I was rude to her, and I deserved it. I was, like, not scared of my mom. But I respected her. I was never rude to her again, you know, in front of people because that just shows disrespect."

While incidents like this one taught her to obey and respect her mother, Corina feels that her mother's reactions are sometimes unwarranted. For example, when her mother hit her after an altercation with her husband, Corina said,

"'That's not right. I don't deserve to get hit because my father was mean to you.' And she apologized to me. I don't blame her, like, that she used her anger. She just shouldn't have used it on me! But that's why I told her."

It is because of her anger that Corina's mother sought individual therapy for herself, a process that helped with the toxic remnants of a difficult childhood. Corina's mother was abused as a child, and her father was a pedophile who molested several children, including his own grandchildren. She tried to kill herself multiple times by taking pills and cutting her wrists. She was "always thinking suicidal thoughts. But basically, what I wanted was some sort of reaction from my mother." Corina's mother married an abusive man, a not uncommon situation among people who were abused as children. They frequently get involved in relationships in which they continued to be victimized. To her credit, Corina's mother was able to stop the cycle of her suicidal behavior, and not "passing it on" to her daughter, showing that suicidal tendencies do not necessarily have to be transmitted to the next generation.

Both Corina and her mother say that their relationship has improved very much since her mother started therapy. Corina notes that it is easier to communicate with her mother. This has helped mother and daughter come to compromises on many issues such as dating. Her mother said that she realized her daughter is no longer "a little kid. You can't make their decisions for your children ."

Her mother's engagement in therapy has not only enhanced the reciprocity in the mother–daughter relationship, but it has also helped Corina and her mother in separate but important ways. Watching her mother make an active decision to improve her life inspired Corina to make changes, such as requesting a transfer of schools so that she could start anew. Corina is now excelling in her new school, volunteers with senior citizens, and is learning to ride horses.

In the end, both Corina and her mother have learned to be a better family through her mother's modeling of disciplined change. Her mother has become more open and flexible, and this has strengthened the mother–daughter relationship. As Corina says, becoming a family is a "growing process." Sometimes, though, you need a little help to learn to grow.

Individual Therapies

What are the starting points for treatment of suicidal Latinas, and what are treatments that we can choose from that have demonstrated effectiveness?

The first point to start from is that therapists cannot rely on only one type of therapy to treat the adolescent suicide attempter and her family. As the old saying goes, if all you have is a hammer, you tend to see all problems as nails. Because no two cases are identical, it is a tool chest with many different tools that is needed. As clinicians we must assess what the best entry point or points are, where the leverage exists in the girl's life for making changes, and what techniques will bring about the most enduring change. While I am a family therapist and believe fully in family therapy's potential to change patterns of family and individual behavior, I am also a psychoanalyst who has seen what a powerful change individual therapy can bring, especially for initiating some behavioral changes that lead to insight and the patient's desire to do more, to be more (Wachtel, 1993; Zayas, 2001; Zayas, Drake, & Jonson-Reid, 2011). Therapists must be willing to move in and out of different therapeutic modalities across cases or within one case.

It is always a blessing to start with patients who are willing participants and with whom one can establish a therapeutic alliance, that important relationship between client and therapist that propels the work, the healing (Horvath & Luborsky, 1993; Meissner, 2007). The reflections that Marietta shared (Chapters Six and Seven) that life is beautiful and that her stepmother wasn't the evil person whom her mother had portrayed can make her an excellent candidate for therapy. For a therapist, there is no better starting point than clients like Corina's mother who decided that therapy for herself would help her work through the problems of her childhood and the effects of her failed marriage. With many such families and individuals, the therapeutic alliance can be achieved quickly. But it is not always the case that the clients come into our consulting rooms willingly. And so our work is made harder. But the rewards are in many ways richer when one takes a resistant or reluctant client on a journey of self-discovery that changes her view of the world, herself and her family, and learns new ways of engaging.

In an examination of a group of 25 girls in our study who attempted suicide (Zayas, Gulbas, Fedoravicius, & Cabassa, 2010), we found that half of them made explicit statements of wanting to die, rationalizing the actions that courted death. This group told us that they were depressed, feeling sad, lonely, guilty, and worthless. They felt an emotional despair that seemed to come from an experience of solitude. As a 16-year-old Ecuadoran girl who attempted suicide by ingesting bleach said, "*No quería existir ya. Nada me valía porque me sentía como que todo el mundo me odia, nadie me quiere, ¿Por qué estoy aquí en este mundo?*" ["I did not want to exist anymore. Nothing was of value to me because I felt that everyone hated me, no one loved me. Why am I here in this world?"] The other half of the group of girls we studied did not express the same level of intent to die. But because of the overwhelming, often conflicting emotions that the girls wanted to manage, their predominant mood was one of anger. They were different from the first group in the absence of statements that they felt depressed or down. Instead, these girls told of the anger and frustration that had built up to such a level that they wanted to escape from them or control the feelings. They spoke almost viscerally of being angry, of hating, and of frustration, stress, and confusion that were unbearable; rather than emotions that came from a place of solitude, their emotions were more seething and explosive in nature. The majority of these girls used knives, razor blades, or other easily available sharp utensils to provide a physical release to an emotional state. Fewer of these research participants ingested pills than the girls in the other half.

What characterized these girls, and many others, was the depression, lack of support and mentoring, and problems in coping. Using this profile as a starting point, it appears that cognitive, ego-building, and interpersonal therapies may be most effective in correcting the girls' passivity or their explosiveness, reactions that limit their abilities to express emotions appropriately. Cognitive interventions are helpful in changing the girls' self-perception of being hopeless, and feeling guilty and worthless (Brent et al., 1997). Past experience with adaptations of cognitive-behavioral and interpersonal treatments for depressed Hispanic adolescents indicates that both of these therapies have equal effects (Rosselló & Bernal, 1999). Interpersonal therapy, however, may contain more of the kinds of social problem-solving skill training that the girls need. Changing their patterns of thinking from "woe is me" to more self-assertive cognitions such as "I can and I will" can initiate the changes that the young suicide attempter needs.

Interpersonal therapy and those therapies that strengthen the ego capacities of adolescents to claim their sense of self and set boundaries on others who infringe on them are essential to depressed Hispanic youth (Zayas & Katch, 1989). Such interventions help strengthen the young persons' social problem-solving skills so that they can assert themselves appropriately and manage interpersonal relationships. The advantages of ego building and interpersonal therapies are their focus on practical approaches to making sense of and tolerating the internal distress they feel. These therapies help the young person learn how to negotiate relations with others that sap their emotional resources. There is no doubt that there are serious depressions that come from endogenous sources, such as neurochemical imbalances or from psychological reactions to physical illnesses and injuries. They assault the girl's self-image and self-efficacy. But more commonly depression is a reaction to unpleasant interactions with others, when others manipulate, insult, mistreat, threaten, belittle, humiliate, or intimidate us. It is worse when these insults to our emotions come from those we love or admire or need the most. Assaults from those closest to us weaken us most when they are sustained and repeated, leaving us feeling helpless to fight back or to undo their hurt.

For the depressions that come from these kinds of interactions, interpersonal therapy is extremely valuable (Mufson, Dorta, Moreau, & Weissman, 2004). Interpersonal therapy takes the position that *role disputes* in a teenager's life cause her to experience a lack of reciprocity from others. Try as she might to engage the other person in a caring, mutual relationship, the young woman is thwarted, rejected, ridiculed, or simply ignored. This was seen in many of our young women: fathers ignored or belittled them; mothers were deaf to the girls' complaints of abuse or plea for their mothers' support and affection, only to be frustrated. The people that she turns to cannot make or do not want to make the connection with her that she seeks. Depression, worthlessness, and suicidal ideation begin to take hold. The interpersonal therapist's job is to help the adolescent girl understand the communicational patterns that fail her and the difficulties that ensue.

Together, they can sensitively explore what the girl is doing and how it is that others relate to her that makes her feel diminished and depressed. In therapy, the clinician and girl work to change the dysfunctional communication. Role playing in the safe environment of therapy helps the depressed adolescent reduce her isolation and find ways to engage with others in ways that do not frustrate her. A key aspect of interpersonal therapy is that of grieving, mourning the loss of the idealized parent or family, something that is needed with some suicidal Latinas whose parents and families simply don't have the emotional capacities to help their daughters. The interpersonal therapist helps the adolescent go through the grieving process, to accept the difficult emotions, and find healthier ways of dealing with people in her life. She may have to be helped to understand that her parents may just be unable or ill-equipped to give her the affection and support that she seeks.

Behavioral and cognitive interventions help improve impulse control, frustration tolerance, and the management of anger and other unpleasant emotions (Rathus & Miller, 2002; Wood, Trainor, Rothwell, Moore, & Harrington, 2001). It is almost axiomatic in adolescent mental health that the most difficult to treat youths are those who act out their emotional turmoil, who have disorders of conduct and behavior, or who lash out verbally and physically. Oftentimes, clinicians and families cannot manage the adolescent in outpatient treatment, and hospitalization or other residential treatment is needed. Sadder still is that the adolescent cannot control herself, and the emotions are manifested in the behaviors that are destructive to relationships and to the person herself. Among the suicide attempters described in this book and that I have seen in my clinical practice, problems of regulating emotions were prominent in some more than others.

Enhancing the girls' emotional self-regulation must be the goal of therapy in cases such as these. Self-regulation refers to how the young Latinas contain and control their emotions, which leads them to decide what the most appropriate behavior is. Self-regulation, an important part of human functioning, helps the the girl choose her actions in accordance with social norms and the context in which she finds herself. When the dysregulation of emotions and behaviors occurs, impulses and thoughts become actions, often inappropriate in their timing, context of expression, and intensity. The principle in the therapy is to promote self-regulation a little at a time, building on small successes in which self-control worked.

One standout among treatments for this kind of dysregulation is dialectical-behavioral therapy (DBT; Linehan, 1987; Miller, Rathus, & Linehan, 2007; Rathus & Miller 2002). DBT is well known to help individuals who have difficulty modulating their emotions and who tend to view the world around them as invalidating. The girls with a suicide attempt history, as evidenced by their higher internalizing and externalizing scores, demonstrate a reduced ability to modulate their emotions. Their lower scores on measures of mutuality, communication, affection, and support suggest that attempters view their parents as not validating their feelings, much less understand them. With its emphasis on regulating emotions, DBT may be effective with suicidal Latinas. DBT views suicidal behaviors as learned behaviors that the person tries to employ in coping with acute emotional suffering. In our model, when we talk about an event, and the trigger that sets off the attempt, it may be the acuteness of the situation that causes the suicide attempt to follow. The person lacks important intrapersonal self-regulation and the capacity to tolerate distress. It is part of a chronic pattern of aversive emotional dysregulation.

DBT addresses several of the issues that are manifest in suicidal Latinas. It teaches them skills to be more effective interpersonally and to regulate their emotions and behaviors, and to tolerate stress. It also allows for individualizing the treatment to the person in such a way as to increase the motivation of the desire to use the skills that are learned (Miller, Rathus, & Linehan, 2007). DBT identifies the sequence of behaviors that the suicidal adolescent has learned and uses repeatedly. The idea behind DBT is to take away the reinforcers and thereby reduce, in time, the dysfunctional behaviors. DBT also helps adolescents extend their learning, that is, generalize it to other situations in which the same stresses and sequence of maladaptive responses or behaviors would appear. Miller, Rathus, and Linehan (2007) recommend that families be included in DBT with suicidal adolescents. Indeed, all of the individual therapies with adolescents benefit from including parents and siblings.

Family-Centered Therapies

For a problem like the suicidal behaviors of Latinas that we can now confidently say is most often rooted in longstanding family problems, the therapeutic approaches that make most sense are family-centered ones. Since the suicide attempt is located in the family system, it is the members of the family system that create and perpetuate the conditions in which suicidality unfolds. The family system may willingly or unwittingly aid and abet the suicide attempt. The family must then be part of the therapy if the girl is to be saved. As in almost any other field of endeavor, returning a rehabilitated organism to a toxic context will likely lead to the return of a deterioration process. However, when the toxic family system is repaired and improved, it provides a better environment for the returning person to thrive. Family-oriented therapy can maximize the effects of interventions to protect the Latina girl from attempting or reattempting suicide. Celia Jaes Falicov (1998) writes that family therapy is about building bridges between parents and their adolescents. In family therapy, Falicov urges that the therapist help clarify expectations, justify conflicts, translate family members' cultural behavior, and encourage compromise and negotiation, particularly when "the developmental clock for dating, curfews, and other freedoms is out of sync between the generations" (p. 235). These are key principles in treating young Latinas—indeed many children of immigrant parents—when the generational gap is complicated by the acculturational gap.

In many of the examples cited in this book, family disorganization, conflict, lack of empathy, and careless, hurtful words and actions prevailed, complicated by the cultural forces affecting the girls and the acculturation gap between them and their parents. The levels of familism among the girls in our study did not differ between attempters and nonattempters and their mothers, indicating that familism is a point of agreement that can be incorporated into tailoring interventions for Hispanic families. However, the significantly lower mutuality, communication, and support found among the girls who attempted suicide compared with nonattempters suggest the need for interventions that tackle family communication and problem solving (Harrington et al., 1998). The concept of "expressed emotion" in families may be a way to conceive of the problems that many of the families of suicide attempters have. Expressed emotion refers to the feelings and behaviors that families display toward someone in the home with a serious psychiatric illness (see Lopez et al., 2009, and Dorian, Ramirez Garcia, Lopez, & Hernandez, 2008, for useful discussions of expressed emotions and Mexican-American caregivers of relatives with a severe mental illness). Thinking of expressed emotions in families as a measure of family "affective climate" can help us better understand the course of adolescent Latina's depression and suicidality as well as the means to treatment (Silk et al., 2009). Expressed emotion is theorized to develop within the context of the family, a larger purview than just parent and child, and is usually characterized by stress, conflict, poor communication across the family, hostility, and sometimes emotional overinvolvement (Boger, Thompson, Briggs-McGowan, Pavlis, & Carter, 2008). In addition to less marital satisfaction and greater family conflict, expressed emotion is strongly associated with poor overall family functioning (Wamboldt, O'Connor, Wamboldt, Gavin, & Klinnert, 2000). Seeing the maladaptive communication that often occurs in the families of young suicide attempters as part of the expressed emotion model can help how we assess the families and how we formulate treatment plans for them. There are several well-defined and tested family-oriented treatments that can be adapted and that show great promise for treating the Hispanic families with daughters who have attempted suicide. In this section, I mention only a few for purposes of illustrating their approach and potential utility in addressing the problems that we see in families of suicidal adolescent Latinas.[17]

One of the best documented approaches is actually a therapy that has been tested many times with Latino families. Brief strategic family therapy that has been advanced by researchers at the University of Miami (Santisteban et al., 2003, 2006; Szapocznik et al., 2002) considers that maladaptive family interactions, alliances, and boundaries create the family's problems. The idea then is to change family functioning by, first, finding a way to "join" the family and supporting its structure, thus permitting the therapist into the malfunctioning system. Once "inside" the family, the therapist can diagnose or assess the patterns in the family that get repeated. This is done through a series of efforts to track interactional patterns and reflect back to the family its style of interacting, its affective climate, and its mood. Most often the problems are those of how power is distributed, the developmental appropriateness of boundaries, and conflict resolution. The technique of "restructuring" involves strategies that change the family, and that promote more adaptive interactions. Many of these techniques are known to clinicians but careful attention to their use in families with suicidal Latinas can have powerful therapeutic impact on the families.

Another well-tested intervention is MultiDimensional Family Therapy (MDFT; Liddle, Rowe, Dakof, Ungaro, & Henderson, 2004), a developmental-ecological treatment developed and used primarily for adolescent drug abuse.

MDFT tries to reduce symptoms and enhance developmental functioning by facilitating change. It has been effective with adolescent substance users in outpatient treatment and with those adolescents who are in the early stages of drug use (Liddle et al., 2004). There are several modules that the therapist follows. The *adolescent module* helps build a therapeutic alliance and improve her problem-solving skills and social competence. In this module, alternative behaviors that the adolescent can use are covered. The *parent module* also builds the alliance with parents and increases their involvement with their adolescent child while also improving parenting skills. The *interactional module* brings parents and adolescents together to enhance their emotional bonding and attachment and change their patterns of communication. The *extrafamilial module* includes collaborative relationships with other social systems that the adolescent encounters (e.g., friends, school, peer, recreational groups). A study of MDFT (Hogue, Dauber, Samuolis, & Liddle, 2006) showed that using family techniques decreased the internalizing problems of adolescents and increased families' cohesion one year after the treatment was completed. The family techniques also reduced externalizing and family conflict and improved family outcomes when the adolescent techniques were maximally used. While MDFT was developed primarily for use with substance abusing teens, its modules and techniques can be effective with Latino families whose daughters have attempted suicide.

The Strengthening Families Program (SFP; Kumpfer, Alvarado, Tait, & Whiteside, 2007) shares many characteristics that are common to evidence-based interventions for youth with substance abuse and behavioral problems. Focusing on groups of parents and separate groups for youth, SFP helps families practice and strengthen their skills of observation, monitoring, communication, and effective discipline. This 14-session *family* skills training program has been used with diverse families in the United States, Canada, Australia, Europe, and Central America. The SFP has shown that it has long-lasting effects in achieving positive results in improved parenting skills and improved child behaviors. Like MDFT and other programs for substance abusing youth, SFP can prove helpful to clinicians treating young Latinas following a suicide attempt.

A very effective and relatively simple intervention for adolescents who have attempted suicide and their parents that can be delivered in an emergency room was developed by Rotheram-Borus and her colleagues (Rotheram-Borus et al., 1996; Rotheram-Borus, Piacentini, Miller, Graae, & Castro-Blanco, 1994; Rotheram-Borus, Piacentini, Cantwell, Belin, & Song, 2000). In this intervention, medical and psychiatric staff members in an emergency room are trained to enhance patients' interactions with others, reinforcing to patients the importance of follow-up outpatient treatment, and recognizing the seriousness of their suicide attempts. Patients are then instructed to watch a 20-minute video-taped "soap opera" that teaches the teens and their parents about what they can expect in outpatient treatment. A Spanish-language video was used for those families who required it in their language. The video reviews the stories of two suicide attempters. (One of the teenagers in the video had attempted suicide multiple times after failing to get outpatient treatment, a concern that commonly arises in emergency rooms given that many patients do not continue in the outpatient treatment that is often recommended.) A bilingual crisis therapist meets with the suicide attempters and their parents, usually mothers, to screen and discuss the videotape, conduct a therapy session, and contract for follow-up outpatient treatment. The crisis therapist also conducts a behavioral assessment of behavioral risk for imminent danger of suicide. The adolescent and parent are asked to identify the positive attributes they and their family have. The intervention ends by designing a plan for the teenager to use to cope with future suicidal feelings. The video of the teenager who repeated her suicide attempts is a way to drive home the importance of families and teens following up in outpatient therapy.

Storytelling and Rituals in Family Therapy

"Initiating conversations with teenagers, in front of their parents, about the cultural tensions they experience . . . usually increases the emotional resonance parents feel regarding their immigrant or minority experience," writes Falicov (1998, p. 237). Falicov's quote reflects the experience of many therapists who work with Hispanic families with an adolescent who is depressed, acting-out, or suicidal. The kind of exchange that Falicov and other therapists employ helps both adolescent and parents appreciate the others' perspective, raising the level of empathy and understanding. The teens can better understand why their parents are the way they are, why they make the demands on them that they do, and why their parents impose the restrictions that they do. Likewise, immigrant parents understand—like that grandmother in the group of women in El Centro, California—that their children's adolescence is a different one from their own, adolescences that occurred in a different country within a cultural system in another time. My clinical experience, like that of Falicov, is that Latino parents are often amenable to suggestions about lending a sympathetic ear to their adolescents to help the teens confide or speak more openly. Immigrant parents often wish to learn the ways that they can be more effective parents in a world in which their children are learning new ways and that require parents' help. However, the therapist must be careful to not alienate parents and other family members by too quickly siding with the adolescent and her pain and making suggestions long before parents are ready to hear them. In this regard, Falicov writes that "it is very important to stress to the whole family that a modified equivalent of *respeto* for parental authority remain in place" (p. 237).

There is reason to think of families of Latinas who have attempted suicide as having lost their way and having lost their protective structural properties. Structural aspects of the family such as boundaries might be too loose or too taut. Voices may be silenced by the roles people are fitted into, in ways that the family members cannot enjoy each other, in which some members can speak and be heard and others cannot. Voices are quieted by secrets, such as the Latina who ate pumice to cleanse herself after being forced to perform fellatio on her mother's boyfriend, and by ridicule and humiliation, such as the girl whose father called her a *puta* (whore) or another whose mother hated her and wanted to strangle her. Communication has been lost, and there is no glue to keep the family together or any positive experiences to motivate them to stay together. We know from the structured interventions for families that I discussed above that the target of these is to improve communication, raise cohesion, reduce negative conflict, and repair the structures of families. For adolescent Latinas who are in the cultural transition, family histories that began in another country and culture may have been lost or untold, not storied or converted into rituals. For this reason, I consider the roles of storytelling and family rituals as ways to promote healing in the families of these girls.

The reason for a focus on stories and rituals is simple: The human mind and cultural groups think and remember by using story lines. That is, the manner in which we think and the memories we hold are formed into stories rather than held as discrete facts (Howard, 1991). In many ways, we *are* our stories and families are a collection of stories. Miller Mair (1988) writes that

> We do not know the world other than as story world. Stories inform life.
> They hold us together and keep us apart. We inhabit the great stories
> of our culture. . . . We are *lived* by the stories of our race and place. . . .
> We are, each of us, locations where the stories of our place and time
> become partially tellable." (p. 127; original emphasis)

And communication in families can come through stories and rituals, for they too tell stories. Restructuring families so that they share stories and rituals can go a long way in improving communication and bonding. In the Latinas we have studied, the impaired communication in families and their broken emotional bonds can begin to heal through storytelling. Take, for instance, those Latinas in our study who had reunited with the parents after having spent many years apart. What was missing in the separation? Time together was missing, and time together is about witnessing and being part of experiences together, experiences of sorrow and joy, trauma and quiescence, defeats and triumphs. Being together is to have shared moments, all sorts of experiences that create shared memories that may be full of emotional meanings. And these experiences get shared orally, reauthored and reexperienced, and made new with meanings that are part of the family unit. (Read the highly instructive book by Janine Roberts (1994), *Tales and Transformations: Stories in Families and Family Therapy,* for a detailed look at the power that stories can have in helping families.)

A case I treated of a single mother of Cuban origin and her U.S.-born daughter who made a suicide attempt (fortunately, the only one in her life) is illustrative of the power of telling stories. The 15-year-old girl, Caridad, lived with her mother, Manuela, in the basement apartment of a luxury high-rise building in Manhattan. Manuela was a live-in janitor of the building and supplemented her income by cleaning the homes of some of the building residents. She worked hard to have Caridad attend an expensive all-girl Catholic school. It was after a major argument between them about Caridad's late nights out with friends that included boys that Caridad made the relatively benign suicide attempt with some aspirin. Immediately, Manuela brought Caridad to treatment with me upon the referral of the emergency room physician who did not find any major physical damage caused by the aspirin.

What became quite evident in the interaction between Manuela and Caridad was the rigidity with which Manuela oversaw her daughter's every move. Manuela had grown up in Cuba in a town outside of Havana, in a devoutly Catholic home. From the history I was able to gather, it appeared that Manuela's mother had suffered a major mental illness, which, although Manuela never learned a specific diagnosis, sounded quite a bit like paranoid schizophrenia. Her mother's illness had been very disruptive to the family: she often accused neighbors of persecuting her, which, understandably, led to arguments and feuds. Manuela's father would then have to move his family to another neighborhood, only to have the scenario replayed. The family's religious devoutness meant that Manuela was restricted from dating, from wearing fashionable or provocative attire, and from any interaction with boys or men that could be interpreted as seductive. Within this backdrop, Manuela grew up anxious and, when she became a mother, imposed many of the same restrictions on her only child, Caridad. (Manuela was divorced from Caridad's father who was, interestingly, diagnosed with paranoid schizophrenia, an interesting choice of spouses in light of Manuela's mother's history of the same illness.)

Caridad was like many young Manhattan adolescents I knew: savvy, streetwise but not street tough, stimulated by all that the city had to offer but cognizant of its dangers. She had close friends whose parents were not quite as strict and she lived vicariously through them. She gradually began to see a few of the boys secretly. When Manuela found out that Caridad was casually dating a boy (an accidental revelation that occurred when her mother over-heard Caridad talking with a friend in an unguarded moment in the privacy of her bedroom), she became upset although not punitive. As Caridad described it, "She just nags and nags and makes nasty comments, like under her breath, about the boys that she sees on the street. And I know she's saying it to get at me."

Most apparent was the lack of communication between mother and daughter, and their inability to understand each other. There were certainly good aspects of their relationship. It was abundantly clear that Manuela loved her daughter and cared for her deeply. The same was true of Caridad toward her mother. It was not anger that Caridad exuded but rather frustration and confusion, not understanding at all why her mother was the way she was.

I had learned a great deal from Manuela and from Caridad about their lives together and their lives apart. But they did not know about each other's lives. Caridad had no idea of her mother's childhood and adolescence in Cuba. Manuela did not understand today's youth and that Manhattan was not the small town she came from and in which she saw parents raising their children. (She was scornful of the permissiveness that the wealthy residents of her build-ing allowed their children.)

In the early stages of our therapy, one which lasted about seven months, my tactic was to focus on the problems in their interactions and their views on life. This had the usual effects of inciting some arguments in the session that became heated at times. Sometimes it caused Caridad to roll her eyes in exasperation, and sometimes it caused Manuela to look at me, imploring me to help her as a fellow adult to convince Caridad that Manuela was in the right. After enough of these, I turned to using a storytelling and narrative approach to the mother–daughter therapy. I structured sessions to focus less on what was going on between them and more on telling each other about their lives. I asked them to simply tell each other about their lives. The rules were simple: "Tell about things in your life that you have lived through and that you are living through but not necessarily about each other." That is, they were not to address the problems that they felt were caused or exacerbated by each other. This meant that Manuela would talk about her childhood and adolescence and her job and the people she met and so on. Caridad was to do the same. The idea was that they not complain about each other; we had already tried that, and we knew the complaints that they each had and they were going nowhere in the exchanges of grievances.

My goal was to open up lines of communication, raise their capacity to see each other through new "lenses," and begin to understand why they were each the person they were. The first step was for Manuela to narrate her childhood to Caridad in my presence and with my assistance. I served mostly as editor to the story, helping Manuela tell her story fully and asking her to interpret her life for her daughter, and doing the same with Caridad.

Manuela recounted in detail what her world was like in Cuba: the familiar sights and sounds, what girls did, the games that boys and girls played, what the adolescents did when they hung out in the town plaza on cool summer evenings. She described the system of chaperoning and how the older women would sit nearby watching carefully their young daughters and the boys they were associating with (judging whether he was from a good family or not). Manuela told of values the girls were taught and how they commiserated about the restrictions of their parents, but a commiseration that was camaraderie: they were all in it together and could laugh about it even under times of serious frustration. And Manuela told of how hard her father struggled to feed his family and to buffer them from their mother's mental illness.

Much of this was entirely new to Caridad. She was taken by the warm manner in which her mother described her childhood and adolescent peers, her friends' parents, and flirtations with friends' older brothers. Caridad listened intently over the period of several sessions. Her mother had seldom spoken about her mother, Caridad's grandmother (a grandmother she had never known), but lavished praise and affection about her father, Caridad's grandfather (a grandfather she had never known either). The details mesmerized Caridad. What she had not been able to learn from her mother at home, voluntarily, was now being disclosed under the watchful eye of a therapist.

In counterpoint, I then had Caridad tell her mother about what it was like to be an adolescent—a female adolescent—growing up in Manhattan. Caridad told of the wonderful experiences she was having in school with caring nuns and lay teachers, educators who cared very much for their students. But Caridad also spoke of the hardships of being extra careful on the streets and subways, having to judge which guy was safe and which one wasn't. It was not at all the safety that Manuela felt on those cool Cuban evenings in the plaza, next to the imposing Catholic Church in the center of the town. Instead, Caridad was growing up in Manhattan, an exciting but sometimes frightening place. There were many times she would have wanted the counsel of a parent who understood the difficulties and could guide her through it.

Almost instinctively, Manuela would begin to suggest that Caridad not do anything else but attend school and come home. Or, she would try to protect Caridad from the possible offenses and dangers that Caridad might experience. But neither of these reactions was realistic, for Caridad had to face these challenges on her own. It was at these moments that I had to intervene to have Manuela listen more carefully to what Caridad was saying, think about what she needed from Caridad (if anything), and know what she needed to understand of what Caridad was saying. When Caridad became frustrated in the sessions with her mother's insistence on upholding certain values and expectations, it was my job to make sure that Caridad listened carefully to her mother, to understand where her mother "was coming from."

It was through this storytelling approach that Manuela and Caridad's level of mutuality was improved and through which their communication improved significantly. Fortunate to live near Central Park, mother and daughter took to scheduling walks together in the park, a plan that was hatched in a session in which they complained about the other's busy schedule that did not allow the other person in. Caridad was more forthcoming than Manuela about what she had learned about her mother's life and her adolescent years. She was able to empathize with the hardships of having a mentally ill mother and to look at that past with some nostalgia. While she had never visited Cuba, Caridad was moved by her mother's descriptions of her life there and took in her mother's nostalgia. Now when her mother played old Cuban music, Caridad understood not just the words but their sentiments. More importantly, she understood the emotions these evoked in her mother.

Manuela did not let go of her rigid ways but certainly became more accommodating and understanding of Caridad. There were moments in which she chided Caridad, but now she had a greater recognition of what Caridad's adolescence was like. This information, transmitted through stories and narratives of their lives, helped raise Manuela's empathy for the challenges Caridad was facing. It resulted in some more freedom for Caridad but not without close supervision, many questions from Manuela, and some reluctance. But trust had been built through this approach. The walks in Central Park once a week, sometimes more but usually on weekends, became an important ritual for Caridad and Manuela, sometimes they held hands while they walked or interlocked their arms to keep warm together on blustery autumn afternoons.

Rituals are activities that are repeated time and again usually the same way or with many of the same steps. The activities become traditions. These rituals provide predictability and stability, like the schedules and activities by which we place our children to bed every night. Naturally occurring family rituals, according to Barbara Fiese and her collaborators (2002), are symbolic communication that create and are reinforced by the emotional commitment family members have to each other and to their collective. Rituals give family members who participate in them a sense of things being "right," familiar, comfortable, warm. Rituals provide a feeling of belonging. Rituals are not to be mistaken for routines; routines are momentary, utilitarian, require little commitment, and do not hold much affective connection after they are done. They are done and forgotten. Putting the garbage cans at the curb on Tuesday mornings is a routine, not a ritual. However, the making of pancakes every Sunday morning and having breakfast together before going to church services constitute rituals if they are important to family members and are imbued with affection, closeness, attachment, and enjoyment.

Important to the rituals in our lives is that after they have been done, we may replay the last time the ritual was performed so as to hold onto the emotional experience and the fulfillment that the ritual and the memory of it gives us (Fiese et al., 2002). Fiese and her colleagues note that rituals have three dimensions. Ritual *communicate symbolically* "this is who we are" as a family. Rituals *demonstrate commitment* to one another, in which our affection endures in our memory. And we seek to return to it as often as we can. And, rituals *provide continuity*, the meanings of the rituals extending across generations. By engaging in family rituals, members of the group are communicating an important message that says, "We look forward to this ritual, to being together and doing this ritual together." That affective experience is then learned and emotionally incorporated by younger generations.

Healthy rituals say about a family, "This is who we are." Stories provide continuity and identity for its members. Many stories may be about the rituals, memorable incidents during rituals that stand out. In some families, stories are forgotten or diminished in importance, and rituals may be eroded or may have never existed. Rituals can be used to protect and to repair. In taking rituals into family therapy, Janine Roberts (1999) suggests three ways in which they influence the therapeutic process. First, therapeutic rituals can be created in the process, so that those families who have lost or never had rituals are now encouraged to do them. Second, rituals can be used to assess families, evaluating what the rituals are that they are doing and how helpful they are to the family and its members. Third, by examining the rituals that families are engaged in, therapists can intervene to modify the rituals when needed. (A fourth, looking at the ritual life of therapists, is important in the training of clinicians who pursue family-oriented practice.)

Roberts' rationale for using rituals gains additional substance when we turn to the work of Dawn Eaker and Lynda Walters (2002), who found that family rituals are beneficial to adolescent psychosocial development. Eaker and Walters revealed in their research that teenagers' satisfaction with family rituals was associated with being more content, less anxious, and less self-conscious. In families with high cohesiveness and respect for the youth's boundaries (i.e., not being intrusive), adolescents reported feeling highly satisfied with the rituals that their families enjoyed. For many of the families we have met in this book, rituals that bond and aid communication, and the stories that they can share and to which they can return time and again, can be important sources for repairing their disrupted systems. Both rituals and stories provide a sense of continuity of "who I am and what I am a part of." Sometimes finding ones way back in the family system through the remembrances of family stories and rituals can be preventive of problems as well as solutions to disruptions.

Starting Prevention in the Middle School Years

Teachers, principals, and school counselors are reminded every day that the behavioral and emotional challenges posed by adolescence starts in middle school. It is a time when children accede to adolescence, driven by puberty, cognitive development, educational advancements, and the need to exert more autonomy. Our schools adapt to the socioemotional and learning needs of the young adolescent, changing their manner of operating to parallel the young person's growth and need for autonomy. The transition from elementary to middle school is demanding for youth, but more demanding still may be the transition from middle school to high school (Rudolph, Lambert, Clark, & Kurlalowsky, 2001). The high school years raise the stakes and demands on youth, requiring students to take more leadership in clubs and general school activities and to make decisions and act as responsible young citizens. It is not surprising that the prevalence of suicidal ideation, planning, and attempts occur mostly among 14- and 15-year-old students, typically in ninth grade. This period in life is crucial, and prevention and treatment efforts for suicidality need to start in the middle school years and continue through the adolescent years. For young Hispanics as with other immigrant and minority youth, the additional stress of minority status, cultural differences, and acculturational disparities between them and their parents (as well as between groups of youth) amplify the demands of negotiating their worlds.

Developmental group therapy with cognitive-behavioral techniques can be effective for Latinas struggling with the autonomy-related struggle of adolescence (Wood et al., 2001). The pressures of negotiating developmental processes and demands of two or more cultures suggest that group therapy with Latinas who face similar challenges—both attempters and nonattempters—can teach skills to modulate emotions and receive external validation of their adolescent experiences. Prevention-oriented groups—psychoeducational groups, support groups, or "rap" groups—are excellent means by which schools can reach the greatest number of adolescents and their parents and identify those in most critical need of intervention. Prevention and early-intervention groups for youth and parents led by social workers in schools that cover similar topics can go a long way in aiding young Latinas and Latinos and their parents.

The primary objectives of such groups are to (a) reduce the chances that teenage Latinas and Latinos will engage in suicidal behaviors through an education program focused on their development in the context of the culture of the home and the culture of the school, handling stress, and healthy living; and (b) enhance Latino parents' understanding and communication with their teenagers through a program that mirrors the content of the group for youth. Overall, the idea is to enhance understanding, communication, mutuality, and perspective taking for Latino youth and their parents. Youth will learn coping skills and more about their development, and they will understand themselves and their parents better. Parents will learn strategies for understanding and mentoring their young teenagers during the impending years of high school. Raising perspective by both youth and parents will lead to adaptable but cohesive interaction that will make suicidal behavior unnecessary.

The youth groups may consist of three or four meetings delivered over the course of 6–8 weeks (every other week). Girls will have their own group and boys a separate one. This recommendation follows from the need to consider developmental and gender issues, when body image, physical maturation, sexuality, and gender specific issues emerge that can be awkward to discuss in mixed groups. Each group session should be long enough (about 2 hours) to allow for the teens to become absorbed into the topic of each session and the content designed to cover the areas that are important to transmit.

Each session must have two or three "take-home" messages (knowledge) and a comparable set of skills (behaviors) and will consist of engaging activities appropriate for the range in ages. One session, "Your Development," might consist of information about what a Latino preteen and teenager can expect with regard to language, immigration, acculturation, ethnic identity, family, autonomy, and other age-related issues. Another session that I call "The Stresses and Strains of Growing up Latina or Latino" can cover the stresses that teenagers face such as the peer group pressure, parental authority, family tensions, and academic demands. Depression and self-injurious behaviors should be included. Lessons about smoking, alcohol, marijuana and other drugs, sexual acting out and safety, dating violence, and other topics can fill out this session. The third and fourth group sessions titled "Living Happy, Living Healthy with Family" combine individual psychological and family-oriented issues and skills. *Parent groups* can follow in similar three- or four-meeting formats, primarily in the evenings at the school for convenience of the many working parents who cannot come during the day. Parent groups will mix fathers and mothers, and the sessions should be designed such that participating parents can bring information home to the other parent who either could not or would not participate.

* * *

Notwithstanding the fact that more research is needed, there are ways to think about preventing the attempts of young Latinas and treating the girls and their families after an attempt. Since there are few interventions that are targeted directly at suicidality and many more treatments that have been developed for other psychosocial problems, I have drawn from these to emphasize their utility for treating young Hispanic women and their families. This discussion was not meant to be an exhaustive look at every possible intervention that is available; clinicians and treatment research have a literature to turn to that can help them take existing treatments and make the right adaptations to make them work for diverse populations (e.g., Cardemil et al., 2010; D'Angelo et al., 2009; Santisteban & Mena, 2009; Zayas, 2010). Rather it represents a starting point by identifying the elements that are pivotal in treating Hispanic families and their daughters.

It is helpful, as many clinicians know to blend empirically based treatments, those with a great deal of scientific testing, with clinical knowledge and experience collected over the span of years in practice. Adapting interventions to match cultural experiences and needs and making them relevant to specific populations, in the case of this book Latino families and daughters, is commonly done in practice. As this chapter has tried to show, there are individual treatments that can be mixed with family treatments, which can be embellished further through the incorporation of culturally relevant stories and rituals. Schools have a major role to play in reducing the despair of young Latinas, and I presented just a few ideas of what they can do.

Around our country there are schools with fine educators and administrators doing unheralded but effective work to help Hispanic youth. There are also community-based program scattered around the American landscape of cities, towns, villages, and counties that are also serving young Latinas and young

Latinos to help them overcome the challenges they face. Besides the widely published descriptions of scientifically rigorous clinical interventions, there are equally rigorous real-world interventions derived from community agencies that deserve our attention and support. We need to continued to bringing those successful community programs to the attention of a wider audience.

Epilogue

As I was putting the finishing touches on the manuscript for this book in the summer of 2010, the CDC released the findings from its youth risks survey of 2009. The results were all too familiar. Although the numbers differed slightly from previous years, the pattern of higher risk for Latinas continued. The prevalence of sadness and hopelessness "every day for 2 or more weeks in a row" among American high school youth was higher among Hispanic students (31.6%) than Black (27.7%) and White (23.7%) students (CDC, 2010, p. 8). Latinas rated their sadness and hopelessness as higher (39.7%) than White female (31.1%) and Black female (37.5%) students.

In 2009, 13.8% of high school students across the nation reported that they had seriously considered attempting suicide during the 12 months before the survey but more girls (17.4%) than boys (10.5%) considered suicide. Suicidal thoughts were higher among Hispanic females (20.2%) than among White females (16.1%) or Black females (18.1%). Generally, the prevalence of seriously considering suicide was higher among Hispanic students (15.4%) than White (13.1%) and Black (13.0%) students.

Suicide plans and attempts reported by youth in 2009 revealed the same pattern that we have become accustomed to (CDC, 2010). In 2009, girls across ethnic and racial groups planned suicides (13.2%) more than boys (8.6%). Among all youth, Hispanics (12.2%) reported making a suicide plan more often than White

(10.3%) and Black (9.85) youth. Latinas again reported higher rates of planning (15.4%) than White female (12.3%) or Black female (13.3%) students.

In actual suicide attempts nationwide, 6.3% of students attempted suicide one or more times in the previous year; the prevalence was higher among girls (8.1%) than boys (4.6%) (CDC, 2010). Among all Hispanic youth the proportion of those who attempted suicide at least once in the preceding year was 8.1% in comparison to 5% among White youth and 7.9% of Black youth. It was certainly good to see that all youth showed lower rates of suicide attempts than in past years. But the concern remains that Hispanic youth are still more likely to attempt suicide than other high school youth: Latinas at a rate of 11.1% compared with 10.4% of Black females and 6.5% of White females. These statistics continue to show that being a young minority female puts you at risk for suicide attempts. These numbers tell us that there is still reason to worry, and we need to step up our treatment and preventive efforts.

Prior to the release of the latest numbers from the CDC in 2010, CNN presented *Latino in America*, a 4-hour, two-part documentary in October 2009 narrated by Soledad O'Brien (with a companion book by O'Brien and Arce, 2009). Millions of people in the United States, throughout Latin America, and beyond watched this first-of-a-kind documentary. It was an important milestone for U.S. Hispanics, for it was the first such occasion that a major network with global reach and reputation had presented a look at what it means to be Latino in America. The public response to the documentary was strong. Some in the Hispanic community were positively impressed with the show. Others were less favorable in their reviews. Regardless of the differences in opinions, *Latinos in America* evoked important reactions and controversies that vivify our diversity in culture, national origin, political orientation, social class, religion, ideology, and geographic regions. The program activated discussions that are important to have in a pluralistic and democratic nation.

The topic of suicide attempts by young Latinas was covered in the documentary and the book by O'Brien and Arce. The topic was new to many viewers, a familiar one to some of us. In particular, the story of a young Dominican girl who had attempted suicide and her mother was told in their words with the immediacy that only images of the speakers and their voices can bring to the viewer. A year later, on October 22, 2010, National Public Radio aired a segment of *Latino USA* on suicide attempts titled "Latina Teen Suicide: Yanira's Story," produced by Laura Starecheski and hosted by Maria Hinojosa, that included excerpts from the recorded interviews with a girl whose case dramatized the plight of many Latinas. The girl's words and her story drove home the point of the developmental and cultural struggles of other teenage women in the Hispanic community. Stories are best told, as I wrote in the preface of this book, by the individuals themselves, in their own words. The stories in both documentaries brought to life all of the arcane details that researchers had reported for so many years.

As a result of the segment on the suicidal teenager in the CNN documentary, I received many e-mail messages. Some were congratulatory messages from colleagues and friends, some from thoughtful strangers offering alternative hypotheses for the suicide attempts. But most were from Latinas who were touched by the story of the young Dominican teenager in O'Brien's piece. Some of the women who sent e-mail to me had attempted suicide as teenagers. I quote them here because their words convey with great richness the ideas that I have touched on in this book.

One wrote, "I am the daughter of Mexican immigrants and completely connected with the struggle shown in the documentary to balance both worlds. Gendered expectations play a huge role in our families, and it's a constant balancing act especially for the daughters of immigrants."

Another Latina spoke for many when she wrote that "I am a 38-year old Hispanic female and survivor of that horrific environment and battle of cultures. My heart aches for the young girls that are suffering through this life crisis. The story brought back heavy memories of my own broken heart and identity. I too was very depressed. On the bright side, though, I managed to be the first female in a very large expanded [sic] family to graduate from college."

Each of these e-mail messages, and others, touched my heart deeply. But the messages were not new since this was not the first time I had borne witness to this kind of reaction. Three years earlier, *The New York Times* (2006) had carried an editorial titled "Young Latinas and a Cry for Help" (July 21, 2006), which prompted national attention. The editorial mentioned the many challenges facing young Latinas, from high rates of dropping out of school, pregnancy, and suicide attempts. In response to the editorial and to interviews that I gave to National Public Radio and other radio programs and newspapers, many Latinas who had overcome their adolescent past, women who had thrived after a suicide attempt, also sent me e-mail. They wanted to tell their stories.

From San Antonio one woman wrote, "I'm 32, educated, mother of 2, married (kept my name) and finally feel like myself. I'd like to share what one Latina thinks. I'm sure it would be good for me too since I attempted in my younger years and never really discussed my actions." From what we learned from the girls in our study, speaking up is healing.

From Los Angeles another woman wrote that the editorial "was so touching to me because I went through a similar childhood. I am Latina and married. It happened to me and happens to a lot of Latinas out there who will not talk about this topic. I never spoke up to protect my parents and myself from embarrassment." That she kept silent to protecting her parents, as we have learned, underscores how important *respeto* and *familismo* are in preserving the integrity of the family unit.

As often as I can, I try to answer these e-mail messages or return the women's calls. I urge them to seek out other Latinas and share their experiences, for in doing so they can help many among them.

They are eloquent messages from women who had survived, rebounded, and are living full, successful lives. But there are voices missing from the e-mail, or letters to the editor, or callers to radio talk shows. Absent from these voices and their messages of hope are those of Latinas whose lives after a suicide attempt in adolescence have not gone as well. They are not among the callers or letter writers. There are many silent women who attempted suicide in adolescence. But they could not write e-mail to say that their lives had gone as well as the women who wrote to tell of recovering from their awful pasts.

The many silent adult Latina who were once victims of adolescent suicide attempts, those who did not write or call, are like the many women I treated in mental health clinics and community health centers during a long career. They are women who are still living troubled lives of domestic violence, dysfunctional families, substance abuse, and unachieved potential. The Latinas I saw in clinics often came in for routine medical care and for services for depression and life stresses. It was in the course of their treatments that the suicide attempts in their biographies were uncovered. Some of these Hispanic women were intelligent, creative persons whose potential had been truncated by their life experiences—not necessarily by their suicide attempts but by the circumstances that incubated their desperation and hopelessness. It didn't help that they had attempted suicide. The women I treated in inner-city clinics often had not received treatment when they were teenagers after the suicide attempts. Many lived in families that did not change after suicide attempts or other major crises to make things better for the young women. They were locked into inflexible, poorly communicating families that were stuck in interactions that were repeated, over and over again, in vicious family interactions, cycles from which they could not break away.

The women in the clinics were once teenagers, daughters of immigrant parents whose imposition of their cultures restricted them; their parents insisted that they follow assiduously the gender roles prescribed for them and that they meet all of the expectations made of traditional Hispanic women. But it was not all immigration- and acculturation-related differences that brought them pain. Many of their families suffered from the dysfunctions I described in Chapter Three where neglect, abuse, lack of empathy, and poor communication pervaded family life. Even in the presence of loving parents and families, they often felt misunderstood, relegated to sacrificing for their families at the expense of their own needs. Some of these women who attempted suicide did so as part of an acting-out process, externalizing in their behaviors the internal stress they felt. They rebelled but only to their own detriment. The suicide attempts were their only acts, or were paired with dropping out of high school, getting pregnant, drug use, and delinquency, thwarting their futures. Other women simply kept it in, internalizing their pain until it was expressed in the suicide attempt. The potential in their lives too was forestalled, too, falling into chasms of depression and low self-worth. Whether the women acted out or "acted in," they did not feel relief from their families. By dint of their own strengths and good use of therapy, some of the women I saw in clinic overcame this past and planned a brighter future. Others could not and did not change. Like the myth of Sisyphus who was doomed to roll an immense boulder up a hill only to see it roll back and start again, many of these women repeated the past in their lives as mothers.

I often think back on these clients. They and many like them are, in my mind, a lost generation of Latinas who still live in poverty, often with the vestiges of their troubled adolescence weighing them down. Many have suffered alone, not knowing that scores of other Latina sisters—and brothers, too—have been caught in similar spirals of desperation to the point of attempting suicide. We can implement preventive and treatment services for young Latinas enduring the situations that foster suicide attempts. For adult women with this event in their past, therapy and support groups are most helpful. It is our responsibility as a society to help move them from their isolation into conversations with other Latinas about what hurts them so deeply. Sharing their private sorrows with each other, not just me, can mean a great deal in healing broken souls.

Acknowledgments

The topic of this book has occupied my thoughts and heart for three decades. As a result of the support of many people and institutions, it became a reality. Elaine Rivera set the book in motion through a series of stories she wrote for *El Diario/La Prensa* in July 2006 that was then cited in an editorial in *The New York Times* calling for attention to the struggles of young Latinas. Maura Roessner of Oxford University Press read the *Times* editorial and urged me to write the story of Latinas and their suicide attempts. Without Elaine's stories and Maura's prompting and support, this book might still be a thought.

Once determined to write the book, I could not have been at a better place to write than at Washington University in St. Louis with its marvelous people and world-class resources. It was through Washington University that I met the truly exceptional people who became my research team and who have earned my eternal gratitude. At the head of this group stands Carolina Hausmann-Stabile, one of the smartest, most energetic, tenacious, and resourceful, people I have ever met. Based in New York City, Carolina opened doors that seem impenetrable, faced hardnosed administrators, soothed suspicious clinicians, and interviewed sad, hurting girls every day for 5 years. Even when she wasn't being paid because of one snafu or another, Carolina kept at it, more hopeful than I at times in making the project a success. Other important members of my team were indispensable, too.

Allyson Pilat Nolle handled the qualitative data, human subjects' protocols (and the seemingly endless modifications that were required), transcriptions, and so much more in our study with her usual aplomb. Jill Kuhlberg came on the scene just as I needed an intelligent and effervescent quantitative analyst with a good sense of humor. Multitalented, unselfish, and considerate Jill worked long days and weekends—always smiling—to make sense of all the numbers that were too overwhelming for me to understand. Juan B. Peña was always there to look at the numbers that Jill produced. Juan found beauty and elegance in the numbers where most of us saw, well, numbers. Lauren Gulbas, a tremendously upbeat and insightful anthropologist, joined the team in the last year of our research, bringing her remarkable talents, knowledge, and energy to the qualitative analyses. Lauren's lasting influence on our research project may be immeasurable, but it is certainly immense. Leo Cabassa was a hardworking doctoral student and coinvestigator who became, with his family, my cherished friends. Jee Yeong Witt earned my unflinching trust and respect as a first-year graduate student when she took on the thankless tasks of proofreading the full manuscript multiple times and finding my mistakes.

Even when there wasn't an agenda or much to discuss in team meetings, I met with this phenomenal group of people just because they were so much fun to be with.

Other colleagues who I thank for their hard work and collegiality are Stavroula "Star" Kyriakakis, Ana Baumann, Lisa Fortuna, Charlotte Bright, Nicole Fedoravicius, Thyria Álvarez-Sánchez, and Luis E. Zayas Rivera. There are many other colleagues, too numerous to list here, who inspired me and influenced this book. To them I give heartfelt thanks. In New York City, special thanks go to the Puerto Rican Family Institute, Holliswood Hospital (Queens), and Lincoln Medical and Mental Health Center (the Bronx) for their support. I am sincerely grateful to the girls and parents who participated in our research.

Good friends surrounded me during the preparation of this book. They seemed to be placed in my life intentionally by an invisible hand to distract me from the all-consuming process of writing. There is the warm, sustaining friendship of my main man Joe Flores who reminds me when I need it that I have to captain my own ship. We shared many beers together in our backyards and bantered. Dave Hernandez perhaps better than many others I know can appreciate the struggles of young Latinos growing up in New York City. Dave read an early draft and lent his keen analytic skills during dark days in his health. Luis R. Torres has been for over 20 years a cheerful and trusted friend. His goodness, insight, and wit have enlarged my life, for which I am grateful. There are great family friends—Mel and Rita Carrozza, and Bill and Betsy

Fisher—whose questions and good-natured ribbing during the months of writing were always filled with affection and genuine interest in the evolution of this book. The love of all these friends made me want to work harder.

Then there is *mi familia*. My wife and best friend, Stephanie, who, whether she understood or not what project it was that I was working on at any given time, has always been supportive and loving, making our house a home for our family. Stephanie was patient and forgiving for the many hours I hid in the Hemingway room. The sense of humor we share keeps our marriage strong. My children—sweet Marissa with her deep sense of responsibility to others, irrepressible Amanda with her wit and compassion, and adventurous Luis-Michael with his generous heart and inquisitive mind—have always made me a proud father. I thank them for their patience while I spent long hours writing or traveling. I hope that by example I can inspire my new daughter, Victoria Valladares, to reach high in her life.

No words can thank my mother Mercedes and my father Luis Antonio for their struggles to raise six children to be closely knit and fiercely loyal to the family. I drew strength from my four sisters—Marta, Maria, Lourdes, and Lillian—whose fortitude during the uncertain times of their own adolescence was truly remarkable. I trust that the men in the family—my father, my brother Nelson, and my son Luis-Michael—will not feel slighted that I dedicated this book to the women who have been so central to our lives.

Finally, I give thanks for my large, raucous, fun-loving extended family—too many to list in just one volume—where *cariño* is expressed with no holds barred. This vast family sustains me with its love.

Credits

Notes

Preface

1 All names and other identifiers of patients and research subjects presented in this book have been changed and all information disguised to protected their privacy.
2 It is worth noting that Fernandez-Marina (1961) was writing about the Puerto Rican syndrome at about the same time that Edgar Trautman (1961a, 1961b) published his work on the suicidal fit. Mehlman (1961) argued against coining terms from cultural experiences that might be psychiatric conditions. Very likely each was aware of the others' work.
3 The Pew Hispanic Center, a leading demographics research project that is part of the Pew Research Center in Washington, D.C., employs a similar usage of the two terms.

Chapter One: First, the Family

4 There is evidence of the existence of an underground network that offers opportunities for these professionals to practice their trade. In some urban centers where undocumented immigrants settle and embed themselves in local communities, those with professional degrees provide services in the shadows of the system. For example, dentists and physicians who cannot practice legally but who have earned the trust of their "patients" (viz., other undocumented

immigrants) may make house calls, provide diagnoses, and treat within the range they can under the circumstances. Former accountants who may in the daytime work as bookkeepers or in stores may moonlight preparing tax returns for other immigrants.

5 Much more research is needed on the impact of immigration and second-generation status among youth from other countries. Anecdotally, I learned from colleagues that first- and second-generation Arab youth, especially girls, in the boroughs of Brooklyn and Queens in New York City were apparently evincing suicidal actions. Immigration and acculturation into an urban culture when coming from a highly traditional, religious cultural origin may help explain this. However, it does not explain what occurred to us when we sought African-American girls in the same emergency rooms and clinics as we recruited the Latinas. In recruiting female African-American teenagers in the Bronx (defined as daughters of African-American families with family history going back to slavery), we only found girls whose parents had immigrated from Africa or the English-speaking West Indies (e.g., Jamaica). Although anecdotes and small indicators do not provide sufficient evidence to establish a trend or a category, we see the need for further exploration of how immigration, acculturation, and the stresses visited on young Latinas may also be affecting youth from other countries and cultural origins.

6 In a paper published in 1974, Emilicia Mizio (1974) commented on the experiences of Puerto Rican families migrating to the places like New York City with their *hijos de crianza* when facing educational, medical, and welfare bureaucracies. Despite deep emotional ties between parents and *hijos de crianza*, these families would not have legal adoption papers and other such documents. This arrangement often caused many misunderstandings and refusals by institutions to enroll the child or provide services for such a child.

Chapter Two: A Brief History

7 The yaxche tree of Mayan mythology is believed to be based on the *ceiba* tree that grows in the Caribbean, Mexico, and Central and South America. The *ceiba* can grow 70 meters or taller and has a distinctive canopy at the top.

Chapter Three: Contexts of Development

8 Ontogeny is elemental to developmental sciences: the study of the origin and development of an organism from fertilized egg to its mature, adult form.

9 Ana Baumann assisted me in the preparation of Yolanda's case.

Chapter Four: Daughters, Familism, and Adulthood

10 I wish to thank George Miranda for introducing me to Imperial Valley and its many kind and helpful people. Special thanks go to Araceli Miranda, Giovanna Casillas, Glenda C. Chavez, and Liliana Sordia-Ramirez for spending a Sunday evening sharing their insights and for permitting me to include their names and comments in this book.

11 The full poem, "Mujercita" ("Little Woman"), appears as "author unknown" in *Naco—O como se diga*, by Andrés Alejandro Cuevas Sosa, Editorial Posada, S.A., Mexico, 1985.

12 Although the group was conducted in Spanish, I present it here fully translated. The names of mothers and daughters have been disguised to protect their identities. I am truly grateful to the women and teenagers for sharing their stories with me. They not only gave words and meanings to growing up Latina; they also left memories and impressions I will never forget.

13 Arguably, defining adulthood in terms of parenthood and milestones (e.g., being of age, graduating, marrying, getting pregnant) may influence the high rates of pregnancies that we see among Hispanics women in the 15- to 19-year age range. The birth rate for Hispanic women in this group is 82 per 1,000 births compared to 27 per 1,000 births for non-Hispanic women and 64 per 1,000 for non-Hispanic Black women (Hamilton, Martin, & Ventura, 2007). This is an area for researchers to explore further in future studies and for public health professionals to continue in their dedicated efforts.

Chapter Five: New Findings

14 We excluded from the study girls who were diagnosed with a major psychiatric disorder such as schizophrenia or other psychotic disorder, girls with mental retardation, and girls living in foster homes.

Chapter Six: Anatomy of the Suicide Attempt

15 Lauren Gulbas assisted in the preparation of the case of Sofia.

16 Allyson Pilat Nolle assisted in the preparation of the cases of Yvonne and Linda.

Chapter Eight: Saving Young Latinas

17 For many more updated lists of empirically validated interventions for youth depression and suicide, visit the National Registry of Evidence-Based Programs and Practices (NREPP) treatments web page of the Substance Abuse and Mental Health Services Administration, Department of Health and Human Services.

References

Achenbach, T.M., & Rescorla, L.A. (2001). *Manual for the ASEBA school-age forms & profiles.* Burlington, VT: University of Vermont, Research Center for Children, Youth, and Families.

Agudelo, A., Cava, M.J., & Musitu, G. (2001). Un análisis intercultural de la socialización familiar y los valores en adolescentes. *Escritos de Psicología, 5,* 70–80.

Alba, R., Logan J., Lutz, A., & Stults, B. (2002). Only English by the third generation? Loss and preservation of the mother tongue among the grandchildren of contemporary immigrants. *Demography, 39*(3), 467–84.

Alvarez, J.A. (1991). *How the Garcia girls lost their accent.* Chapel Hill, NC: Algonquin Books.

Alvarez, J.A. (1999). *Something to declare.* Chapel Hill, NC: Algonquin Books.

Alvarez, J.A. (2007). *Once upon a quinceañera: Coming of age in the USA.* New York: Plume.

Alvarez, L. (2007). Derecho u obligación? Parents' and youths' understanding of parental legitimacy in a Mexican origin familial context. *Hispanic Journal of Behavioral Sciences, 29,* 192–208.

American Psychiatric Association (2000). *Diagnostic and statistical manual of mental disorders (text revision).* Washington, DC: Author.

Arciniega, G.M., Anderson, T.C., Tovar-Blank, Z.G., & Tracey, T.J.G. (2008). Toward a fuller conception of machismo: Development of a traditional Machismo and Caballerismo Scale. *Journal of Counseling Psychology, 55,* 19–33.

Asencio, M.W. (1999). Machos and sluts: Gender, sexuality, and violence among a cohort of Puerto Rican adolescents. *Medical Anthropology Quarterly, 13*(1), 107–26.

Barber, B.K. (1996). Parental psychological control: Revisiting a neglected construct. *Child Development, 67*, 3296–3319.

Barber, B.K., & Harmon, E.L. (2002). Violating the self: Parental psychological control of children and adolescents. In B.K. Barber (Ed.), *Intrusive parenting: How psychological control affects children and adolescents* (pp. 15–52). Washington, DC: American Psychological Association.

Barber, B.K., Olsen, J.E., & Shagle, S.C. (1994). Associations between parental psychological and behavioral control and youth internalized and externalized behaviors. *Child Development, 65*, 1120–36.

Bell, D. (1975). Ethnicity and social change. In N. Glazer & D.P. Moynihan (Eds.), *Ethnicity: Theory and experience* (pp. 100–117). Cambridge, MA: Harvard University Press.

Berne, J.E. (1983). The management of patients post-suicide attempt in an urban municipal hospital. *Psychoanalytic Quarterly, 57, (Psychiatria Fennica Supplementum)*, 45–54.

Betancourt, H., & López, S.R. (1993). The study of culture, ethnicity, and race in American psychology. *American Psychologist, 48*(6), 629–37.

Biehl, J., Good, B., & Kleinman, A. (Eds.) (2007). *Subjectivity: Ethnographic investigations.* Berkeley, CA: University of California Press.

Blos, P. (1967). The second individuation process of adolescence. *The Psychoanalytic Study of the Child, 22*, 162–86.

Boger, K.D., Tompson, M.C., Briggs-Gowan, M.J., Pavlis, L.E., & Carter, A.S. (2008). Parental expressed emotion toward children: Prediction from early family functioning. *Journal of Family Psychology, 22*(5), 784–88.

Bornstein, M.H., Putnick, D.L., Heslington, M., Gini, M., Suwalsky, J.T.D., Venuti, P., et al. (2008). Mother-child emotional availability in ecological perspective: Three countries, two regions, two genders. *Developmental Psychology, 44*(3), 666–80.

Boss, P. (2004). Ambiguous loss research, theory, and practice: Reflections after 9/11. *Journal of Marriage and Famiy, 66*, 551–66.

Bowlby, J. (1969). *Attachment and loss: Vol. 1. Attachment.* New York: Basic Books.

Bowlby, J. (1973). *Attachment and loss: Vol. 2. Separation: Anxiety and anger.* NewYork: Basic Books.

Bowlby, J. (1980). *Attachment and loss: Vol. 3. Sadness and depression.* New York: Basic Books.

Bowlby, J. (1988). *A secure base: Clinical applications of attachment theory.* London: Routledge.

Brener, N.D., Billy J.O.G., & Grady, W.R. (2003). Assessment of factors affecting the validity of self-reported health-risk behavior among adolescents: Evidence from the scientific literature. *Journal of Adolescent Health, 33*(6), 436–57.

Brener, N.D., Collins, J.L., Kann, L., Warren, C.W., & Williams, B.I. (1995). Reliability of the youth risk behavior survey questionnaire. *American Journal of Epidemiology, 141*(6), 575–80.

Brener, N.D., Kann, L., McManus, T., Kinchen, S.A., Sundberg, E.C., & Ross, J.G. (2002). Reliability of the 1999 youth risk behavior survey questionnaire. *Journal of Adolescent Health, 31*(4), 336–42.

Brent, D.A., Holder, D., Kolko, D., Birmaher, B., Baugher, M., Roth, C., et al. (1997). A clinical psychotherapy trial for adolescent depression comparing cognitive, family, and supportive therapy. *Archives of General Psychiatry, 54,* 877–85.

Bronfenbrenner, U. (1979). *The ecology of human development.* Cambridge, MA: Harvard University Press.

Brumariu, L.E., & Kerns, K.A. (2010). Parent–child attachment and internalizing symptoms in childhood and adolescence: A review of empirical findings and future directions. *Development and Psychopathology 22,* 177–203.

Cabassa, L.J. (2003). Measuring acculturation: Where we are and where we need to go. *Hispanic Journal of Behavioral Sciences, 25*(2), 127–46.

Cable News Network (CNN). (2009, July 13). *Sonia Sotomayor faces members of Senate in Supreme Court Confirmation Hearings* [Television broadcast]. Washington, DC: Cable News Network.

Calkins, S.D., Hungerford, A., & Dedmon, S.E. (2004). Mothers' interactions with temperamentally frustrated infants. *Infant Mental Health Journal, 25*(3), 219–39.

Candelaria, N. (1988). *The day the Cisco Kid shot John Wayne.* Tempe, AZ: Bilingual Press/Editorial Bilingüe, Arizona State University Press.

Canino, G., & Roberts, R.E. (2001). Suicidal behavior among Latino youth. *Suicide and Life-Threatening Behavior, 31,* 122–31.

Canino, I.A., & Canino, G. (1980.). Impact of stress on the Puerto Rican family: Treatment considerations. *American Journal of Orthopsychiatry, 50,* 535–41.

Cardemil, E.V., Kim, S., Davidson, T., Sarmiento, I.A., Zack, R., Sanchez, M., et al. (2010). Developing a culturally appropriate depression prevention program: Opportunities and challenges. *Cognitive & Behavioral Practice, 17,* 188–97.

Centers for Disease Control and Prevention. (2004). Methodology of the Youth Risk Behavior Surveillance System. *Morbidity and Mortality Weekly Report, 53*(RR-12), 1–13.

Centers for Disease Control and Prevention. (2006a). *Trends in HIV-related risk behavior among high school students, United States, 2003.* Atlanta, GA: U.S. Department for Health and Human Services.

Centers for Disease Control and Prevention. (2006b). Youth risk behavior surveillance—United States, 2005. *Morbidity and Mortality Weekly Report, 54*(SS-5), 1–108.

Centers for Disease Control and Prevention. (2008). Youth risk behavior surveillance—United States, 2007. *Morbidity and Mortality Weekly Report, 57*(SS-4), 1–131.

Centers for Disease Control and Prevention (2009). *2009 State and local youth risk behavior survey.* Retrieved from http://www.cdc.gov/HealthyYouth/yrbs/.

Centers for Disease Control and Prevention. (2010). Youth risk behavior surveillance—United States, 2009. *Surveillance Summaries, Morbidity and Mortality Weekly Report, 59*(SS-5).

Chant, S.H. (2003). Gender in a changing continent. In S.H. Chant & N. Craski (Eds.), *Gender in Latin America* (pp. 1–18). New Brunswick, NJ: Rutgers University Press.

Cisneros, S. (1987). *My wicked, wicked ways.* Bloomington, IN: Third Woman Press.

Cisneros, S. (1988). *The house on Mango Street.* Houston, TX: Arte Publico Press.

Conger, R.D., & Elder, G.H. (1994). *Families in troubled times: Adapting to change in rural America.* Hawthorne, NY: Aldine de Gruyter.

Conger, R.D., Wallace, L.E., Sun, Y., Simons, R.L., McLoyd, V.C., & Brody, G.H. (2002). Economic pressure in African American families: A replication and extension of the family stress model. *Developmental Psychology, 38*(2), 179–93.

Coohey, C. (2001). The relationship between familism and child maltreatment in Latino and Anglo families. *Child Maltreatment, 6*(2), 130–42.

Cotterell, A. (1979). *A dictionary of world mythology.* New York: Oxford University Press.

Cuéllar, I., Nyberg, B., Maldonado, R., & Roberts, R.E. (1997). Ethnic identity and acculturation in a young adult Mexican-origin population. *Journal of Community Psychology, 25*(6), 535–49.

D'Angelo, E.J., Llerena-Quinn, R., Shapiro, R., Colon, F., Rodriguez, P., Gallagher, K., et al. (2009). Adaptation of the Preventive Intervention Program for Depression for use with predominantly low-income Latino families. *Family Process, 48*(2), 269–91.

Díaz, J. (2007). *The brief wondrous life of Oscar Wao.* New York: Penguin Books Ltd.

Dickstein, D.P., & Leibenluft, E. (2006). Emotion regulation in children and adolescents: Boundaries between normalcy and bipolar disorder. *Development and Psychopathology, 18,* 1105–1131.

Dillon, C.O., Liem, J.H., & Gore, S. (2003). Navigating disrupted transitions: Getting back on track after dropping out of high school. *American Journal of Orthopsychiatry, 73*(4), 429–40.

Dorian, M., García, J.I., López, S.R., & Hernández, B. (2008). Acceptance and expressed emotion in Mexican American caregivers of relatives with schizophrenia. *Family Process, 47*(2), 215–28.

Dunn, M.S.A., Bartee, R.T., & Perko, M.A. (2003). Self-reported alcohol use and sexual behaviors of adolescents. *Psychological Reports, 92*(1), 339–48.

Durkheim, E. (1897/2006). *On suicide.* New York: Penguin.

Dyche, L., & Zayas, L.H. (1995). The value of curiosity and naiveté for the cross-cultural psychotherapist. *Family Process, 34*(4), 389–99.

Dye, J.L. (2005). Fertility of American women: June 2004. *Current Population Reports, P20–555.* Washington, DC: U.S. Census Bureau.

Eaker, D.G., & Walters, L.H. (2002). Adolescent satisfaction in family rituals and psychosocial development: A developmental systems theory perspective. *Journal of Family Psychology, 16*(4), 406–414.

Eccles, J.S., Buchanan, C.M., Flanagan, C., Fuligni, A., Midgley, C., & Yee, D. (1991). Control versus autonomy during early adolescence. *Journal of Social Issues, 47*(4), 53–68.

Egeland, B., & Carlson, E.A. (2004). Attachment and psychopathology. In L. Atkinson & S. Goldberg (Eds.), *Attachment issues in psychopathology and intervention* (pp. 27–48). Hillsdale, NJ: Erlbaum.

El-Sheikh, M., Hinnant, J.B., Kelly, R.J., & Erath, S. (2010). Maternal psychological control and child internalizing symptoms: vulnerability and protective factors across bioregulatory and ecological domains. *Journal of Child Psychology and Psychiatry, 51*(2), 188–198.

Elkin, J.L. (1998). *The Jews of Latin America.* Teaneck, NJ: Holmes & Meier.

Erikson, E.H. (1950). *Childhood and society.* New York: Norton.

Falicov, C.J. (1998). *Latino families in therapy: A guide to multicultural practice.* New York: Guilford.

Fernández-Marina, R. (1961). The Puerto Rican syndrome: Its dynamics and cultural determinants. *Psychiatry: Journal for the Study of Interpersonal Processes, 24*(1), 79–82.

Fiese, B.H., Tomcho, T.J., Douglas, M., Josephs, K., Poltrock, S., & Baker, T. (2002). A review of 50 years of research on naturally occurring family routines and rituals: Cause for celebration? *Journal of Family Psychology, 16*(4), 381–90.

Finerman, R. (1989). The burden of responsibility: Duty, depression, and *nervios* in Andean Ecuador. In D.L. Davis & S.M. Low (Eds.), *Gender, health and illness: The case of nerves* (pp. 49–65). New York: Hemisphere.

Fix, M., & Zimmerman, W. (2001). All under one roof: Mixed-status families in an era of reform. *International Migration Review, 35*(2), 397–419.

Flores, E., Eyre, S.L., & Millstein, S.G. (1998). Sociocultural beliefs related to sex among Mexican American adolescents. *Hispanic Journal of Behavioral Sciences, 20*, 60–82.

Ford, D.H., & Lerner, R.M. (1992). *Developmental systems theory: An integrative approach.* Newbury Park, CA: Sage.

Friedman, J.H, Asnis, G., Boeck, M., & DiFiore, J. (1987). Prevalence of specific suicidal behaviors in a high school sample. *American Journal of Psychiatry, 144*(9), 1203–1206.

Garcia, C., Skay, C., Sieving, R., Naughton, S. & Bearinger, L.H. (2008). Family and racial factors associated with suicide and emotional distress among Latino students. *Journal of School Health, 78*(9), 487–95.

Garofalo, R., Wolf, R.C., Wissow, L.S., Woods, E.R., & Goodman, E. (1999). Sexual orientation and risk of suicide attempts among a representative sample of youth. *Archives of Pediatrics and Adolescent Medicine, 153*(5), 487–93.

Genero, N.P., Miller, J.B., Surrey, J., & Baldwin, L.M. (1992). Measuring perceived mutuality in close relationships: Validation of the Mutual Psychological Development Questionnaire. *Journal of Family Psychology, 6*(1), 36–48.

Gil, M.R., & Vazquez, C.I. (1997). *The Maria Paradox: How Latinas can merge Old World traditions with New World self-esteem.* New York: Putnam.

Goldsmith, S.K., Pellmar, T.C., Kleinman, A.M., & Bunney, W.E. (Eds.) (2002). *Reducing suicide: A national imperative.* Washington, DC: National Academies Press.

Gonzales, N.A., Knight, G.P., Morgan-Lopez, A., Saenz, D., & Sirolli, A. (2002). Acculturation and the mental health of Latino youths: An integration and critique of the literature. In J.M. Contreras, K.A. Kerns, & A.M. Neal-Barnett (Eds.), *Latino children and families in the United States: Current research and future directions* (pp. 45–74). Westport, CT: Greenwood Publishing Group.

Gonzales, N.A., Pitts, S.C., Hill, N.E., & Roosa, M.W. (2000). A mediational model of the impact of interparental conflict on child adjustment in a multiethnic, low-income sample. *Journal of Family Psychology, 14*(3), 365–79.

Gonzales, N.A., Tein, J-Y., Sandler, I.N., & Friedman, R.J. (2001). On the limits of coping: Interaction between stress and coping for inner-city adolescents. *Journal of Adolescent Research, 16,* 372–95.

Granic, I., & Dishion, T.J. (2003). Deviant talk in adolescent friendships: A step toward measuring a pathogenic attractor process. *Social Development, 12*(3), 314–34.

Gray, M.R., & Steinberg, L. (1999). Unpacking authoritative parenting: Reassessing a multidimensional construct. *Journal of Marriage & the Family, 61,* 574–87.

Greenway, C. (1998). Hungry earth and vengeful stars: Soul loss and identity in the Peruvian Andes. *Social Science and Medicine, 47*(8), 993–1004.

Griffith, J.D., Joe, G.W., Chatham, L.R. & Simpson, D.D. (1998). The development and validation of a simpatia scale of Hispanics entering drug treatment. *Hispanic Journal of Behavioral Sciences, 20,* 468–83.

Guarnaccia, P.J., Canino, G., Rubio-Stipec, M., & Bravo, M. (1993). The prevalence of ataques de nervios in the Puerto Rico Disaster Study: The role of culture in psychiatric epidemiology. *Journal of Nervous and Mental Disease, 181*(3), 159–67.

Guarnaccia, P.J., & Farias, P. (1988). The social meanings of nervios: A case study of a Central American woman. *Social Science and Medicine, 26*(12), 1223–31.

Guarnaccia, P.J., Lewis-Fernández, R., & Marano, M.R. (2003). Toward a Puerto Rican popular nosology: Nervios and ataque de nervios. *Culture, Medicine, and Psychiatry, 27*(3), 339–66.

Guarnaccia, P.J., Rivera, M., Franco, F., & Neighbors, C. (1996). The experiences of ataques de nervios: Towards an anthropology of emotions in Puerto Rico. *Culture, Medicine, and Psychiatry, 20*(3), 343–67.

Guarnaccia, P.J., & Rogler, L.H. (1999). Research on culture-bound syndromes: New directions. *American Journal of Psychiatry, 156*(9), 1322–27.

Guarnaccia, P.J., Rubio-Stipec, M., & Canino, G. (1989). *Ataques de nervios* in the Puerto Rican Diagnostic Interview Schedule: The impact of cultural categories on psychiatric epidemiology. *Culture, Medicine, and Psychiatry, 13*(3), 275–95.

Gutmann, M.C. (1996). *The meanings of macho: Being a man in Mexico City.* Berkeley, CA: University of California Press.

Hakimzadeh, S., & Cohn, D. (2007). *English usage among Hispanics in the United States.* Washington, DC: Pew Hispanic Center.

Hamilton, B.E., Martin, J.A., & Ventura, S.J. (2007). Births: Preliminary data for 2006. *National vital statistics reports, 56*(7). Hyattsville, MD: National Center for Health Statistics.

Hankin, B.L., Kassel, J.D., & Abela, J.R.Z. (2005). Adult attachment dimensions and specificity of emotional distress symptoms: Prospective investigations of cognitive risk and interpersonal stress generation as mediating mechanisms. *Personality and Social Psychology Bulletin, 31*(1), 136–51.

Harkness, S., & Super, C.M. (Eds.) (1996). *Parents' cultural belief systems: Their origins, expressions, and consequences.* New York: The Guilford Press.

Harrington, R., Kerfoot, M., Dyer, E., McNiven, F., Gill, J., Harrington, V., et al. (1998). Randomized trial of a home-based family intervention for children who have deliberately poisoned themselves. *Journal of the American Academy of Child & Adolescent Psychiatry, 37*(5), 512–18.

Heller, P., Briones, D., Aguirre-Hauchbaum, S., & Roberts, A. (2004). Source of support and mastery: The interaction of socioeconomic status and Mexican-American ethnicity. *Sociological Spectrum, 24*(2), 239–64.

Hernandez, D.J. (2004). Demographic change and the life circumstances of immigrant families. *The Future of Children, 14*(2), 17–47.

Hingson, R., Heeren, T., Levenson, S., Jamanka, A., & Voas, R. (2002). Age of drinking onset, driving after drinking, and involvement in alcohol related motor-vehicle crashes. *Accident Analysis and Prevention, 34*(1), 85–92.

Hogue, A., Dauber, S., Samuolis, J., & Liddle, H.A. (2006). Treatment techniques and outcomes in multidimensional family therapy for adolescent behavior problems. *Journal of Family Psychology, 20*, 535–43.

Hollan, D. (2004). Self systems, cultural idioms of distress, and the psycho-bodily consequences of childhood suffering. *Transcultural Psychiatry 41*, 1, 62–79.

Horvath, A.O., & Luborsky, L. (1993). The role of the therapeutic alliance in psychotherapy. *Journal of Consulting and Clinical Psychology, 61*, 561–73.

Howard, G.S. (1991). Culture tales: A narrative approach to thinking, cross-cultural psychology, and psychotherapy. *American Psychologist, 46*(3), 187–97.

Itzigsohn, J., & Dore-Cabral, C. (2001). The manifold character of panethnicity: Latino identities and practices among Dominicans in New York City. In A. Laó-Montes & A. Davila (Eds.), *Mambo montage: The Latinization of New York City.* New York: Columbia University Press.

Johnson, J.G., Cohen, P., Gould, M.S., Kasen, S., Brown, J., & Brook, J.S. (2002). Childhood adversities, interpersonal difficulties, and risk for suicide attempts during late adolescence and early adulthood. *Archives of General Psychiatry, 59,* 741–749.

Johnston, L.D., O'Malley, P.M., Bachman, J.G., & Schulenberg, J.E., (2007). *Monitoring the future national results on adolescent drug use: Overview of key findings, 2006.* (NIH Publication No. 07-6202). Bethesda, MD: National Institute on Drug Abuse, U.S. Department of Health and Human Services.

Jones, J.M. (1991). Psychological models of race: What have they been and what should they be? In J.D. Goodchilds (Ed.), *Psychological perspectives on human diversity in America* (pp. 5–46). Washington, DC: American Psychological Association.

Kao, H.S., McHugh, M.L., & Travis, S.S. (2007). Psychometric tests of Expectations of Filial Piety Scale in a Mexican-American population. *Journal of Clinical Nursing, 16,* 1460–67.

Keller, H., Borke, J., Yovsi, R., Lohaus, A., & Jensen, H. (2005). Cultural orientations and historical changes as predictors of parenting behavior. *International Journal of Behavioral Development, 29,* 229–37.

Keller, H., & Lamm, B. (2005). Parenting as the expression of sociohistorical time: The case of German individualization. *International Journal of Behavioral Development, 29,* 238–46.

Kincaid, J. (1996). *The autobiography of my mother.* New York: Farrar, Strauss, & Giroux.

King, K.M., & Chassin, L. (2007). A prospective study of the effects of age of initiation of alcohol and drug use on young adult substance dependence. *Journal of Studies on Alcohol and Drugs, 68*(2), 256–65.

Kirmayer, L.J. (2001). Cultural variations in the clinical presentation of depression and anxiety: Implications for diagnosis and treatment. *Journal of Clinical Psychiatry, 62*(Suppl. 13), 22–28.

Kirmayer, L.J., & Sartorius, N. (2007). Cultural models and somatic syndromes. *Psychosomatic Medicine, 69,* 832–40.

Knight, G.P., Jacobson, R.P., Gonzales, N.A., Roosa, M.W., & Saenz, D.S. (2009). An evaluation of the psychological research on acculturation and enculturation processes among recently immigrating populations. In R.L. Dalla, J. DeFrain, J. Johnson, & D. Abbot (Eds.), *Strengths and challenges of new immigrant families: Implications for research, policy, education, and service* (pp. 9–31). Lanham, MD: Lexington Books.

Koss, J. (1990). Somatization and somatic complaint syndromes among Hispanics: Overview and ethnopsychological perspectives. *Transcultural Psychiatric Research Review, 27*(1), 5–29.

Krug, E.G., Dahlberg, L.L., Zwi, A, Mercy, J.A., & Lozano, R. (Eds.) (2002). *World report on violence and health.* Geneva, Switzerland: World Health Organization.

Kuhlberg, J.A., Peña, J.B., & Zayas, L.H. (2010). Parent-adolescent conflict, family, self-esteem, internalizing behaviors and suicide attempts among adolescent Latinas. *Child Psychiatry and Human Development, 41,* 425–40.

Kumpfer, K.L., Alvarado, R., Tait, C., & Whiteside, H.O. (2007). The Strengthening Families Program: An evidence-based, multicultural family skills training program. In P. Tolan, J. Szapocznik, & S. Sambrano. (Eds.), *Preventing youth substance abuse: Science-based programs for children and adolescents* (pp. 159–181). Washington, DC: American Psychological Association.

Lamm, B., & Keller, H. (2007). Understanding cultural models of parenting: The role of intracultural variation and response style. *Journal of Cross-Cultural Psychology, 38*(1), 50–57.

Leinonen, J.A., Solantaus, T.S., & Punamäki, R. (2002). The specific mediating paths between economic hardship and the quality of parenting. *International Journal of Behavioral Development, 26*(5), 423–35.

Lerner, R.M. (2002). *Concepts and theories of human development.* Mahwah, NJ: Lawrence Erlbaum Associates.

Lester, R.J. (2007). Critical therapeutics: Cultural politics and clinical reality in two eating disorder treatment centers. *Medical Anthropology Quarterly,* 21, 369–87.

Lewis-Fernandez, R. (1994). Culture and dissociation: A comparison of ataques de nervios among Puerto Ricans and possession syndrome in India. In D. Speigel (Ed.), *Dissociation: Culture, mind and body* (pp. 123–167). Washington, DC: American Psychiatric Press.

Lewis-Fernández, R., Garrido-Castillo, P., Bennasar, M.C., Parrilla, E.M., Laria, A.J., Ma, G., et al. (2002). Dissociation, childhood trauma, and ataque de nervios among Puerto Rican psychiatric outpatients. *American Journal of Psychiatry, 159*(9), 1603–1605.

Lewis-Fernández, R., Guarnaccia, P.J., Martínez, I.E., Salmán, E., Schmidt, A., & Liebowitz, M. (2002). Comparative phenomenology of ataques de nervios, panic attacks, and panic disorder. *Culture, Medicine, and Psychiatry, 26*(2), 199–223.

Lewinsohn, P., Rohde, P., & Seeley, J. (1994). Psychosocial risk factors for future adolescent suicide attempts. *Journal of Consulting and Clinical Psychology, 62*(2), 297–305.

Liddle, H.A., Rowe, C.L., Dakof, G.A., Ungaro, R.A., & Henderson, C.E. (2004). Early intervention for adolescent substance abuse: Pretreatment to posttreatment outcomes of a randomized clinical trial comparing multidimensional family therapy and peer group treatment. *Journal of Psychoactive Drugs, 36*(1), 49–63.

Liebowitz, M.R., Salman, E., Jusino, C.M., Garfinkel, R., Street, L. Cardenas, D. L., et al. (1994). Ataques de nervios and panic disorders. *American Journal of Psychiatry, 151,* 871–75.

Linehan, M.M. (1987). Dialectical behavior therapy: A cognitive behavioral approach to parasuicide. *Journal of Personality Disorders, 1*(4), 328–33.

López, S.R., Ramírez García, J.I., Ullman, J.B., Kopelowicz, A., Jenkins, J., Breitborde, N.J.K., et al. (2009). Cultural variability in the manifestation of expressed emotion. *Family Process, 48*(2), 179–94.

Lugo Steidel, A., & Contreras, J.M. (2003). A new familism scale for use with Latino populations. *Hispanic Journal of Behavioral Sciences, 25*(3), 312–30.

Lundberg, S., & Pollak, R.A. (2007). American family and family economics. *Journal of Economic Perspectives, 21*, 3–26.

Mair, M. (1988). Psychology as storytelling. *International Journal of Personal Construct Psychology, 1*(2), 125–37.

Marín, G.S., & Gamba, R.J. (1996). A new measurement of acculturation for Hispanics: The Bidimensional Acculturation Scale for Hispanics (BAS). *Hispanic Journal of Behavioral Sciences, 18*(3), 297–316.

Marttunen, M.J., Aro, H.M., & Lönnqvist, J.K. (1993). Precipitant stressors in adolescent suicide. *Journal of the American Academy of Child & Adolescent Psychiatry, 32*(6), 1178–83.

McLoyd, V.C. (1998). Socioeconomic disadvantage and child development. *American Psychologist, 53*(2), 185–204.

Mehlman, R.D. (1961). The Puerto Rican Syndrome. *American Journal of Psychiatry, 118*, 328–32.

Meissner, W.W. (2007). Therapeutic alliance: Theme and variations. *Psychoanalytic Psychology, 24*, 231–54.

Mikulincer, M., Shaver, P.R., & Pereg, D. (2003). Attachment theory and affect regulation: The dynamics, development, and cognitive consequences of attachment-related strategies. *Motivation and Emotion*, Vol. *27*(*2*), 77–102.

Miller, A.L., Rathus, J.H., & Linehan, M.M. (2007). *Dialectical behavior therapy with suicidal adolescents.* New York: The Guilford Press.

Mizio, E. (1974). Impact of external systems on the Puerto Rican family, *Social Casework, 55*(2), 76–83.

Moos, R.H., & Moos, R. (1981). *Family environment scale manual.* Palo Alto, CA: Consulting Psychologist Press.

Moscicki, E.K. (1999). Epidemiology of suicide. In D.G. Jacobs (Ed.), *Harvard Medical School guide to suicide assessment and intervention* (pp. 40–51). San Francisco, CA: Jossey-Bass.

Moscicki, E.K., & Crosby, A. (2003). Epidemiology of attempted suicide in adolescents: Issues for prevention. *Trends in Evidence-Based Neuropsychiatry, 5*(2): 36–44.

Mufson, L, Dorta, K.P., Moreau, D., & Weissman, M.M. (2004). *Interpersonal psychotherapy for depressed adolescents.* New York: Guilford Press.

National Center on Addiction and Substance Abuse. (2002). *Substance use and sexual health among teens and young adults in the U.S.* New York: Columbia University.

Nencel, L. (2001). *Ethnography and prostitution in Peru.* London: Pluto Press.

The New York Times (2006, July 21). Editorial: Young Latinas and a Cry for Help. p. A22.

Ng, B. (1996). Characteristics of 61 Mexican Americans who attempted suicide. *Hispanic Journal of Behavioral Studies, 18*, 3–12.

Nichter, M. (1981). Idioms of distress: Alternatives in the expression of psychological distress: A case study from South India. *Culture, Medicine, and Psychiatry 5*, 379–408.

Nolle, A.P., Gulbas, L., Kuhlberg, J.A., & Zayas, L.H. (2011). Sacrifice for the sake of the family: Expressions of familism by Latina teens and mothers in the context of suicide. *American Journal of Orthopsychiatry, 81.*

Norborg, B., & Sand, B. (Producer & Director). (1995). *Socialism or Death* [Film]. Stockholm: Sveriges Television.

O'Brien, S., & Arce, R.M. (2009). *Latino in America.* New York: Penguin.

O'Carroll, P.W., Berman, A.L., Maris, R.W., & Moscicki, E.K. (1996). Beyond the tower of Babel: A nomenclature for suicidology. *Suicide and Life-Threatening Behavior, 26*(3), 237–52.

Ojito, M. (2005). *Finding Mañana: A memoir of a Cuban exodus.* New York: Penguin.

Olson, D.H. (2000). Circumplex model of marital and family systems. *Journal of Family Therapy, 22*(2), 144–67.

Oquendo, M.A. (1994). Differential diagnosis of ataque de nervios. *American Journal of Orthopsychiatry, 65,* 60–65.

Oquendo, M.A., Horwath, E., & Martinez, A. (1992). Ataques de nervios: Proposed diagnostic criteria for a culture specific syndrome. *Culture, Medicine, and Psychiatry, 16*(3), 367–76.

Organista, K.C. (2007). *Solving Latino psychosocial and health problems: Theory, practice, and populations.* Hoboken, NJ: John Wiley & Sons, Inc.

Ornduff, S.R., Kelsey, R.M., & O'Leary, K.D. (2001). Childhood physical abuse, personality, and adult relationship violence: A model of vulnerability to victimization. *American Journal of Orthopsychiatry, 71,* (3), 322–331.

Ortiz Cofer, J. (1990). *Silent dancing: A partial remembrance of a Puerto Rican childhood.* Houston, TX: Arte Público Press.

Padilla, F. (1985). *Latino ethnic consciousness: The case of Mexican Americans and Puerto Ricans in Chicago.* South Bend, IN: University of Notre Dame Press.

Passel, J.S., & Cohn, D. (2009). *A portrait of unauthorized immigrants in the United States.* Washington, DC: Pew Hispanic Center.

Pena, M. (1991). Class, gender, and machismo: The "treacherous-woman" folklore of Mexican male workers. *Gender and Society, 5,* 30–46.

Pew Hispanic Center. (2009). *Between two worlds: How young Latinos come of age in America.* Washington, DC: Pew Hispanic Center.

Pfeffer, C.R., Klerman, G.L., Hurt, S.W., & Kakuma, T. (1993). Suicidal children grow up: Rates and psychosocial risk factors for suicide attempts during follow-up. *Journal of the American Academy of Child & Adolescent Psychiatry, 32*(1), 106–113.

Phinney, J.S. (1989). Stages of ethnic identity development in minority group adolescents. *Journal of Early Adolescence, 9*(1-2), 34–49.

Popp, T.K., Spinrad, T.L., & Smith, C.L. (2008). The relation of cumulative demographic risk to mothers' responsivity and control: Examining the role of toddler temperament. *Infancy, 13*(5), 496–518.

Portes, A., & Hao, L. (1998). E Pluribus Unum: Bilingualism and loss of language in the second generation. *Sociology of Education, 71,* 269–94.

Poss, J., & Jezewski, M.A. (2002). The role and meaning of susto in Mexican Americans' explanatory model of type 2 diabetes. *Medical Anthropology Quarterly*, 16(3), 360–77.

Prout, R. (1999). Jail-house rock: Cuba, AIDS, and the incorporation of dissent in Bengt Norborg's *Socialism or Death*. *Bulletin of Latin American Research*, 18(4), 423–36.

Quintana, S.M. (1998). Children's developmental understanding of ethnicity and race. *Applied and Preventive Psychology: Current Scientific Perspectives*, 7(1), 27–45.

Quintana, S.M., & Scull, N.C. (2009). Latino ethnic identity. In F.A. Villarruel, G. Carlo, J.M. Grau, M. Azmitia, N.J. Cabrera, & T.J. Chahin (Eds.), *Handbook of U.S. Latino psychology: Developmental and community-based perspectives* (pp. 81–98). Thousand Oaks, CA: Sage.

Quintero, G.A., & Estrada, A.L. (1998). Cultural models of masculinity and drug use: "Machismo," heroin, and street survival on the U.S.-Mexico border. *Contemporary Drug Problems*, 25, 147–68.

Ramos, J. (2002). *The other face of America: Chronicles of the immigrants shaping our future*. New York: HarperCollins.

Rathus, J.H., & Miller, A.L. (2002). Dialectical Behavior Therapy adapted for suicidal adolescents. *Suicide and Life-Threatening Behavior*, 32(2), 146–57.

Razin, A.M., O'Dowd, M.A., Nathan, A., Rodriguez, I., Goldfield, A., Martin, C., et al. (1991). Suicidal behavior among inner-city Hispanic adolescent females. *General Hospital Psychiatry*, 13, 45–58.

Rebhun, L.A. (2004). Culture-bound syndromes. In C.R. Ember & M. Ember (Eds.), *Encyclopedia of medical anthropology: Health and illness in the world's cultures* (pp. 319–327). New York: Kluwer.

Rew, L., Thomas, N., Horner, S., Resnick, M.D., & Beuhring, T. (2001). Correlates of recent suicide attempts in a triethnic group of adolescents. *Journal of Nursing Scholarship*, 33(4), 361–67.

Roberts, J. (1994). *Tales and transformations: Stories in families and family therapy*. New York: Norton.

Roberts, J. (1999). Beyond words: The power of rituals. In D.J. Wiener (Eds.), *Beyond talk therapy: Using movement and expressive techniques in clinical practice* (pp. 55–78). Washington, DC: American Psychological Association.

Roberts, R.E., & Chen, Y. (1995). Depressive symptoms and suicidal ideation among Mexican-origin and Anglo adolescents. *Journal of the American Academy of Child and Adolescent Psychiatry*, 34(1), 81–90.

Robin, A.L., & Foster, S.L. (1989). *Negotiating parent-adolescent conflict: A behavioral family systems approach*. New York: The Guilford Press.

Robles, F. (1995, December 18). Concern mounts over middle school suicides. *Miami Herald*. p. 4B.

Rosenberg, M., Schooler, C., & Schoenbach, C. (1989). Self-esteem and adolescent problems: Modeling reciprocal effects. *American Sociological Review*, 54(6), 1004–1018.

Rosselló, J., & Bernal, G. (1999). The efficacy of cognitive-behavioral and interpersonal treatments for depression in Puerto Rican adolescents. *Journal of Consulting and Clinical Psychology, 67,* 734–45.

Rothbart, M.K., & Bates, J.E. (2006). Temperament. In W. Damon & N. Eisenberg (Eds.), *Handbook of child psychology: Vol. 3. Social, emotional, personality development* (5th ed.). (pp. 619–700). Hoboken, NJ: Wiley & Sons.

Rotheram-Borus, M.J., Piacentini, J., Cantwell, C., Belin, T.R., & Song, J. (2000). The 18-month impact of an emergency room intervention for adolescent female suicide attempters. *Journal of Consulting and Clinical Psychology, 68*(6), 1081–93.

Rotheram-Borus, M.J., Piacentini, J., Miller, S., Graae, F., & Castro-Blanco, D. (1994). Brief cognitive-behavioral treatment for adolescent suicide attempters and their families. *Journal of the American Academy of Child and Adolescent Psychiatry, 33*(4), 508–517.

Rotheram-Borus, M.J., Piacentini, J., Van Rossem, R., Graae, F., Cantwell, C., Castro-Blanco, D., et al. (1996). Enhancing treatment adherence with a specialized emergency room program for adolescent suicide attempters. *Journal of the American Academy of Child and Adolescent Psychiatry, 35*(5), 654–63.

Rubell, A.J. (1964). The epidemiology of a folk illness: *Susto* in Hispanic America. *Ethnology, 3*(3), 268–83.

Rubell, A.J., O'Nell, C.W., & Collado-Ardón, R. (1991). *Susto: A folk illness*. Berkeley, CA: University of California Press.

Rudolph, K.D., Lambert, S.F., Clark, A.G., & Kurlakowsky, K.D. (2001). Negotiating the transition to middle school: The role of self-regulatory processes. *Child Development, 72*(3), 929–46.

Rumbaut, R., & Ima, K. (1988). *The adaptation of Southeast Asian refugee youth: A comparative study*. Washington, DC : U.S. Office of Refugee Resettlement.

Saetermoe, C.L., Beneli, I., & Busch, R.M. (1999). Perceptions of adulthood among Anglo and Latino parents. *Current Psychology, 18*(2), 171–84.

Salgado de Snyder, V.N., Diaz-Perez, M., & Ojeda, V.D. (2000). The prevalence of nervios and associated symptomatology among inhabitants of Mexican rural communities. *Culture, Medicine, and Psychiatry, 24*(4), 453–70.

Sameroff, A.J. (1983). Developmental systems: Contexts and evolution. In P.H. Mussen & W. Kessen (Ed.), *Handbook of child psychology: Vol. 1. History, theory, and methods* (4th ed.). (pp. 237–94). New York: Wiley & Sons.

Sanson, A., Hemphill, S.A., & Smart, D. (2004). Connections between temperament and social development: A review. *Social Development, 13*(1), 142–70.

Santiago, E. (1993). *When I was Puerto Rican*. Cambridge, MA: DaCapo Press.

Santiago, E. (1999). *Almost a woman*. New York: Vintage.

Santisteban, D.A., Coatsworth, J.D., Perez-Vidal, A., Kurtines, W.M., Schwartz, S.J., LaPerriere, A., et al. (2003). Efficacy of brief strategic family therapy in modifying Hispanic adolescent behavior problems and substance use. *Journal of Family Psychology, 17,* 121–33.

Santisteban, D.A., & Mena, M.P. (2009). Culturally informed and flexible family-based treatment for adolescents: A tailored and integrative treatment for Hispanic youth. *Family Process, 48*(2), 253–68.

Santisteban, D.A., Suarez-Morales, L., Robbins, M.S., & Szapocznik, J. (2006). Brief strategic family therapy: Lessons learned in efficacy research and challenges to blending research and practice. *Family Process, 45*(2), 259–71.

Shaffer, D., & Craft, L. (1999). Methods of adolescent suicide prevention. *Journal of Clinical Psychiatry, 60,* 70–74.

Shapiro, J., & Simonsen, D. (1994). Educational/support group for Latino families of children with Down syndrome. *Mental Retardation, 32,* 403–415.

Silk, J.S., Morris, A.S., Kanaya, T., & Steinberg, L. (2003). Psychological control and autonomy granting: Opposite ends of a continuum or distinct constructs? *Journal of Research on Adolescence, 13,* 113–128.

Silk, J.S., Ziegler, M.L., Whalen, D.J., Dahl, R.E., Ryan, N.D., Dietz, L.J., et al. (2009). Expressed emotion in mothers of currently depressed, remitted, high-risk, and low-risk youth: Links to child depression status and longitudinal course. *Journal of Clinical Child and Adolescent Psychology, 38*(1), 36–47.

Silverman, M.M., Berman, A.L., Sanddal, N.D., O'Carroll, P.W., & Joiner, T.E. (2007). Rebuilding the Tower of Babel: A revised nomenclature for the study of suicide and suicidal behaviors: Part II: Suicide-related ideations, communications and behaviors. *Suicide and Life-Threatening Behavior, 37*(3), 264–77.

Smith, B.D., Sabin, M., Berlin, E.A., & Nackerud, L. (2009). Ethnomedical syndromes and treatment-seeking behavior among Mayan refugees in Chiapas, Mexico. *Culture, Medicine, and Psychiatry, 33*(3), 366–81.

Smokowski, P., & Bacallao, M. (2011). *Becoming bicultural: Risk, resilience, and Latino youth.* New York: New York University Press.

Smokowski, P., Buchanan, R.L., & Bacallao, M.L. (2009). Acculturation and adjustment in Latino adolescents: How cultural risk factors and assets influence multiple domains of adolescent mental health. *Journal of Primary Prevention, 30*(3-4), 371–93.

Sommers, L.K. (1991). Inventing Latinismo: The creation of "Hispanic" panethnicity in the United States. *Journal of American Folklore, 104*(411), 32–53.

Spinrad, T.L., Eisenberg, N., Gaertner, B., Popp, T., Smith, C.L., Kupfer A., et al. (2007). Relations of maternal socialization and toddlers' effortful control to children's adjustment and social competence. *Developmental Psychology, 43*(5), 1170–86.

Spirito, A., Sterling, C.M., Donaldson, D.L., & Arrigan, M.E. (1996). Factor analysis of the Suicide Intent Scale with adolescent suicide attempters. *Journal of Personality Assessment, 67,* 90–101.

Steinberg, L. (1990). Autonomy, conflict, and harmony in the family relationship. In S. Feldman & G. Elliott (Eds.), *At the threshold: The developing adolescent* (pp. 255–276). Cambridge, MA: Harvard University Press.

Steinberg, L. (2007). *Adolescence* (8th ed.). New York: McGraw-Hill.

Substance Abuse and Mental Health Services Administration. (2003). *Summary of findings from the 2000 National Household Survey on Drug Abuse (DHHS Publication No. SMA 01-3549, NHSDA Series: H-13)*. Rockville, MD: Author.

Szapocznik, J., Robbins, M.S., Mitrani, V.B., Santisteban, D.A., Hervis, O., & Williams, R.A. (2002). Brief strategic family therapy with behavior problem Hispanic youth. In F.W. Kaslow & J. Lebow (Eds.), *Comprehensive handbook of psychotherapy: Vol. 4: Integrative/eclectic* (pp. 83–109). New York: John Wiley & Sons.

Tannen, D. (2006). *You're wearing that? Understanding mothers and daughters in conversation*. New York: Random House.

Taylor, J.M., Veloria, C.N., & Verba, M.C. (2007). Latina girls: "We're like sisters—Most times!" In B.J. Leadbeater & N. Way (Eds.), *Urban girls revisited: Building strengths* (pp. 157–174). New York: New York University Press.

Tinker-Salas, M. (1991). El imigrante Latino: Latin American immigration and pan-ethnicity. *Latino Studies Journal, 2*, 58–71.

Tolin, D.F., Robison, J.T., Gaztambide, S., Horowitz, S., & Blank, K. (2007). Ataques de nervios and psychiatric disorders in older Puerto Rican primary care patients. *Journal of Cross-Cultural Psychology, 38*(6), 659–69.

Torres, J.B., Solberg, V.S.H., & Carlstrom, A.H. (2002). The myth of sameness among Latino men and their machismo. *American Journal of Orthopsychiatry, 72*, 163–81.

Tortolero, S.R., & Roberts, R.E. (2001). Differences in nonfatal suicide behaviors among Mexican and European American middle school children. *Suicide and Life-Threatening Behavior, 31*(2), 214–23.

Trautman, E.C. (1961a). The suicidal fit: A psychobiologic study on Puerto Rican immigrants. *Archives of General Psychiatry, 5*(1), 76–83.

Trautman, E.C. (1961b). Suicide attempts of Puerto Rican immigrants. *Psychiatric Quarterly, 35*(3), 544–45.

Triandis, H. C., Bontempo, R., Villareal, M. J., Asai, M., & Lucca, N. (1988). Individualism and collectivism: Cross-cultural perspectives on self-ingroup relationships. *Journal of Personality & Social Psychology, 54*(2), 323–338.

Triandis, H., Lambert, W., Berry, J., Lonner, W., Heron, A., Brislin, R., et al. (Eds.). (1980). *Handbook of cross-cultural psychology, Vols. 1–6*. Boston, MA: Allyn & Bacon.

Turner, S., Kaplan, C., Zayas, L.H., & Ross, R. (2002). Suicide attempts by adolescent Latinas: An exploratory study of individual and family correlates. *Child and Adolescent Social Work Journal, 19*, 357–74.

Ungemack, J., & Guarnaccia, P.J. (1998). Suicidal ideation and suicide attempts among Mexican Americans, Puerto Ricans and Cuban Americans. *Transcultural Psychiatry, 35*(2), 307–27.

Unger, J.B., Shakib, S., Gallaher, P., Ritt-Olson, A., Mouttapa, M., Palmer, P.H., et al. (2006). Cultural/interpersonal values and smoking in an ethnically diverse sample of Southern California adolescents. *Journal of Cultural Diversity, 13*(1), 55–63.

U.S. Census Bureau. (2006). *American Community Household Survey: 2006.* Retrieved from http://www.census.gov.

U.S. Census Bureau. (2007a). *American Community Household Survey: 2007.* Retrieved from http://www.census.gov.

U.S. Census Bureau. (2007b). *Single-parent households showed little variation since 1994.* Retrieved from http://www.census.gov.

U.S. Census Bureau. (2008a). *Countries and areas ranked by population: 2008.* Retrieved from http://www.census.gov.

U.S. Census Bureau. (2008b). *Household income rises; poverty rate unchanged; number of uninsured down.* Retrieved from http://www.census.gov.

U.S. Census Bureau. (2008c). *Older and more diverse nation by midcentury.* Retrieved from http://www.census.gov.

U.S. Census Bureau. (2008d). *One third of young women have bachelor's degrees.* Retrieved from http://www.census.gov.

U.S. Census Bureau. (2008e). *School enrollment in the United States: 2006.* Retrieved from http://www.census.gov.

U.S. Census Bureau. (2008f). *Statistical abstract of the United States: 2009, Table 596.* http://www.census.gov.

U.S. Department of Health and Human Services (2005). *Healthy People 2010: The cornerstone for prevention.* Rockville, MD: Office of Disease Prevention and Health Promotion.

Valenzuela, A., & Dornbusch, S.M. (1994). Familism and social capital in the academic achievement of Mexican origin and Anglo adolescents. *Social Science Quarterly, 75*(1), 18–36.

Valle, M.E. (1991). The quest for ethnic solidarity and a new public identity among Chicanos and Latinos. *Latino Studies Journal, 2,* 72–83.

Varela, R.E., Vernberg, E.M., Sanchez-Sosa, J.J., Riveros, A., Mitchell, M., & Mashunkashey, J. (2004). Anxiety reporting and culturally associated interpretation biases and cognitive schemas: A comparison of Mexican, American, and European American families. *Journal of Clinical Child & Adolescent Psychology, 33*(2), 237–47.

Vega, W.A., Gil, A., Zimmerman, R., & Warheit, G. (1993). Risk factors for suicidal behavior among Hispanic, African-American, and non-Hispanic white boys in early adolescence. *Ethnicity and Disease, 3,* 229–41.

Viramontes, H.M. (1995). *Under the feet of Jesus.* New York: Penguin.

Vygotsky, L.S. (1978). *Mind in society: The development of higher psychological processes.* Cambridge, MA: Harvard University Press.

Wachtel, P.L. (1993). *Therapeutic communication: Knowing what to say when.* New York: Guilford Press.

Wagner, B.M. (1997). Family risk factors for child and adolescent suicidal behavior. *Psychological Bulletin, 121,* 246–98.

Wamboldt, F.S., O'Connor, S.L., Wamboldt, M.Z., Gavin, L.A., & Klinnert, M.D. (2000). The Five Minute Speech Sample in children with asthma: Deconstructing the construct of expressed emotion. *Journal of Child Psychology and Psychiatry, 41*(7), 887–98.

Ware, N.C., & Kleinman, A. (1992). Culture and somatic experience: The social course of illness in neurasthenia and chronic fatigue syndrome. *Psychosomatic medicine, 54*, 546–60.

Wood, A., Trainor, G., Rothwell, J., Moore, A., & Harrington, R. (2001). Randomized trial of group therapy for repeated deliberate self-harm in adolescents. *Journal of the American Academy of Child and Adolescent Psychiatry, 40*(11), 1246–53.

Zayas, L.H. (1987). Toward an understanding of suicide risks in young Hispanic females. *Journal of Adolescent Research, 2*(1), 1–11.

Zayas, L.H. (1989). A retrospective on the "suicidal fit" in mainland Puerto Ricans: Research issues. *Hispanic Journal of Behavioral Sciences, 11*(1), 46–57.

Zayas, L.H. (1995). Family functioning and child rearing in an urban environment. *Journal of Developmental and Behavioral Pediatrics, 16* (Suppl.), 21–24.

Zayas, L.H. (2001). Incorporating struggles with racism and ethnic identity in therapy with adolescents. *Clinical Social Work Journal, 29*, 361–73.

Zayas, L.H. (2010). Seeking models and methods for cultural adaptation of interventions: Commentary on the special section. *Cognitive and Behavioral Practice, 17*, 198–202.

Zayas, L.H., Bright, C., Alvarez-Sanchez, T., & Cabassa, L.J. (2009). Acculturation, familism and mother-daughter relations among suicidal and non-suicidal adolescent Latinas. *Journal of Primary Prevention, 30*, 351–69.

Zayas, L.H., & Bryant, C. (1984). Culturally sensitive treatment of adolescent Puerto Rican girls and their families. *Child and Adolescent Social Work Journal, 1*(4), 235–253.

Zayas, L.H., Drake, B., & Jonson-Reid, M. (2010). *Overrating or dismissing the value of evidence-based practice: Consequences for clinical practice.* Manuscript submitted for publication.

Zayas, L.H., & Gulbas, L.E. (2011). *Are suicide attempts by adolescent Latinas a cultural idiom of distress?* Unpublished manuscript.

Zayas, L., Gulbas, L.E., Fedoravicius, N., & Cabassa, L.J. (2010). Patterns of distress, precipitating events, and reflections on suicide attempts by young Latinas. *Social Science and Medicine, 70*, 1773–79.

Zayas, L.H., Hausmann-Stabile, C., & Pilat, A.M. (2009). Recruiting urban Latina adolescents and their families: Challenges and lessons learned in suicide attempts research. *Youth & Society, 40*(4), 591–602.

Zayas, L.H., Kaplan, C., Turner, S., Romano, K., & Gonzalez-Ramos, G. (2000). Understanding suicide attempts by adolescent Hispanic females. *Social Work, 45*(1), 53–63.

Zayas, L.H., & Katch, M. (1989). Contracting with adolescents: An ego–psychological approach. *Social Casework, 70*(1), 3–9.

Zayas, L.H., Lester, R.J., Cabassa, L.J., & Fortuna, L.R. (2005). Why do so many Latina teens attempt suicide? A conceptual model for research. *American Journal of Orthopsychiatry, 75*(2), 275–87.

Zhang, L., Wieczorek, W.F., & Welte, J.W. (1997). The impact of age of onset of substance use on delinquency. *Journal of Research in Crime and Delinquency, 34*(2), 253–68.

Zimmer-Gembeck, M.J., Siebenbruner, J., & Collins, W.A. (2004). A prospective study of intraindividual and peer influences on adolescents' heterosexual romantic and sexual behavior. *Archives of Sexual Behavior, 33*(4), 381–94.

Zimmerman, J.K. (1991). Crossing the desert alone: An etiological model of female adolescent suicidality. In C. Gilligan, A.G. Rogers, & D.L. Tolman (Eds.), *Women, girls, and psychotherapy* (pp. 223–240). New York, NY: Haworth Press.

Zuckerman, M. (1990). Some dubious premises in research and theory on racial differences: Scientific, social, and ethical issues. *American Psychologist, 45*(12), 1297–1303.

Index

215